LOVE THY NEIGHBOR

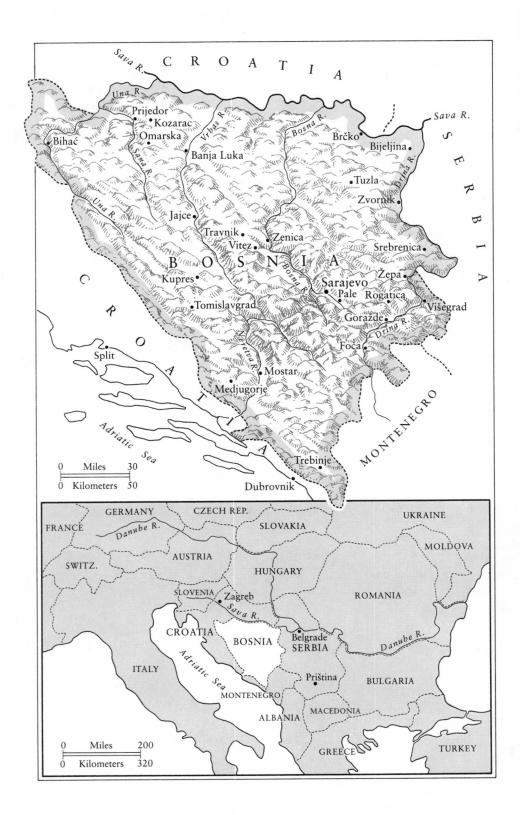

LOVE THY NEIGHBOR

A Story of War

PETER MAASS

ALFRED A. KNOPF   NEW YORK   1996

THIS IS A BORZOI BOOK
PUBLISHED BY ALFRED A. KNOPF, INC.

Library of Congress Cataloging-in-Publication Data
Maass, Peter, [date]
Love thy neighbor : a story of war / by Peter Maass. — 1st ed.
p.   cm.
Includes bibliographical references and index.
ISBN 0-679-44433-5
1. Yugoslav War, 1991– —Personal narratives, American.
2. Yugoslav War, 1991– —Bosnia and Hercegovina.
3. Bosnia and Hercegovina—History—1992–
4. Maass, Peter, [date]. I. Title.
DR1313.8.M33   1996
949.702'4—dc20   95-39250   CIP

Manufactured in the United States of America
First Edition

Only part of us is sane: only part of us loves
pleasure and the longer day of happiness, wants to
live to our nineties and die in peace, in a house that
we built, that shall shelter those who come after us.
The other half of us is nearly mad. It prefers the
disagreeable to the agreeable, loves pain and its darker
night despair, and wants to die in a catastrophe
that will set back life to its beginnings and leave
nothing of our house save its blackened foundations.

Rebecca West,
Black Lamb and Grey Falcon

Note to the Reader

This book describes people and events anchored in the Bosnian war but is neither a history of the conflict nor a prediction of its final outcome. On questions of war and peace, it is best to resist the urge to make predictions. The latest twists and turns are of secondary importance to this book, and in any event they follow a trajectory set in 1992 and 1993, when I reported on the Bosnian war. The tragedies and pathos of the people described in the following pages have not changed since then: the dead have not risen from their graves; suspicion has not evolved into trust. Moreover, what happened to these people has happened to other people in other countries, and will happen yet again. There is a universal character to war and its companions, cowardice and heroism. I have tried to explore them in this book, tried to explore the maddening question "Why?" That, rather than Bosnia, is the true subject of my story of war.

P.M.
December 1995

Contents

LOVE THY
NEIGHBOR

THE WILD BEAST

WHEN YOU GROW up in America, you don't really learn how foul humans can smell, just as you don't learn about the smell of death. Taking a crowded bus in the summer exposes you to unpleasant odors, but that is a transitory experience. If you turn your head or move a few steps away from an offending commuter, the smell is gone.

No amount of journeys on buses, however, can prepare you for the stink of refugees. When you enter a sports hall filled with women and children who have not washed for a month, or when you enter a cowshed filled with male prisoners who have not washed for two or three months, you smell something new, and it is terrible. You think that somebody has wrapped a discarded dishrag around your face, and that you must inhale air through it. Of course the smell is disgusting. It is the smell of filth, the smell of animals. We have an easy time thinking of animals as animals in part because they smell like animals. That's a difference between us and them. But what are you supposed to think when you find a group of humans who smell no better than cows, even worse? It reminds you that humans are animals, with the ability to stink like pigs, and kill like wolves.

The sports hall in Split reeked of sweat, not from athletes but from refugees. The basketball floor was jammed full of Bosnians, mostly women and children who had just straggled into town. They slept on blankets, one family per. The court was too small for all of them, so a few hundred refugees were living on the bleacher seats. It was May 1992. Many of the Bosnians had not showered since the war began a month earlier, having been trapped in basements all the time or scrambling through forests. The wait for the gym showers was so long that, days after arriving in Croatia, most had not begun the first step of cleansing their bodies. Just six weeks before, some of them had been well-groomed doctors and lawyers, but now they smelled like livestock. It was only the smallest insult the war had bestowed on them.

Split is a city along the Adriatic Sea, the main port of Croatia's Dalmatia region and the only place in Europe that makes me feel like I am in California. It is a land of abundant food, great wines and bronzed women who look like goddesses. The people are relaxed in Dalmatia, tinged more by the carefree attitude of the Italians who face them on the other side of the Adriatic, and who ruled them intermittently in the past centuries, than the dark passions of the Balkans. Even when Croatia declared independence from Yugoslavia in 1991 and fought a six-month war, Split was left virtually untouched—just a few protest marches, a small amount of bloodshed, and then it was over, leaving no physical scars. It suited my needs perfectly, a comfortable classroom where I could learn about Bosnia before making the journey inland, over the mountains and into the real world of war.

I sat down on the gym floor with Munevera, who had just arrived with her two children, a daughter of seven, a son of five. She had come on foot from Foča, a Bosnian town that's about a six-hour drive from Split, in normal times. She had to leave Foča in the middle of the night, when attacks by bands of Serb paramilitary soldiers became too frightening, and then she had to sneak from one safe village to the next, never in a direct line, avoiding roads, walking through forests and mountains, sneaking past Serb villages, occasionally being shot at. She was on Bosnia's underground railroad, and it was a rough ride. She could rest for no more than a day at safe villages, because other refugees were arriving and food was running out. I asked how long it took to get from Foča to Split.

"Forty-five days," she said.

"Excuse me?"

"Forty-five days."

"You have been walking for forty-five days?"

"Yes. But only at night. It was too dangerous to walk during the day."

I wrote it down in my notebook but I didn't believe it. How could she have been on the run with two children for forty-five days? During World War II people wandered for that long, even longer, but Bosnia's war was a small-time affair, a few people killed, a few thousand refugees, it would be over in a couple of months, when the politicians would come to their senses again. She wasn't marching from Russia to Poland. The year was 1992, not 1942, and Bosnia had smooth roads and fast cars with antilock braking systems and double-overhead cam engines. What was going on? I looked at Munevera's feet for an answer. She was wearing a pair of blue snow boots. They had been the best thing to put over her feet when she fled into mountains still covered with snow. She had run for so long that by the time she arrived in Split, in late May, the seasons had changed. It was 72 degrees outside. I was wearing a T-shirt. And she was wearing snow boots, her only shoes.

Munevera had been "cleansed." That word, cleansed, had not yet entered the American vocabulary. It was a learning process, and I was at the start of it. Like an infant trying to speak, you had to learn the building blocks of cleansing before you could understand its meaning. First the syllables, then the word; articles of speech, then grammar. So you had to learn about mass arrests, torture, rapes and expulsions, and you needed to understand that it was a system rather than a series of random incidents. Then you could understand what cleansing meant. It took time. You digested the patterns reluctantly rather than intuitively, because it made no sense that Europe was falling into madness again at the end of the twentieth century. When I met Munevera, I was struggling with the ABCs of atrocities.

During the interview Munevera said Muslim and Croat men were rounded up in Foča and put into a "concentration camp" on the town's outskirts (her words, not mine). I wrote down the words and forgot about them. Concentration camps were a Nazi invention, and in 1945 we buried the machine that created them. Munevera was being hysterical. Munevera spoke of a girl who lived next door, seventeen years old, who was dragged off by Serb soldiers one day and dumped back at home a few days later, bleeding from her groin. She had been raped an unimaginable number of times, Munevera said, and she died at home. I jotted it down. Munevera was being hysterical. Attack helicopters of the Yugoslav National Army floated in the air over Foča, directing artillery shots and strafing houses below with machine-gun fire, she said. I jotted it down. Munevera was being hysterical.

"I tried to call a friend in Foča today," Munevera said. "She stayed behind. I told her not to. When I called, a strange man answered the phone. I asked for my friend, and he said, 'This is a Serb apartment now.' "

I felt a tug at my sleeve.

"Hey, mister, come here, this man, my cousin, he had seven brothers killed."

My visit was turning into a freak show. I couldn't refuse to see the next exhibit, free of charge, satisfaction guaranteed. The guy with seven dead brothers. I said good-bye to Munevera and her sorrows and moved over to the next blanket. A farmer named Adem sat in the corner, hunched over, face toward the ground. His cousin, the one who lured me over, coaxed Adem to life, barely. Adem extended one of his hands, a big, muscle-bound paw of a man of the earth. I shook the hand, and it was limp. It had gone limp, like his spirit, on the night when thirty-five men from his village were rounded up by Serbs from a neighboring village and had their throats slit. He told the story in a whispered mumble. They were killed by Serbs who had been their friends, people who had helped harvest their fields the previous autumn, people with whom they shared adolescent adventures and secrets, skinny-dipping in the Drina River on hot summer days, groping with the naughty girls of the village at night. All of a sudden, seemingly without reason, they had turned into killers.

Adem, who was twenty-eight, fled in time, just as the roundup started on an evening in the first week of April. There were others who got out, fleeing to the forests and fields around the village. The Serbs chased after them, shooting wildly into the darkness with assault rifles and hollering like drunken hillbillies, which they were, "Muslim scum, hah, we'll get you tomorrow. We've got your women for tonight. We're going to fuck them real good. Did you hear that? *We're going to fuck them real good tonight!*" Some of the men were injured while fleeing. They begged their friends to kill them so they would not be captured by the Serbs, who were sure to comb the fields once dawn broke. Adem didn't say whether their wishes were granted, but his silence was ominous. His face hung toward the ground, his eyes staring at a spot on the blanket that only he could see. His hands started to shake.

"Mister," the cousin said. "Do you want to hear more? I know another man who . . ."

I didn't really listen to the rest. What could be done with more stories of death and thuggery, none of it reliable, most of it beyond the realm of credibility? From the sound of it, Bosnia was alight with atrocities. But who knows? The Serbs said it wasn't. Which side do you believe? A teenage girl explained to me how one of the Muslim men in her village had been nailed to the front door of the mosque, his arms spread out, so that he was like Christ on the cross, and he was still alive at the time. "Excuse me," I said. "He was *nailed* to the door?" Yes, she replied, she saw it herself, as the women of her village were marched past the mosque, being herded toward buses that would take them to train stations where they were loaded into cattle cars, yes, cattle cars, and expunged from their homeland, because it was no longer their homeland. The prettiest girls were taken off the trains at one of the stations. "They were all raped," she said. "I was lucky because I wasn't one of them." Girls did their best to avoid becoming war booty by cutting their hair into a crew cut, by smearing their faces with dirt, by binding up their breasts so that they could pass as boys. It worked, some of the time.

I needed a breath of fresh air. The stories, the smells, it was enough for one day. I stepped outside and was blinded by a bright sun that repudiated everything I heard in the dim bowels of the sports hall. When you are in pleasant Split, the wretchedness of Bosnia seems impossible, as unlikely as nighttime enveloping your neighbor's home while your house is soaked in sunshine. If you wanted to find the truth, to find out whether men would act like animals as well as smell like them, you had to leave the sunshine and head for the darkness. There, you would learn that the refugees you felt such pity for in Split were among the luckiest Bosnians of all, because they had escaped the darkness.

▶ *Two*

FOR MORE THAN four centuries, Višegrad has been dominated by two things, its bridge and its Muslims. The bridge was
built over the Drina River during the reign of Süleyman the Mag-
nificent, the Ottoman sultan. In its day and even now, the bridge is
an Eiffel Tower–like achievement, horizontally. Commerce between
Bosnia and Serbia was routed over its white stones, worn down over
the centuries to a surface nearly as smooth as a baby's skin. It trans-
formed Višegrad into a crossing point between the Ottoman empire
and the Christian world, and when there was peace between the two
giants, Višegrad thrived. When not, it suffered miserably, for Višegrad lay on top of a historical fault line.

In the summer of 1992, when I visited Višegrad, the bridge stood
strong and secure as always. It was easy to understand why the first
love of some village boys might be the bridge rather than a girl.
Even as adults, the town's inhabitants retained a special fondness
for their bridge, and they boasted about it as though it were an only
son. It is so handsome, they said, it is so strong, there can be no
better. In 1992, the bridge was a witness rather than a victim of the
young war, which touched Višegrad lightly, just a few burned buildings here, a chipped façade there. The war came and went quickly,
yet it took something away from the city. The Muslims.

Višegrad had been cleansed, not of garbage, of which there was
a neglected mess on its streets and alleys, but of people. It felt like
a ghost town in a western movie, minus the tumbleweeds rolling
down Main Street. Shutters clanged open and shut with every
breeze, wild dogs roamed around, snarling and licking open sores
on their haunches. They made good target practice for bored soldiers
wandering about. Front doors were ajar, left that way by looters
and soldiers, and you could walk into any Muslim home in Višegrad, and what you saw changed little from one to another. The
floorboards were ripped up by intruders searching for jewelry or
German marks, the preferred reserve currency in Yugoslavia. Mat-
tresses were knifed open like pigs for slaughter, drawers were emptied onto the ground, and copies of the Koran were urinated on.
Dried blood might be splattered on one of the walls, or several.
Everything of any value, including lightbulbs, had vanished.

For the Serbs who inherited the town, this was progress.

"I don't know what you mean by ethnic cleansing," said Mojmilo Marković, who called himself executive mayor, although the Beretta pistol tucked into his pants indicated he was being modest. "The Muslims left voluntarily. Why, we even supplied the buses. We didn't force them to leave. I swear."

A few hundred yards from City Hall, a mosque had been dynamited out of existence, and the rubble carted away. All that remained was a patch of black earth, and Marković said it would be turned into a park once life returned to normal. The town doesn't have enough parks, he said, as though the destruction of a house of worship was an inspired act of civic improvement. The "mujahadeen" of Višegrad were using the minaret as a machine-gun nest, he said, so, sadly, the mosque had to be destroyed. Marković, a brutal man but not very smart, remained silent when asked why, if the mujahadeen were shooting from the mosque, there was not a bullet mark on any building around it. He was an amateur at rewriting history.

The cleansing of Višegrad was an ordinary affair, according to refugees who survived it. Paramilitary soldiers, most of them from Serbia, came to town soon after the war began and rounded up the Muslim men, who were unarmed, going from house to house, apartment to apartment. The Serbs cruised around in several trucks, including a refrigerated meat truck. An old Muslim, forced to push corpses into the river, managed to escape and later talked to my *Washington Post* colleague Blaine Harden. "The Serbs took the prisoners to the railing of the bridge," he said. "They forced them to lean forward. Sometimes they would shoot them and sometimes they would cut their throats. They threw them all into the river. . . . They ordered me and a man who was even older than me to walk toward the bridge. We came across the body of an old man with a mutilated head. They ordered us to drag him toward the bridge. As we were dragging the old one, his skull was falling open and the brain came out. We dragged the body to the bridge and they ordered us to throw it into the Drina. There were two more bodies on the bridge. They had their throats cut. We were ordered to throw them into the river as well. On one of the bodies, four fingers on the left hand were freshly cut off."

The bridge's white stones were colored red with blood, but not for the first time. Brutality feels at home in Višegrad, and the bridge has been at the center of Balkan intrigue for centuries. The stones cannot speak, but their stories have been told in an epic novel that earned its author, Ivo Andrić, the Nobel Prize for Literature in 1961. Andrić was raised in Bosnia and understood its people and history better than anyone else. His masterpiece, *The Bridge over the Drina*, is a literary blueprint of the passions that plunge the Balkans, and the rest of the world, into madness every few generations, sometimes more often than that. The novel begins four hundred years ago with a gruesome scene in which a rebellious Serb is impaled on a stake at the bridge. He had made the mistake of trying to prevent the bridge from being built.

A Balkan impaling is not a simple matter of ramming a short wooden stake through a victim's midsection. It's much more delicate than that, and much more painful, if done properly. An oak stake, about eight feet long, is tipped with a sharp iron head and greased with lard for its entire length. It is shoved into the victim's anus, widened for the ritual by being sliced open with a knife. The executioner, who gets a bonus if the victim survives for a long time, moves the stake up into the abdomen quite slowly and quite carefully with blows to its base with a wooden mallet, and does his best to avoid puncturing any vital organs. The stake is coaxed through the midsection, sliding past the liver and spleen, the diaphragm and lungs, brushing past the heart, and then, triumphantly, exits the skin via the shoulder muscles in the victim's back. The victim should still be alive, and at this point the pole is raised up to a half-vertical position so that everyone can see. The victim hangs up there, a writhing statue, until he breathes his last. His enemies spit at him, and the village dogs lick up his dripping blood. In Andrić's book, the Serb stays alive for nearly a day, and his last words are defiantly aimed at the tormentors around him: "Turks on the bridge . . . may you die like dogs . . . like dogs."

It is a brutal practice, and it is a brutal scene, but Andrić is honest and wants his readers to understand the worst, and best, about humanity. If you can understand everything that Andrić wants you to understand, you become far wiser than the warlords and diplomats who make a mess of our world. The events of 1992 begin to make sense after a reading of Andrić's novel. The violent passions unleashed in 1992, and the horrific results they brought, were identical to previous convulsions of the human spirit, such as the ones of

1914, when a Serb nationalist in Sarajevo named Gavrilo Princip assassinated Austrian Archduke Franz Ferdinand, setting off World War I. With the abruptness of the first roar of thunder, the peace in Višegrad tore apart in that doomed summer of 1914. Andrić's explanation of it is timeless, placeless:

> The people were divided into the persecuted and those who persecuted them. That wild beast, which lives in man and does not dare to show itself until the barriers of law and custom have been removed, was now set free. The signal was given, the barriers were down. As has so often happened in the history of man, permission was tacitly granted for acts of violence and plunder, even for murder, if they were carried out in the name of higher interests, according to established rules, and against a limited number of men of a particular type and belief. . . . In a few minutes the business quarter, based on centuries of tradition, was wiped out. It is true that there had always been concealed enmities and jealousies and religious intolerance, coarseness and cruelty, but there had also been courage and fellowship and a feeling for measure and order, which restrained all these instincts within the limits of the supportable and, in the end, calmed them down and submitted them to the general interest of life in common. Men who had been leaders in the commercial quarter for forty years vanished overnight as if they had all died suddenly, together with the habits, customs and institutions which they represented.

I ran into an honest man in Višegrad, and his name was Vladimir Radjen, a carpenter, a Serb. I was exploring a looted Muslim house when I spotted him in a narrow street with a broom, an odd sight in a town without souls or soul. Vladimir was about forty-five years old and chubby, but he had a boyish face that made him seem younger and innocent. He lived in the neighborhood and was trying to tidy it up during a few days of leave he had from the front line. He wore a T-shirt over his belly and his chin was covered with two days of stubble. "We all lived in Višegrad like a big family, the Muslims and Serbs," he reminisced, leaning on the broom. "Everyone had mixed marriages. We never tried to find out who was a Serb or Muslim. We didn't look for differences. You know, it wasn't the people who wanted to fight. It was the politicians who prepared this stew, and now we can never go back."

I wanted to know more about the family that lived in the looted house. The floorboards had been torn out, of course, and holes punched in the walls, too. The family's belongings, the ones that weren't worth anything to the people who ransacked the place, were tossed around the rooms like rubbish at a dump. By walking on top of their clothes, their books, their pictures, I felt like I was walking on top of the family, and that this home of theirs was no longer a home but an unlocked tomb into which I was trespassing, perhaps desecrating it. Papers and books were lying everywhere, and I picked some of them up. Who were these people? One piece of paper was an application to the local authorities to make an extension on the house. Another piece of paper notified one of the daughters in the family that she had won a scholarship to study in Sarajevo. A train conductor's hat was crushed in a corner; it belonged to the father, a railway man. I found a diary, a high school diary, full of the daughter's adolescent thoughts about love. What happened to her? Had she been raped? Tortured? Killed? Or merely cleansed, the best fate of all, considering the options?

I asked Vladimir. He looked extraordinarily sad, on the verge of tears, and his confused expression made me think of Lennie, the simpleminded farmworker in John Steinbeck's *Of Mice and Men*. Vladimir did not fully understand the things that had happened around him, so quickly and so violently, in the past months. "Yes, they were wonderful people," he said. "They ran away because they were scared of what was happening. Lots of Muslims had to run. It makes me feel poor and sad. I want to cry every day."

I learned more about Višegrad a few months later, when I met a girl named Mersiha, who was the same age, seventeen, as the daughter of the looted house, whose diary I have kept. Mersiha was very beautiful, which was a great drawback when the war broke out. The Višegrad warlord took a fancy to her and one night dragged her and her younger sister away from their mother, who of course was crying hysterically and holding onto the legs of the warlord, who kicked her away and shouted, "I am the law!" The warlord's name was Milan, and human rights groups have thick dossiers on him, because he was the chief cleanser of Višegrad. Milan took Mersiha and her sister to the Vilina Vlas Motel, which had been turned into a party house for the thugs; Bosnians called such places rape camps. Mersiha was locked into a room, and her sister was locked into a room across the hall. Mersiha overheard Milan laughingly tell a soldier in the corridor to "question her but not too much," and then Mersiha heard an eruption of laughter from other soldiers as one of them went into her sister's room. A few hours later, Mersiha heard the sobs of a young girl waft into her room, and realized that the sobs came from her sister. It was the last time Mersiha, or anyone else, heard from her sister. She was fifteen years old.

Milan came into Mersiha's room, relocked the door and put a table in front of it. He told her to undress.

"He said that if I didn't do what he wanted, I would never go home," Mersiha told me, speaking in a nervous but constant voice. "Then he ordered me to take off my clothes. I didn't want to do that. He said I must, that it would be better to take my clothes off myself or else he would do it, and he would be violent. I started to cry. He said I was lucky to be with him. He said I could have been thrown into the river with rocks tied around my ankles. But I didn't want to do it. He got angry and cursed and said, 'I'm going to bring in ten soldiers.'"

Mersiha paused in her narration. She tightened her hold on the hand of her elder sister, who sat next to her throughout the interview, which went on for two hours but seemed much longer. We were in an empty basement pizzeria in Zenica, where Mersiha had fled to once her ordeal in Višegrad ended. She stared at the same type of spot, hers on a tablecloth, that Adem, the refugee in Split, stared at as he told me of the murder of his seven brothers. I could not see it. Mersiha told me that she tried to stop crying as she was raped by a man who called himself the law. After he finished the rape—or, as he liked to say, finished the "questioning"—Mersiha cried again. "What do you want to do to me?" Milan sneered. "Stuff me into a big artillery gun and shoot me to Turkey?"

He fell asleep. Some soldiers later knocked on the door and one of them shouted to Milan, "We know what you've got in there and we want it, too." Milan told them to go away. At about five in the morning, he woke and ordered Mersiha to get dressed, and then, much to her surprise, drove her home. Mersiha's mother was waiting in front of the apartment building. Mersiha did not mention what happened, and her mother never asked. They walked upstairs, both crying. They stayed in Višegrad for a month more, until they could no longer stay, hoping the younger sister would be returned to them. Mersiha's mother went to the police station almost every day, but it did no good. During one visit, a Serb aimed his gun at her and said, "Leave." Another time, she saw Milan. "What do you want?" he sneered. "At least I returned one of your daughters." And so it went in Višegrad, as elsewhere.

What intrigued me most about Bosnia was the question it posed about human beings—how could they do such monstrous things? How could a man wake up one morning and shoot his neighbor in the face and perhaps rape the neighbor's wife for good measure? How could they forget, as though it never existed, the commandment to love thy neighbor? How could this happen on a massive scale, and how could good people like Vladimir Radjen go along with it? The explanation I hung on to for the first few months of the war was simple enough. This is the Balkans, it's ethnic rivalry, tribal warfare, the people are uncivilized, they've been doing it for centuries. It was a comforting explanation because it defined the violence as an antimodern and anti-Western phenomenon—an exception. These people are different from the rest of us, I said to myself, they are like animals in a strange zoo. It was convincing but not more enlightening than repeating the memorable words spoken by a British officer one day as he and I watched a pensioner, on an orange bicycle, pedal calmly through a sniper zone. The Brit just shook his head and said, "Bosnian mind fuck."

If you spend much time in Bosnia, even in its wrecked state, you learn very quickly that it was a relatively sophisticated place before the war. The living standard in Yugoslavia was similar to poorer regions of Western Europe and America. The country had an open socialist economy that delivered a decent standard of living, including Levi's jeans and Madonna records. Yugoslavia broke from the Soviet orbit in 1948, so its citizens enjoyed unheard-of freedoms for a socialist country, such as the ability to travel where they wanted. Yugoslavia was not America, but neither was it Africa. Many of the cleansers in Bosnia were lawyers and engineers who, in peacetime, wore ties to work and had Sony televisions in their living rooms.

I couldn't figure it out. My journey into the depths of the human spirit had just begun, and I could not yet make sense of the things I was seeing. I was still too curious about them to be repulsed; all I knew at the time was that the Muslims of Višegrad had been mistaken to think that everything was okay and that barbarism was behind them because they had university diplomas and poetry readings and skiing vacations in the Alps. They forgot Andrić's warning, that when the call of the wild comes, the bonds of civilization turn out to be surprisingly weak, professors turn into nutcases and everything that a generation built up can be destroyed in a day or two, often by the generation that built it. The wild beast had not died. It proved itself a patient survivor, waiting in the long grass of history for the right moment to pounce.

▶ *Three*

TIME TRAVELING in Bosnia is an involuntary event that can occur at any moment. It happens, for instance, when a Serb farmer invites you to his house, serves a glass of slivovitz, homemade plum brandy, and then serenades you with a lecture on the Battle of Kosovo Polje, a historic defeat in 1389 that led to almost 500 years of Turkish domination over Serbs. The brandy is the same stuff that was drunk back then, the Serb who is your host carries the same genes of the warriors he evokes, the song he sings after the first bottle is emptied might be the same one that Serbs sang as they fought to their deaths five centuries earlier, and he might be playing the *gusle*, a one-stringed musical instrument that existed back then, too. If you ignore the refrigerator in the kitchen and the running water in the bathroom, you are back in 1389.

On a scorching summer day in 1992, the machine that took me back into time was a four-door BMW. The day began in the lap of modernity, the Hyatt Hotel in Belgrade, where the television offerings included a dozen satellite channels ranging from CNN to Eurosport. An American colleague persuaded me to join him on a search for a secret Serb prison camp in Bosnia, and he picked me up at nine in the morning. The outside world had just been hit with the first news that Serbs were running their own gulag, so concentration camps were the story of the month. We drove out of Belgrade on a freeway, crossed over a railroad bridge into the Serb-controlled part of Bosnia and then, just before reaching the city of Bijeljina, we turned off the main road and headed down a country lane.

The scenery was ageless, cornfields on either side of the road, a fat sun overhead. Shirtless farmers slashed at cornstalks with sickles, loading their harvest into wagons. The map said the lane ended at a village called Batković, our destination, but a mile before Batković, we had to stop at a roadblock. It was not the usual roadblock with soldiers wearing army fatigues and holding Kalashnikovs. Those are the good roadblocks, because the guys with the guns are under a military chain of command in which, usually, there is somebody who is not insane. The Batković roadblock was different, manned by four guys who had hunting rifles and tempers hotter than asphalt at noon. They were resting in the shade of a tree, chatting with a couple of village women. They didn't wear normal uniforms, they didn't have many teeth, and they didn't want us there.

"What are you doing here?" their leader said, a barrel-chested guy whose belly flopped over his belt. He was the only one with a uniform of any sort, but his uniform was from the World War II era. It might have been his father's, or perhaps his own. He was at least sixty years old, his wavy gray hair partly covered by a military cap that I had seen in history books about the Chetniks, royalist fighters. His attitude was rooted in 1389.

"We're here to visit the prison camp."

"There's no prison camp here. Get out."

"If there's no prison camp, then why is there a roadblock?"

They said there was fighting ahead, and that we would not be safe if we proceeded. We knew this was a lie, because the area was firmly under Serb control, but our attempt to ask more questions came to a sudden finish. Three rifles took aim at us, and the trigger fingers belonged to drunks.

"Out! Now!"

We obeyed. Among the many rules of survival in Bosnia is one that says you never talk back to the barrel of a gun. The Serbs wanted us to leave, so we left. If they had wanted the flak jackets in the trunk of the car, we would have surrendered them. If they had wanted the car itself, we would have surrendered it, too. Those are the rules. The car, the flak jackets, the money in your wallet, it can all be written off on expenses. It is surprising just how much a journalist can write off on expenses. But there is one thing you certainly cannot write off, and that is your life.

We drove a mile back down the road and stopped. We had spent two hours getting to this dump, and we were not going to leave empty-handed. If we couldn't reach the camp, perhaps we could at least confirm its existence by talking to some of the locals. It would be a decent story, though hardly the scoop we had hoped for. A few non-Serbs still lived in the area, so we stopped at a Gypsy house, where the first thing the woman said was, "Oh, are you here to see the prison camp?" She explained that buses full of prisoners with shaved heads rumbled toward Batković every day. Everyone knew what was at the end of the road. She pointed out a nearby dirt track that, she said, traversed the cornfields and bypassed the roadblock. We went to a neighboring Gypsy house and got the same story from another woman, whose husband pedaled away on his bicycle soon after we arrived.

We returned to the car and discussed the desirability of heading down the dirt track. Should we give it a shot? The answer was obviously no. Our presence was not desired in these parts, and if we drove down the track we probably would run into another road-block presided over by men who were even more drunk on liquor and prejudice than the ones we had just met. If the guys at the first roadblock heard that we were still snooping around the neighbor-hood . . . It wasn't a pleasant thought. We should drive back to Belgrade, repair to the air-conditioned Hyatt Hotel and drain a few beers from my minibar. It was time to return to the twentieth century.

And so we headed down the dirt road.

The Bosnian war has led to good and courageous reporting by American and West European journalists. It also has led to the deaths of dozens of them and serious injuries to scores of others. That's because the best stories are often ones that somebody is trying to hide, or that are difficult to reach because of fighting. The jour-nalists who get to them are usually the ones willing to run the most risks, which means the scoops often go to the craziest SOB rather than to the best writer or the best analyst. That was part of my unease about working in a war zone; I was competing against loon-ies. I was also dismayed by the realization that I had the capacity to act like a crazy SOB, despite my better judgment. The situation is simple. Journalists have the same instincts as bloodhounds on the scent of a fox. They chase after the story at full speed, and the closer they get, the more determined they are to sink their teeth into it, and the scent drives them nearly mad, so that they do things they should not. Bloodhounds will run until they drop dead of exhaus-tion, and in the heat of pursuit they will jump off cliffs to their death. It is the same with journalists; in a war, we can be a menace to our own well-being.

The degree of stupidity in heading down that dirt track cannot be measured. It was way off the chart. Even if we reached the prison camp, what did we expect? The camp commandant was unlikely to greet us at the front gate, shake our hands and say, "Gee whiz, I thought you'd never get here. Good job." This is not a story that I am proud to recount—it reflects stupidity rather than bravery or cleverness—but it became my first awakening to the fact that the longer I stayed in Bosnia, the more likely I was to die there.

We got only a few hundred yards down the dirt road. The husband who had pedaled off on his bicycle when we arrived at the second Gypsy house turned out to be an informer rushing off to alert his buddies at the roadblock. Jonathan Landay, the colleague at the wheel of the BMW, was the first to notice the red Yugo car that scooted up behind us. I recall his first words as being "Oh fuck." The gang from the roadblock was in the chase car, and their guns were sticking out the windows, a Keystone Kops sight that would have been comical if it weren't so scary. They flashed their headlights, honked their horn and ordered us to halt.

I do not know what it is like to have the AIDS virus, but I think I know what it is like to be told that you have it. While sitting in the car trying to look as unconcerned as possible, I got this sick feeling in my stomach, half regret, half foresight. It's a feeling that always came to me at moments of terror, those times when I stumbled into a battle or drove into sniper fire and could do little but pray for deliverance, and I imagine it's the same feeling that someone gets when he is told that he has the AIDS virus. All of a sudden you feel horribly unwell and look back in time and pinpoint the moment when you made the stupid mistake that is going to mean death. For someone with AIDS, the moment might be a one-night fling with a stranger in New York City. You locate the fateful moment in your mind, and you curse yourself. It doesn't make you feel less sick, but it distracts you from the immediate threat of death. You make wishes or pleas, you pray to a god you may not believe in, and you think, *If only I could go back in time, I would not make the same mistake again.* You mean it.

I had that AIDS feeling. I began sweating, not from the heat, but from the fear. There seemed to be little doubt about what was going to happen. We were in the middle of nowhere, surrounded by eight-foot-tall cornstalks and a soft wind that would not carry the sound of gunshots very far. The Serbs have a word for an isolated place like that, *vukojebina*, which means "where the wolves fuck." It was the perfect place for a killing. And that's pretty much what I expected when the roadblock gang piled out of their car and ran toward us with their guns leading the way, veins bulging out of their necks as they screamed at us. We coughed up our passports and United Nations press passes and obeyed their order to follow them.

They drove deeper into the cornfield. I don't recall any conversation in our car. Jonathan, myself and our female interpreter, Vlatka Mihelić, knew that the odds were against us and there was nothing we could do to change them. If we suddenly reversed gear and tried to back out of the cornfield at full speed, the guys in the Yugo would just start blasting away. In moments like that you want to close your eyes, hang your head and sob. You've blown it, no doubt about it, everything is finished. You feel weak, like you've just been punched in the groin and the guy who did it is winding up for another huge blow. You feel like a defenseless, scared child—like a Bosnian. You just want to survive, and you figure cooperation is the best option. Perhaps your captors will take pity, perhaps they don't really want to kill you, perhaps the cavalry will arrive. Nobody in the BMW argued for ramming it into reverse and trying to escape.

The Yugo began slowing down and made a U-turn, a glorious U-turn which meant that they, and us, were heading back to the main road. We followed. This was great news. Perhaps as they drove deeper into the cornfield they realized that they should probably get permission to punish us. "Damn journalists," the barrel-chested leader might have said. "They deserve to die, but, shit, we better get the commander to approve it first." He might have then stared at one of the guys in the back. "Hey, Bogdan, stop hogging the brandy, and goddamnit, stop farting." The U-turn didn't mean a pardon, just an appeal.

One of the mysteries of Bosnia's war is why so many good people stood by as evil deeds were committed in their name—people like Vladimir, the Serb in Višegrad who cried over what had been done to his neighbors. It is a universal mystery. Why, when the would-be dictators of the world start barking their songs of hate, do so many people sing along rather than stand up and say, simply, "No"? It's a cliché to point to the "good Germans" who followed Hitler into his madness because their duty was not to question but to obey. What about the Americans who buckled under to McCarthyism? Or what about the joggers in Central Park who fearfully run past someone being mugged?

I was hardly alone in feeling righteous about Serbs who supported, in their silence, a dirty war. If I was in their shoes, I would speak out. Or so I thought until I was put into their shoes.

The Serbs led us back to the main road and stopped in front of a run-down café. One of them went inside and made a phone call, apparently to their commander. The leader, whose nickname was Voja Chetnik, had gotten out of his car and didn't seem to mind that we did the same. He wandered onto the café patio and suddenly started shouting at a thin, middle-aged Muslim who was sipping a cup of coffee in the shade. It was one of the odd features of Serb-controlled territory that while Muslims were being tortured at a prison camp a mile down the road, others who had sworn their loyalty to the local Serb warlords remained at liberty, though precariously.

"Ramiz!" Voja roared, "I told you never to come here! Get out of here, you filth!"

Voja grabbed a beer bottle and slammed it against Ramiz's shoulder. Broken glass flew in all directions, dripping bits of blood. The shirtless Ramiz didn't even have a chance to get out of his chair because Voja started punching his head, kicking him, keeping him down. Ramiz tried to raise his hands to protect his face, but it did no good. Voja kept slugging away. When he got tired of that, he slammed the muzzle of his rifle into Ramiz's chest and undid the safety catch. An execution was moments away.

This was happening ten yards from me. I did not plead with Voja to spare Ramiz's life. Neither did Jonathan or Vlatka. I don't think any of us considered doing so. We fell silent. Voja was going to do what Voja wanted to do, and anyone who got in the way, especially journalists who were only one order away from their own execution, would likely be shot alongside the Muslim. Jonathan and Vlatka looked on. I turned around and walked toward the car, preferring not even to watch. Witnesses to war crimes rarely survive to tell about it. If my back was turned, perhaps Voja would think I hadn't seen the killing and wouldn't write about it, or perhaps he would think I simply wasn't interested in the fate of a "filthy" Muslim. Ramiz was on his own.

In the end, Voja decided not to shoot. Ramiz's wife appeared out of nowhere and threw herself between Voja and her husband. Voja cursed and kicked Ramiz a bit more and then let him scamper away, like a tormented mouse freed from the claws of a bored cat. We had made the right decision not to intervene, but it didn't feel very good. I told myself that journalists are not supposed to get involved in events they cover, which is true. It's also an alibi. A man was on the verge of being executed in cold Balkan blood, and we stood aside because it was the prudent thing to do. Was it much different from the Serbs who prudently kept quiet as their Bosnian neighbors were shot or packed off to prison camps?

One of Voja's men marched out of the café and whispered that the commander wanted us taken to the headquarters. This was wonderful news. Voja barked out the order for us to follow him, which we did, and he duly delivered us to the warlord of Bijeljina, the town where, on April 1, 1992, the Serb attack on Bosnia can be said to have started.

On that first day in April, a Belgrade gangster who called himself Arkan, and whose real name was Željko Ražnjatović, led his private militia into Bijeljina, a strategic gateway into Bosnia, and rounded up the town's leading Muslims, executing several in front of the main mosque. After a few days of pillaging in Bijeljina, Arkan and his militia, known as the Tigers, headed south and attacked the strategic border town of Zvornik. Arkan, who would later be elected to Serbia's Parliament, was replicating in Bosnia a campaign of looting and murder that he carried out during the war in Croatia a year earlier. His activities, which became known as "ethnic cleansing," illustrate the fact that outsiders from Serbia—operating with the support of Serbian authorities—organized and initiated the war in Bosnia.

Arkan was no longer in charge of Bijeljina when we were marched into military headquarters. "These people are enemies whom we caught near Batković," Voja told the new warlord, Dušan Djukić, a kindly-looking fellow who reminded me of the actor Richard Dreyfuss. Djukić thanked Voja and dismissed him. Voja was not finished with us. As he strode past, he snarled under his breath, "Never come back again." At the time, a return trip was the last thing on my mind.

Djukić chastised us for wandering around a "war zone" without proper authorization. Instead of throwing us into a cell, he drove us to his requisitioned house, served us coffee and Cokes and instructed us to watch an hour of hideously gory videos about the historical crimes committed against Serbs by Muslims and Croats. Bijeljina was in the midst of a daily blackout to conserve energy, so it was impossible for him to turn on the television and VCR. Djukić called the power-station chief and ordered him to turn on the juice for the whole town. The electricity was on in five minutes. It was a masterful display of warlordly clout. We watched his videos avidly and interviewed him afterward, scribbling down every word he uttered, like students anxious to please the teacher. The point was to get out of Bijeljina, and if that meant toadying to the warlord, we would toady.

We gently asked whether there was a prison camp at Batković.

"Of course not," Djukić replied. "There is no prison camp in this area. I have no reason to lie to you about it."

He let us go. We had one act of foolishness left in us. Instead of heading straight out of town for the relative safety and sanity of Serbia, we dawdled in Bijeljina and went into a two-chair barbershop next to a mosque. We still wanted to get the whole story and needed more information about the camp that our friendly warlord insisted did not exist. Vlatka struck up a conversation with the two men in the shop, the barber and his client.

"Are you Muslim?" she asked casually.

They looked at each other and nodded yes.

"These men with me are American journalists," she said.

The barber slipped the scissors off his fingers, went to the door, slid the lock shut and pulled the window shades down.

"What can you tell us about the prison camp?" Vlatka asked.

"Everything," he whispered.

An hour later we were finally on the road out of Bijeljina. The bridge we needed to cross into Serbia was temporarily closed because a train was passing over it. We had to wait. I was nervous. We had made few friends in Bijeljina, and our discussion at the barbershop (which, along with the adjacent mosque, was later demolished and turned into a parking lot) was a final act of defiance that would not go unpunished if the warlord or Voja became aware of it. I just wanted to get out of Bosnia. Our car was second in line to cross the bridge. The Serbs behind us noticed we were foreigners by our special license plates and started chatting with us. Then they started cursing us, the usual stuff about foreigners trying to crush the Serbs. One of them, who was drunk, got carried away with his curses, forgetting the target of his vulgarities—us—and reveling instead in the great Serb pastime of inspired swearing about anything that popped into his head. Serbs have many talents, one of which is a gift for coming up with oaths that combine amusing portions of imagination and smut. It is the opposite of political correctness, and I admired them for it, because they said what was on their minds, and said it in the most colorful way they could find, rather than in the blandest. Restraint is alien to Serbs, and this is good if a Serb is your friend, bad if he is your rival.

Vlatka started chuckling and even blushed a bit, an unusual act for one of the most seasoned war interpreters in the Balkans. I asked what the Serbs were saying. Oh, she replied, they are no longer swearing about us. Good, I said, so what are they swearing about? Oh, Vlatka giggled, they are saying something about Jesus' mother being fucked with a horse's prick. Oh, now they are saying that Milošević (the Serbian president) doesn't care about ordinary Serbs because he's living in Belgrade and fucking fashion models every night. Oh, now they are saying the weather was so hot today that cows didn't even have the energy to shit.

I loosened up. It was classic stuff. One moment a Serb has you sweating in fear, the next moment he is trying to make you laugh. I almost forgot about getting across the bridge, which reopened a few minutes later. We got back into the car, crossed into Serbia, and within ninety minutes I was back at the Hyatt Hotel in Belgrade, draining the minibar.

▶ *Four*

AT THE TIME, I didn't think there was anything strange about flying through the air with 35,000 pounds of feta cheese. I was going to Sarajevo for the first time. The United Nations airlift had just gotten under way, and I hitched a ride on a Belgian Air Force transport plane. The flight was routine until we entered Bosnian airspace and the crew put on parachutes, flak jackets, fireproof gloves, goggles, helmets and oxygen masks. The loadmaster offered me a parachute. I hesitated, not knowing whether he was serious.

"Okay, but if we get hit by a shell and must jump, we won't wait for you to put on a 'chute," he said. I replied that I had never jumped out of a plane, and he reassured me that he'd never been in a plane that got hit, but just in case something happened, I should put on the parachute and, after jumping, count to three before pulling the rip cord.

The notion of jumping out of a plane was just as alien as the assignment to cover a Balkan war. I had been living in Budapest and reporting on Eastern Europe for two years but never visited Bosnia until the fighting started. It was someone else's job until then. In these early months, the fighting seemed to be a brushfire conflict that would be put out quickly. I was adapting to it easily enough, perhaps because it was a welcome break from stories about recession in the post-Communist world. My rusty knowledge of Russian was helping me get a grip on a language that used to be called Serbo-Croat but had been Balkanized by the war; each side claimed the language as their own, so the Bosnians spoke Bosnian, the Croats spoke Croatian, and the Serbs spoke Serbian. The difference is minimal, like British and American English, but a lapse could cost you dearly. Croats have a special word for good-bye—*bog*, which also means "God"—and a cheery "Bog!" at a Serb checkpoint could get you a windshield of bullet holes. (Showing a Croat press pass, or being in a car with Croat license plates, would yield similar results.)

A grasp of history came rapidly. In the Balkans, you don't need to ask for history lessons, because they come at you all the time, uninvited and long-winded, with the same kind of odd enthusiasm that a stranger in America might tell you about his children, pulling a picture out of his wallet. I listened as Serbs lectured about the barbarism of the Turkish empire and their suffering under Croatia's Ustashe regime. Ustashe, which means "uprising," is the name of the World War II pro-Nazi movement that Hitler set up in power in Croatia. It earned international notoriety by slaughtering hundreds of thousands of Serbs, Jews and Gypsies. The efficiency of Germany's gas chambers was substituted for in Croatia with the raw enthusiasm of Ustashe soldiers who killed with knives, axes and their bare hands. The Ustashe leader, Ante Pavelić, was so beloved by his troops that on one occasion they presented him with a basket of Serb eyeballs. He was delighted. Even German officers stationed in Zagreb were horrified by the viciousness of the Ustashe.

The Croats, who are Roman Catholic, had a different history lesson to impart. To them, Yugoslavia was dominated by Serbs, who are Orthodox Christians and who, in the Croat view, made life miserable for them. The Croats had a point. Although Josip Broz Tito, the longtime Yugoslav leader, was part Croat, he suppressed Croat nationalism because he viewed it as a danger to Yugoslav unity; Croat nationalists were routinely thrown into jail. Also, much of the income from Croatia's lucrative tourist industry was siphoned into Serbia and other Yugoslav republics. However, the Croats failed to appreciate that Tito was well aware of the dangers of Serb nationalism, and he suppressed it, too.

What was to be made of it all? This much was clear: The blade of Balkan history was sharpened by the flint of myth, and it became a deadly knife that men with names like Slobodan Milošević and Franjo Tudjman were using to carve up territory and people. Serbs and Croats had at least one thing in common as Yugoslavia fell to pieces—leaders who spared no excess in pursuing violent agendas. Bosnia, sandwiched in the middle, was the principal victim. Flying into Sarajevo, I was interested in deeds rather than history, for I had a quaint notion that the statute of limitation had long ago expired on settling old grudges, and that barbarism in the name of historical justice is still barbarism. It was, I must repeat, a very quaint notion.

The rip cord dangled seductively on my chest, like a piece of broken glass that you want to run your finger over to see if it's sharp. Does the parachute really pop open when the rip cord is pulled?

"We're at eleven thousand feet," the pilot said. "The idea is to stay high for avoiding ground fire and descend steeply at the last moment. The only problem is if there are tailwinds."

"Are there tailwinds today?" I asked.

"*Bien sûr.* There are always tailwinds here."

The grin on his face reflected the fact that pilots of transport planes wanted to be fighter aces but didn't make the cut at flight school. Instead of commanding the hot rods of the Air Force, they were stuck with the eighteen-wheel trucks. I always felt a bit sorry for them and understood why they got a kick out of dive-bombing into Sarajevo airport. Cheap thrills. It was no surprise that the fleet of military transport planes that flew into Sarajevo was known as Maybe Airlines—maybe you get there, maybe you don't.

There was something fitting about flying into Sarajevo with a

crew of Belgians. Belgium, a simpler version of Yugoslavia, is split
between people who speak Flemish (never say Dutch) and people
who speak French. A slight majority of Belgians call themselves
Flemings, and the rest call themselves Walloons. These are not birds.
They have lived together half peacefully, half contentiously for more
than 150 years. Theirs is a loveless marriage, but they have the wisdom to know that divorce would be foolish. As we descended into
Sarajevo, the Belgian pilot saw more than the dead cities below us.
"The idea of a big united Europe is falling apart," he sighed. "This
is like Africa."

Alarms bleated madly in the cockpit because the rules of flying a
Hercules transport plane were being broken. One alarm buzzed like
a police siren because the plane was descending too quickly. Another
alarm sounded because the pilot had not lowered the landing gear;
he was waiting until the last moment, wanting to reduce the chance
of the tires being shot up. My first glimpse of Sarajevo, from behind
his shoulder, consisted of several smoldering houses near the runway, surrounded by hundreds of other homes that were skeletons,
their rafters exposed to the sky like the white bones of a long dead
prairie animal. It looked desolate, and I felt a bit of envy for the
Belgians who would not even get out of their seats while the plane
was on the tarmac. The engines would stay on and, after the cheese
was unloaded, they would head for the skies again. I would be left
behind in Africa.

In a sense, the war that I was stepping into had begun in 1980,
when Tito died and the pillars of the Yugoslav federation began
falling apart. His iron-fisted leadership was replaced with a rotating
presidency designed to ensure unity by making the leaders of Yugoslavia's six republics and two autonomous provinces compromise
with one another. Instead, it led to deadlock and economic decay.
With the old ideas discredited, political opportunists began using
nationalism as a lever to gain power. In Serbia, the largest republic,
a little-known official named Slobodan Milošević took control in
1987 and told Serbs it was time to stand up for their rights. This
sent a shiver through the rest of Yugoslavia. Milošević's virulence
helped ignite sparks of nationalism elsewhere, particularly in Croatia
and the Serbian province of Kosovo, inhabited by Albanians.

In 1990, it was clear that the political earthquakes in Eastern
Europe would have a different impact in Yugoslavia, where the

debate was not about ditching socialism but about ditching Yugoslavia. The key issue was whether Yugoslavia's republics would separate peacefully (into a looser federation or confederation) or violently (into war). The answer came in 1991, when the standoff between Serbia and Croatia turned to war. Milošević co-opted the nationalists' program and insisted that Croatia, which was home to 600,000 Serbs, could become independent only if it gave up territory where those Serbs lived. After several months of minor incidents, war started in the summer of 1991, and, after more than 10,000 deaths, a United Nations–brokered truce was agreed upon in January 1992. At the time, one third of Croatia was under the control of Serbs despite the deployment of thousands of U.N. peacekeepers. Slovenia, the smallest republic, gained independence at the same time with little bloodshed and no loss of territory because it had few Serb residents.

This was a prelude to the war in Bosnia. The secession of Croatia and Slovenia meant that Yugoslavia was, more than ever, a constitutional shell controlled by Milošević, who was driving it into economic ruin and political extremism. Bosnia wanted out. In its population of 4.4 million people, 44 percent were Muslim, 31 percent were Serb, and 17 percent were Croat. These statistics tell a misleading story, for dividing lines could not be drawn so starkly. The Muslims, rather than being interlopers, were native Slavs who adopted the religion of the invading Turks centuries ago. Everyone spoke the same language, dressed alike and intermarried frequently (18.6 percent of all marriages recorded from 1981 to 1991 were between people of different nationalities). In a February 29, 1992, referendum, 99 percent of the ballots were cast in favor of independence, and Bosnia gained international recognition as a sovereign country. There was a catch, though. Most Serbs obeyed their nationalist leaders, who were puppets of Milošević, and boycotted the poll. The argument against Bosnian independence was the same as it had been in Croatia: Serbs, as a minority, would be persecuted to the point of genocide. A month after the referendum, Serb paramilitary groups began their campaign of cleansing and conquest.

The crucial question is whether Serbs had justifiable reasons for taking up arms against Bosnia's government. If, indeed, they faced genocide at the hands of a radical Muslim dictatorship, then armed opposition would be understandable. But all evidence points to the contrary. The leaders of Bosnia's government—most of them Muslim, but many of them Serbs and Croats and people of mixed parentage—believed in the idea of a pluralistic country, refrained from creating an army (or acquiring weapons) and repeatedly pledged to defend minority rights. Western diplomats viewed their pledges as genuine. Bosnia's Muslims showed no signs of the religious intolerance that Milošević and his nationalist followers claimed to fear. In fact, these were the world's worst Muslims; most of them drank liquor, ate pork and rarely visited a mosque. Few made religious pilgrimages to Mecca, while many made shopping trips to Austria.

So why, if there was nothing to fear, did Milošević stir up so much trouble and send troops and weapons into Bosnia? This is, of course, the source of great debate, and my answer is this: Milošević and his followers used the specter of Islamic persecution as a smoke screen. The reason they started the war and pursued it with a brutality unseen in Europe since Nazi times is that they wanted to enlarge the borders of Serbia to include parts of Bosnia (and Croatia), thereby creating a "Greater Serbia." For Milošević, an apparatchik without a future in a democracy, it was a matter of staying in power by playing the nationalist card. For hard-core nationalists, it was a matter of achieving a historical dream. And for the Bosnians, it was a nightmare.*

As I landed in Sarajevo, America and Western Europe were taking their first steps toward ending the fighting. Serb rebels, who had gained control of two thirds of the country, would be persuaded to leave the remaining third to Bosnia's government. The government's reluctance to embrace the notion of surrender was, at the time, understandable but not discouraging. It might take a while to convince the Bosnians that ethnic cleansing would be tolerated by America and Western Europe, and that because we would accept it, so must they. In the meantime, we would take pity on them and supply feta cheese and pasta but not guns or ammunition. We wanted peace at any cost, and that meant we wanted the Bosnians to surrender, not fight. A U.N. arms embargo against all former Yugoslav republics, designed to prevent the outbreak of war, would stay in place even

---

* In this book, "Bosnian" refers to anyone who lived in Bosnia and supported the notion of a unified country. This means virtually every Muslim and any Serb, Croat or "mixed" person who opposed the nationalists trying to carve up the country.

though it crippled Bosnia, which had few weapons when the war started. In contrast, Serbia had plenty of weapons and a large arms industry that could replace whatever was captured or destroyed. Throughout the war, Bosnia's government begged for the arms embargo to be lifted.

Sarajevo's airport, like the country, was chaotic. The control tower had served as an irresistible target for Serb gunners in the hills, and it had more gouges than a dart board. Mortars landed within fifty yards of the perimeter as I arrived, wrecking houses that clearly didn't need any more wrecking. U.N. armored personnel carriers rumbled to and fro along the tarmac, motorized armadillos with gun turrets whirling around in reaction to cracks of sniper fire. The airport was sandwiched between Serb and Bosnian front lines.

I looked around and realized that this might be my lucky day. General Lewis MacKenzie, the first U.N. commander in Sarajevo, was standing on the tarmac's edge for a souvenir photo with a couple of departing soldiers. MacKenzie loved the spotlight and agreed to an interview on the spot. Literally. We sat on lawn chairs astride the tarmac, as though at a garden party, and shouted at each other over the occasional blasts of shells and the constant roar of airplanes. Two of his French bodyguards stood beside us, scanning the perimeter for danger, their assault rifles at the ready. If surrealism had not existed, Bosnia would have invented it.

General MacKenzie came from central casting. He is tall, beefy, handsome, a champion amateur race-car driver in his spare time. He wore his flak jacket like an oversized badge of honor, and he shined his own boots. He had served in U.N. operations in Vietnam, the Gaza Strip and Central America. Canada is known for producing hockey stars rather than war heroes, but MacKenzie was becoming one, and if a movie is ever made about Sarajevo, he should be cast to play himself. He was a user-friendly general whose remarks were sound-bite quality, and he genuinely liked journalists. "I hear there's a good story in town about one of the female Olympic sharpshooters," he advised me. "She claims sixty-five kills."

General MacKenzie had charmed journalists but was having a tougher time with the residents of Sarajevo. They despised him. I was baffled. How could a straight-talking U.N. general be so hated by the city he saved from starvation? The people of Sarajevo had been delighted when MacKenzie and his Canadian troops rolled into

town with more firepower than they could dream of possessing, and
they threw flowers in his path and figured, Great, the knight in shining armor has arrived. It was a mirage. MacKenzie's job was to open
the airport and start an airlift of food. He was there to feed people,
not help them fight. From the Bosnian viewpoint, this was hypocrisy.
What, they asked, was the point in feeding us but not protecting us?
So we can die on a full stomach? There was truth to this; the main
humanitarian problem for Sarajevo was not a lack of decent food
but a surplus of incoming shells.

"When people give you the finger walking down the street, I guess
you could say relations are not exactly ideal," MacKenzie said with
a shrug. "Nobody is saying thank you."

His good times in Sarajevo were coming to an end as we talked.
Death threats trickled into his office by phone and fax, his troops
came under hostile fire from all sides, and General MacKenzie had
just made the mistake of lashing out at the only side whose behavior
he had any hope of influencing—the Bosnians. They were the weakest ones. Without knowing it, he set in motion a pattern that the
United Nations would follow for the rest of the war. He wanted the
fighting to cease, which of course was laudable, but he wanted it to
cease at any price, which was not so laudable. Because the Serbs
couldn't be forced to accept a just peace, the Bosnians eventually
must accept an unjust one, and until the papers were drawn up, they
should stop fighting. But the Bosnians were not going along with it,
and so MacKenzie dropped his own bomb on them.

"We have evidence that both sides shell themselves in order to
create a particular image," he told journalists a few days before we
met. "I got so frustrated about this a month ago that I said to both
sides, 'If you'll stop shelling yourselves, maybe we'll have peace
around here.' "

It was a great quote, and it was zapped across the global village
in no time at all. It helped shape the world's impression of Bosnia
as a crazed place where all the people were nuts and all they wanted
to do was kill, kill, kill. At the time, journalists like myself treated
his bombing accusation as credible. If anybody could make sense
out of the mess, it was General Lewis MacKenzie, the voice of
sanity. After all, neither the rebel Serbs who were shelling Sarajevo
nor the hysterical Bosnians defending it seemed particularly well-
balanced. The Bosnians might be the underdogs, but most of their
frontline soldiers were crooks.

A key commander of Sarajevo's defense in the early days of the war was an underworld thug whose uniform consisted of little more than a sweat suit, Reebok tennis shoes and a bad attitude. Jusuf Prazina, known to his friends as Juka, had a narrow face, dirty black hair and an angular nose that looked like it had been twisted to Belgrade and back. A "debt collector" in peacetime, he swiftly evolved into a war rat, thriving in the murkiness of battle. Bosnia's government was not a criminal regime, but it did not have an army when it declared independence, so in desperation it gave the few weapons it had to the few people who knew how to use them— hoodlums like Juka.

MacKenzie, like any decent human being, had trouble dealing with Juka and his ragtag followers. We all did. Juka's men weren't the kind of soldiers who snapped to attention for the commander of U.N. forces, and they broke promises quite easily, like the bones of their prisoners. Patton would have arrested them, shaved their heads and thrown them into the cooler. On the other side of the front lines, Serb leaders might be war criminals in the making, but their names were preceded by words like "general" or "colonel" or "doctor," they showed up at meetings on time and they might have taken a shower in the preceding week. MacKenzie had an easier time dealing with the professional Serb soldiers who were besieging Sarajevo than the amateur Bosnian crooks who were defending it. He thought they were all nuts, which they were, but this is a minor part of the overall picture.

The Bosnian government hit the roof over MacKenzie's comment because, as he later admitted, it was directed at them. He suggested that the Bosnians themselves were responsible for the infamous "Breadline Massacre" of May 27, 1992, when at least twenty civilians died and dozens were wounded after an explosion in the middle of a Sarajevo breadline. The incident woke up the world with shocking television footage of pensioners cradling their shredded limbs and lying in pools of their own blood. The war was still young, but those scenes were as horrifying as anything else the West would see in the following years. Serbs accused the Bosnians of trying to provoke Western military intervention by planting a bomb and then blaming the blast on a Serb shell. MacKenzie backed them up with his comment.

General MacKenzie was booted out of Sarajevo a few days after my interview. He remained a media hero. When he returned to

North America, he hit the lecture circuit, going from *Nightline* to the National Press Club to the White House with a message that never changed—don't intervene in Bosnia, it's a quagmire, they're all madmen over there, the Bosnians are almost as bad as the Serbs. "Dealing with Bosnia is a little bit like dealing with three serial killers," he told the House Committee on Armed Services. "One has killed fifteen. One has killed ten. One has killed five. Do we help the one that has only killed five?" His opinion carried weight, as is understandable, because very few people had hands-on experience in Bosnia, and few spoke as forcefully or articulately as MacKenzie. He provided politicians with the alibi they sought. Even the U.N. general says the Bosnians commit atrocities. Look, they bomb their own people. They massacre Serbs. We'd be foolish to intervene. Those people are animals, all of them.

We learned much later that MacKenzie had gotten it wrong. Nobody has produced any credible evidence that links the Bosnian Army to killings of its people, least of all the Breadline Massacre. More than 10,000 civilians have been killed in Sarajevo since the war began, and the Serbs contend that almost all of these deaths were caused covertly by the Bosnian Army. When sixty-eight people were killed more than a year later by a shell in Sarajevo's main marketplace, the Serbs initially said the whole thing was faked, that the bodies we saw on television were blood-smeared dummies. When that excuse failed to impress, the Serbs said, Yes, perhaps a bombing took place, but the Bosnians did it. It was almost laughable. Even so, whenever a child was killed in Sarajevo the U.N. command was almost as likely to blame Bosnians as Serbs. It was the U.N.'s queer version of impartiality, and it was the legacy of General Lewis MacKenzie.

"When the Serbs kill me," Bosnian President Alija Izetbegović has said, "the U.N. will probably say I committed suicide."

MacKenzie was flat wrong about the math of war crimes, too. According to a comprehensive assessment by the Central Intelligence Agency, Serbs carried out 90 percent of the acts of ethnic cleansing in Bosnia. In a front-page article disclosing the CIA report, *The New York Times* noted that "the report makes nonsense of the view—now consistently put forward by Western European governments and intermittently by the Clinton administration—that the Bosnian conflict is a civil war for which guilt should be divided between Serbs, Croats and Muslims rather than a case of Serbian aggression." MacKenzie, whose area of command was confined to Sara-jevo, made the error of viewing Bosnia's capital as a microcosm of the entire country. In the war's first months, Sarajevo was a mis-leading sideshow, one of the few places where Serb rebels were held at bay by scrappy Bosnian fighters. Elsewhere, Serbs were cleansing and killing as a matter of policy rather than happenstance, racking up a huge lead in the atrocity sweepstakes. MacKenzie had a poor grasp of the scale of the carnage and he failed to understand that it amounted to a war of aggression orchestrated by a neighboring country—Serbia—against an essentially unarmed and unthreatening civilian population in Bosnia. It's a pity MacKenzie wasn't based in Višegrad.

MacKenzie's credibility has diminished since he made the rounds in Washington and published his memoirs. It turns out that his speaking tour in America was paid for, in part, by $15,000 from a pro-Serb lobbying group. When this fact was unearthed, MacKenzie blamed his agent for not paying enough attention to who was underwriting the speeches. The general can at least take comfort in the fact that he fared better than Juka, his nemesis. The famous hoodlum-turned-defender-of-Sarajevo was tossed out of town after the Bosnian government formed a real army. Juka joined a militia outside the capital, but that didn't go so well, and he was forced to leave the country altogether. He resurfaced in 1993 near a freeway in Belgium. He had been dead for two weeks when his body was found by hitchhikers. Two bullets were in the back of his head. The United Nations did not issue an opinion about whether he commit-ted suicide.

My tarmac interview with General MacKenzie came to a close. I jogged to a semi-obliterated hangar where U.N. soldiers and relief workers were hanging out. I wanted to talk with them, but before doing that, I wanted to go to the bathroom. A British soldier, lying on a cot, gave me directions to the john. "Go to the back of the hangar, through that door there, take a left, and it's the second door on the left side of the corridor. Don't go through the door on the right side of the corridor. There's sniper fire coming into that room." These were directions that I didn't want to get wrong, so I repeated them back to the soldier, who groaned, grabbed his assault rifle and said, "Okay, just follow me." It was the first time I had been es-corted to a toilet since I was a child.

I was learning one of the dirty truths of journalism—reporting on a war can be an adventure. For me, for a while, it was. The journalists who flocked to Bosnia were not watching a movie about a dramatic war, they were in it. Like film stars, it got to their heads. Press passes became fashion accessories, strung around the neck like pearls, the more the better. It had not yet gotten to my head, if only for the reason that I didn't know what was going on. These were my days of innocence, and my clothing was the first giveaway. In the early days of the war, bullet-proof vests were optional, and I was borrowing one from the Budapest police department. It was a lovely shade of baby blue, very light and fluffy, and it had a little tag on the inside that outlined the cleaning instructions (machine washing okay, don't tumble dry). U.N. soldiers laughed at it. The basic rule in the realm of flak jackets is that the heavier it is, the better it is. Mine weighed less than five pounds. The soldiers poked it and asked whether it was filled with straw. I became worried that it was.

As the war dragged on and became a deadly serious affair for journalists, the flak jackets got heavier. Within a few months of my maiden visit to Sarajevo, I had spent $1,500 of the *Washington Post*'s money on something called Body Armor, Level II, at a survivalist shop in a seedy part of London. The thing weighed twenty-five pounds, had an internal cushion of Kevlar, bullet-stopping ceramic plates in the front and back, a Kevlar collar to protect your neck and a flap that you pulled down from the waist to cover your groin. Its color was a menacing shade of dark blue. It was the real thing, and U.N. soldiers took me more seriously, but Bosnians still laughed, because they knew how many ways there are to die in a war, and that a few pounds of overpriced metal won't often make much difference.

I had planned to spend just a few hours at the airport to check out the relief operation, and at the end of the day I was relieved to hop aboard a plane heading back to Zagreb, Croatia. I saw and heard enough to convince myself, like General MacKenzie, that Sarajevo was a nuthouse, to hell with them all, they just want to kill one another. Maybe it was the French sentry at the airport perimeter who responded to a few explosions by grunting, nonchalantly, "RPG," military shorthand for rocket-propelled grenade. The explosions were good news, he said, because if the Serbs and Bosnians were busy bombing each other, they wouldn't bomb the U.N. forces.

Or maybe it was the frantic Greek television reporter, a tiny woman with frizzy black hair, encased in an oversized flak jacket, who rushed around the airport saying, "Have you seen my cameraman, have you, have you?" No, I hadn't, I told her on the first pass. Five minutes later, she was back again. "Have you seen my cameraman, have you, have you?" Or perhaps it was the odd wisdom of a Swedish soldier who had just finished a three-week tour in Sarajevo and was waiting for a flight out. His feet propped up on his duffel bag, he popped open a can of Tuborg in the hangar. "The scariest thing about this place is that you don't feel frightened," he said.

I filed his words of wisdom into the back of my mind. They would be useful when I returned to Sarajevo five months later, in the middle of a winter siege.

GROUND ZERO

M ILAN KOVAČEVIĆ wanted to pray. It was Sunday, he shouted, a goddamn holy day, and he wanted to go to church.

Kovačević weighed about 225 pounds and was built like a heavyweight boxer whose muscle was turning to fat but who could still send you flying to the other side of the Balkans with a single punch. He sat at the head of a table in a dingy room in a dingy municipal building in Prijedor, a town swept virtually clean of non-Serbs. Under a wary military escort, I arrived in town with a small group of journalists on a Sunday morning in August 1992, and our first duty was to meet Kovačević. We wanted to see his gulag.

He wouldn't hear of it. He cursed the military officer who escorted us to Prijedor from Banja Luka, forty miles away. Why the fuck were we so concerned about these camps? Why didn't we fucking investigate the murders of Serb babies? His forces needed "collection centers" to hold captured Muslim soldiers, Kovačević shouted. What was so unusual about that? A war was going on. And didn't we know that the Serbs were good friends of the Americans? When the war was completed and Bosnia under total Serb control, perhaps it could become the fifty-first American state! Kovačević was not joking. He wore a combat-colored T-shirt that had "U.S. Marines" emblazoned across the front and back. The guy loved America.

He was a real piece of work. An anesthesiologist by profession, Kovačević had a walrus mustache that, in other times, would lend him a look of grandfatherly charm, but these were times of war, and the gray mustache served as little more than a storage facility for the remnants of his breakfast toast. He was bursting with crudeness and chutzpah. You could love him and be repulsed by him at the same time, like a comic who belches onstage and draws waves of laughter. What could be more hilarious than the idea that a cleansed Bosnia might want to join not Serbia but the United States? But Kovačević was not doing funny things. His right hand was on intimate terms with the pistol strapped to his waist.

"This is a great moment in the history of the Serbian people," he chanted, priestlike.

Kovačević was a madman from birth, and I mean it literally. He was born in a World War II Croatian concentration camp, the notorious Jasenovac slaughterhouse where tens of thousands—perhaps hundreds of thousands—of Serbs, Jews and Gypsies met their end. Imagine the stories his mother told him as he grew up, assuming his mother survived Jasenovac. Kovačević would tell visitors in Prijedor that they should never forget where he came from, and this was one piece of advice that was both truthful and revealing. There was a certain vulgar justice to the fact that a man who was born in a concentration camp ended up ruling his own string of camps as an adult.

Evil has two faces. There is the banal face that Hannah Arendt wrote about in her classic book *Eichmann in Jerusalem*, which chronicled the life and trial of a senior Nazi official sentenced to death in Jerusalem for crimes against humanity. Arendt wrote that Adolf Eichmann was a dull man, neither intelligent nor venal, a bureaucrat whose hands were bloodied only by paper cuts. He personified the "banality of evil." If you want to pursue an evil policy, you need people like Eichmann. The leaders are a different breed. They are deranged geniuses, the vulgar face of evil, the Hitlers and Stalins, the ones who come up with final solutions. In Bosnia, they were the ones who resurrected the notion of ethnic cleansing and fired the first shots or committed the first rapes. In the disturbed universe of evil, they are the "brave" ones who shout the unspeakable and perform the undoable and snap everyone else into line.

The fact that Kovačević had a disturbed childhood was not a happenstance. This was not a reasonable war led by reasonable men.

If you take a close look at the well-educated politicians and generals who led ordinary Serbs into the war, you'll see that they have troubled histories. Look at Slobodan Milošević, the Serbian president. His father failed in the priesthood and committed suicide. His mother was a fervent Communist who committed suicide. Look at General Blagoje Adžić, the chief of staff of the Yugoslav National Army who plotted the war against Croatia. As a child in World War II, Adžić scampered into a tree when Croat Ustashe troops attacked his village, and he watched as his family was hacked to death. Look at General Ratko Mladić, the commander of Serb forces in Bosnia. His father was killed by the Ustashe in World War II, and his daughter committed suicide during the Bosnian war. Mladić invented a new military argot, including "clobber," "torch" and "beat them senseless," all of them orders that he shouted over military airwaves. Kovačević was in their class.

Before Kovačević got to work, Prijedor was the second largest city in northern Bosnia, with a population of 112,000 in which Muslims constituted a slim majority over Serbs and controlled the city council. Nationalist Serbs staged a nighttime coup against the elected Muslim authorities when the war started. There wasn't much fighting because the Serbs were well armed and the Muslims offered no resistance to speak of. They weren't prepared for war. Kovačević organized the takeover. His official title depended on the mood he was in when journalists came to visit. On the day I met him, Kovačević gave his title as "executive mayor." Other journalists had been told he was the "city manager" or "president of the municipal council." He was the warlord, and warlords can call themselves whatever they want.

After most of Prijedor's Muslim men were shipped to prison camps, the cleansing campaign focused on cracking a final nut called Kozarac, a town of 25,000 people, mostly Muslims, just six miles down the road. The cleansing of Kozarac turned into one of the most vicious campaigns of civilian slaughter in the entire war. Mary Battiata, my colleague from the *Washington Post*, wrote a lengthy investigative story about the cleansing of Kozarac, and I am drawing on her article for details about the town's virtual obliteration.

The shelling began on May 24 after Kozarac had been surrounded by Serb tanks. Up to fifteen shells hit the town every minute from twelve directions. After a few hours, the shelling stopped and the

Serbs used loudspeakers to tell the people of Kozarac that they would not be harmed if they left their basements and surrendered. The people complied, and almost as soon as the streets filled up with surrendering Muslims, the shelling resumed. It was a trick, and the street became littered with severed limbs and human gore. The survivors fled back to their basements or into the hills. After two days of continued bombardments, another order to surrender was issued, and the Muslims of Kozarac complied once more.

This time, the Serbs played a different trick. As Kozarac's beaten population filed down the main road toward the soccer stadium, one of the Serbs who lived in the town stood on a balcony and pointed out every important Muslim—the mayor, police chief, doctors, lawyers, judges, businessmen, even sports heroes. Most were shot on the spot by Serb soldiers or taken to a nearby house where their throats were slit. One man had his legs tied to a tank that dragged him through town. He was finished off when the tank ran over him. It was a scene out of *Schindler's List*, except this was no movie, and until Steven Spielberg makes a movie about it, few Americans will know, or believe, that it happened. This was eliticide, the systematic killing of a community's political and economic leadership so that the community could not regenerate. At least 2,500 civilians were killed in Kozarac in a seventy-two-hour period. It was a slaughterhouse. The survivors were sent to the prison camps I wanted to visit.

Kovačević continued to talk about going to church. Fine, we said, go to church, but please give us permission to visit your camps. If you have nothing to hide, then why not let us go there? It went on like this for nearly an hour. He got tired of it and finally assigned Prijedor's "police chief," Simo Drljača, to escort us to the three camps in the area—Keraterm, Trnopolje and Omarska. We would not be the first journalists to visit them. A handful of reporters had been there a few days earlier, so the world had been alerted, and Kovačević had begun cleaning up his gulag, washing away bloodstains, carting away bodies and body parts and closing down the worst camps. He could now afford to let us have a sanitized glimpse of his camps. I was almost glad for this, because the Potemkinized tour was chilling enough; the real thing would have been devastating.

Drljača, our tour guide, was the second most unsavory character in Prijedor. Over six feet tall and dressed in all-black combat fatigues, Drljača had the obligatory pistol at his waist and a bad poker player's instinct for deception. Why do you want to go to Keraterm, he inquired? It's just a factory, nothing's there. Yes, some prisoners were held there, but that was just for a couple of days, and the last ones left more than a month ago. Fine, we said, but please take us there anyway. He shrugged his shoulders and we drove in a convoy to the Keraterm ceramics factory on the outskirts of town. Word had leaked out that some of the worst atrocities had been committed there. Bosnians were locked into storage rooms without food, water or fresh air, and many died from thirst as they lay in a stinking mixture of their excrement and urine. When they cried out for help, guards fired shots through the doors; prisoners taken out of the storage rooms usually ended up tortured to death.

Our van pulled into the factory grounds. It was deserted, not a soul in sight. Drljača led the way into a building and said it had been used to hold prisoners for a few days in the month of June. "See, no blood," he smiled. We were given five minutes to wander around. The building was the size of a football field and housed the main furnace in which ceramic goods were baked into hardened form. The area around the furnace was empty, covered by a thin layer of white dust. There was not a human smudge mark on the floor or any of the walls. There wasn't as much as a discarded shoelace. It had no smell, not even a hint of sweat or antiseptic. It was much too clean. Prisoners had never been held in the building. The ruse had begun.

Drljača led the way out of the building and told us to get back into the van. We asked to visit a brick warehouse that was less than fifty yards away. It was, of course, the building where prisoners had been held and tortured—and evacuated from a day before we arrived, as we learned later. No, he said, you cannot go there, it is a military facility. There was not a soldier or piece of military hardware in sight. A television cameraman swung his lens toward the building, and one of Drljača's men jumped in the way. No filming of the building, the soldier shouted. Drljača smiled again. Time to leave, he said. We followed his orders. We were his guests, and if we got out of line, we might become his prisoners. Simple.

We drove into the countryside and within fifteen minutes arrived at a former elementary school that had an English-language banner draped over its entrance: "Trnopolje Open Reception Center." When the first journalists had arrived there a few days earlier, barbed wire surrounded the place and there was no welcoming banner. But Trnopolje had changed only superficially since then; it was fundamentally the same place. A few thousand Bosnians were penned in, not by barbed wire but by the roaming presence of armed guards and the knowledge that they had nowhere to flee to. The entire countryside was in the hands of Serbs, so the inmates could not run, they could not hide, they could only stay put and hope for deliverance.

I never thought that one day I would talk to a skeleton. That's what I did at Trnopolje. I walked through the gates and couldn't quite believe what I saw. There, right in front of me, were men who looked like survivors of Auschwitz. I remember thinking that they walked surprisingly well for people without muscle or flesh. I was surprised at the mere fact that they could still talk. Imagine, talking skeletons! As I spoke to one of them, I looked at his arm and realized that I could grab hold of it and snap it into two pieces like a brittle twig. I could do the same with his legs. I saw dozens of other walking skeletons of that sort. I could break all of their arms, all of their legs. Snap. Snap. Snap.

I have visited America many times since my reporting in Bosnia, and I often faced the same question: Did you visit those camps? Were they really so bad? I still find it hard to believe that Americans and West Europeans are confused about Bosnia and, in particular, confused about the camps. Yes, I visited them, and yes, they were as bad as you could imagine. Didn't you see the images on television? Don't you believe what you see? Do you give any credence to the word of Radovan Karadžić, the Bosnian Serb leader, who said the pictures were fakes? Chico Marx had a great line in *Duck Soup* as he tried to fool an unsuspecting woman (Margaret Dumont) into believing a preposterous put-on: "Well, who you gonna believe, me or your own eyes?" It was like that with Karadžić and the camps.

Trnopolje was the repository for men who had been released from the hard-core concentration camps of Omarska and Keraterm. That's where the skeletons came from. Also, women and children who had been cleansed from nearby villages came to Trnopolje voluntarily. Yes, voluntarily. It was one of the strangest situations in Bosnia—people seeking safety at a prison camp. Trnopolje was no picnic, but the known brutalities dished out there were preferable to the fates awaiting Bosnians who tried to stay in their homes. Women might be raped at Trnopolje but probably not gang-raped. They might be beaten but probably not killed. Ironically, the first television images that shocked the world came from Trnopolje, the "best" camp. No one ever saw the worst camps when they were at their worst.

The luckiest prisoners at Trnopolje had found a spot on the floor in the school building, which stank of urine and unwashed humanity. You could not walk inside without tripping over someone. The less fortunate inmates lived outside, baking in the August sun and shivering in the cool nights. Their latrine was an outhouse over a ditch; people camped out within a few feet of it. Drljača gave us 15 minutes to wander around, and technically speaking, we were free to talk with whomever we wished. But guards with Kalashnikov assault rifles and Ray-Ban sunglasses sauntered through the grounds, and I could talk for no more than a minute or so before one of them would creep up behind me and start listening to the conversation. A few guards had slung their rifles across their backs and started snapping pictures of us as we talked with prisoners. They were not subtle; they were in charge, and they wanted us to know it. If there's one thing that all bullies have in common, it's the fact that they want you to know they are bullies. One skeletal prisoner had just enough time to unbutton his shirt, showing off a mutilated chest with a few dozen fresh scars from God-knows-what torture, before a look of horror came over his face. He was staring, like a deer caught in a car's headlights, at a spot just above the top of my head. I looked around. A guard stood behind me.

I walked on. A prisoner tugged at my sleeve. *Follow me.* I followed, trying to pretend as though I wasn't following. He led me to the side of the school building and, after glancing around, darted through a door. I followed. Where was he taking me? Why? I feared not only the trouble that I might be getting into, but the trouble that he might be getting into. The door closed behind me. The room was small, dark. My eyes took a moment to adjust. People were whispering beside me. I looked at the floor. Two bodies on the ground. Corpses? Not yet. I was in the infirmary, the sorriest infirmary you could imagine. No medicine, no beds. I was not supposed to be there.

The doctor, also a prisoner, motioned for me to crouch down so that guards could not see me through the window. He began peeling off a filthy bandage from the leg of one of the two men. Puss oozed out. The man had an infected hole the size of a baseball just under his knee. A bone-crushing blow from a rifle butt. In a few days, the leg would turn gangrenous, and the man would die. The doctor whispered his explanations to Vlatka, my interpreter, who whispered them to me. I handed my notebook and pen to her. Ask the questions, write down the answers, I told her, we don't have time for translation. Vlatka had worked for me and other journalists long enough to know the right questions. She was the best.

I looked at the other body, barely alive. The man seemed to be in his late thirties or early forties. It was hard to tell. His face was cut and bruised, colored black and red, and swollen, as though I was looking at the kind of grossly expanded reflection you get from a trick mirror at a circus. I looked at his naked torso—more bruises, more swelling, more open wounds. He didn't move, and I doubted that he was still alive. I didn't need to ask questions about what had happened to this poor man, or what was going to happen to him. His agony would be over soon, for if his wounds didn't finish him off in the next twenty-four hours, then the guards would. As I learned later, guards routinely killed prisoners who could not recover quickly from the beatings. Prisoners who could neither talk nor walk were of no use.

We slipped out after a few minutes, Vlatka first, me a few seconds later. An eighteen-year-old youth came up to us. He had just arrived at Trnopolje after two months at Omarska, the worst camp of all. His skin was stretched like a transparent scarf over his ribs and shoulder bones. "It was horrible," he whispered. "Just look at me. For beatings, the guards used hands, bars, whips, belts, chains, anything. A normal person cannot imagine the methods they used. I am sorry to say that it was good when new prisoners came. The guards beat them instead of us."

I slipped into his hand a sandwich from my shoulder bag. It was a ham sandwich.

"I'm sorry, it's all I have," I said. "Will you eat it?"

He stared at me, as though I was a naked fool. Of course he would eat it. It was food. Allah would look the other way as he devoured the forbidden pork.

I approached another skeleton, this one too afraid to talk, turning away after whispering a single word, "Dachau."

It was time to go. The guards started rounding up the journalists. We boarded the van. There were about six of us: a reporter and camera crew from an American television network, a reporter from *Newsweek*, myself, a French photographer. We were staying at the same hotel in Banja Luka and, thrown into a hard situation together, we had quickly become friends, chatting all the time. But the van was silent as we pulled away from Trnopolje. We were thinking the same thing. "Fucking hell, I can't believe this."

I forget my parting words as I broke off my conversation with the last prisoner. What do you say in a situation like that? See you later? Good luck? You are leaving the condemned, the half-dead, and the fact that you spoke to them probably puts them into greater peril than they already were. You had a good breakfast that morning, a couple of eggs, some toast, lots of jam. He had half a slice of stale bread, if he was lucky. Your money belt contains five thousand dollars, and there is always more where it came from. He has nothing. You have an American passport that allows you to walk into the camp and walk out unmolested. He has no passport, only two eyes that watch you perform this miracle of getting out alive. You have a home somewhere that has not been dynamited. You have a girlfriend who has not been raped. You have a father who has not been killed in front of your eyes.

Whenever I returned to a normal place after an assignment in Bosnia friends would ask me what it was like to suddenly leave a war zone and then be in a place where bombs are not falling. I would say that it was no big deal, which was the truth. Going from Sarajevo to London in a day is a piece of cake in psychological terms. I would feel relief, splendid relief. It didn't compare to the experience of mixing with death camp inmates and then walking away, a free man with a future. The misery of Bosnia is not half a world away at places like a prison camp; it is staring right at you, less than a foot away, watching you as you get into a van and drive away, and it notices that you don't look back.

The next stop was Omarska. I was to have the privilege, if you can call it that, of meeting some of the worst torturers of the twentieth century.

During its heyday, Omarska was ground zero of atrocities. The existence of the camp and of the horrors there had become known a few days before we arrived. As a result, the Serbs had begun playing a shell game: most prisoners were shipped off to other locations or executed, the camp was cleaned up, food rations were improved for those left behind, and then foreign journalists were ushered in. When we pulled up to the camp gates, no more than 250 prisoners remained of the thousands who had been there, and those on display were recent arrivals, not yet emaciated or bloodied. They were kept there for the benefit of journalists like myself, so that we would report to the outside world that the camp was small and conditions tolerable. Omarska was a changed place, and it was going out of business, but one thing was unaltered, the terror in the prisoners' eyes. They had plenty of reason to be afraid.

Every imaginable degradation had been played out at Omarska during the previous months. It was not a death camp on the order of Auschwitz. There was no gas chamber to which the prisoners were marched off every day. What happened at Omarska was dirtier, messier. The death toll never approached Nazi levels but the brutality was comparable or, in some cases, superior, if that word can be used. The Nazis were interested in killing as many Jews as possible, and doing it as quickly as possible. The Serbs, however, wanted to interrogate their Bosnian prisoners, have sadistic fun by torturing them in the cruelest of ways and then kill them with whatever implement was most convenient, perhaps a gun, perhaps a knife or scissors, perhaps a pair of strong hands wrapped around an emaciated neck. If the Germans had used the same approach, they would have needed decades to kill 6 million Jews.

Omarska was an abandoned mining compound. The prisoners were kept primarily in two places—an open pit mine and a huge storage shed. Many interrogations ended with execution in a building the prisoners called the "White House," and there was another building, known as the "Red House," where, in addition to more executions taking place, the torn corpses were kept until being buried outside Omarska or thrown down a disused mine shaft. Between twenty-five and fifty people were killed on a daily basis. Some prisoners never made it as far as the White or Red Houses, dying of thirst or starvation or asphyxiation (because they were crowded so tightly) while awaiting their formal torture, or dying when they made the mistake of asking a guard for water and received a bullet

in the head instead. In a way, they were the lucky ones for whom
death came quickly and painlessly.

Our van halted on a strip of asphalt next to the White House. A
group of about fifty prisoners were washing themselves at an open
spigot at a side of the building. They were surrounded by guards
with sub-machine guns. It is a neutral term, "guards," and it implies
a certain amount of discipline, a sense that the camp had rules, and
that these men whom we call "guards" enforced the rules. Nothing
could be further from the truth. There were no rules at Omarska
except for one: the guards were omnipotent. It might be accurate
therefore to refer to them as gods rather than guards. They could
kill as they please, pardon as they please, rape as they please. Their
subjects, the prisoners, prayed to them for forgiveness, for a favor,
for life.

We were marched into the building and up a dark stairwell to the
second floor. Into that room, Drljača told us, motioning toward a
door at the end of the hallway. We went. It was a stuffy office, with
stacks of papers in the corners, a few books in a shelf, a table, chairs,
a desk. A calendar hung behind the desk. It showed a half-nude
woman who had a pair of huge breasts. The camp's "chief investigator" was sitting behind the desk. I had brought an instamatic
camera on this trip, an idiot-proof apparatus, and during the half
hour that the "chief investigator" talked to us, I tried to line up a
picture that would show him and the nude girl in the background.
The interview was a piece of obscenity, so what could be better than
a visual touch of obscenity to go with it?

The session was forgettable, and so I have forgotten much of it,
even the face of the "chief investigator." That sounds strange, because it's not often that you get to question a man who, in all probability, spent the previous months overseeing a frenzy of cruelty.
Imagine, how could an interview with Dr. Josef Mengele be forgettable? But this man, like dozens of other war criminals whom I
interviewed during my time in Bosnia, was not going to pour his
heart out to us. Of course not. He said the prisoners were interro-
gated to learn what role they played in the "Islamic insurrection,"
and that they were released if the investigators decided they played
no role. The ones who were involved in the fabled insurrection were
transferred to "other facilities" for trial. Torture? He laughed. Of
course not.

"Interrogation is being done in the same way as it is done in America and England," he said.

I looked up from my notebook. The nude girl in the calendar was smiling.

What I find most remarkable about the session is that I cannot recall the chief investigator's face. It is a total blank, gone from my memory, or sealed in a corner I cannot reach, no matter how long and hard I think about Omarska, no matter how firmly I close my eyes and try to recall. It is as though my subconscious is playing a trick on me, perhaps trying to send me a message, that the man's identity is not important, he is just another human being, faceless, he is you, he is my friend, he is me.

It was show time. We were led downstairs to the cafeteria, a small one of the institutional, stainless steel variety. Bean soup was being served. Inmates were shepherded into the room in groups of two dozen, heads bent down in supplication, shuffling one after another, hunched over. They knew the drill. After getting their lunchtime soup and piece of bread—the only meal of the day—they shuffled to the few tables and spooned the muck into their mouths as quickly as possible. They had about a minute or two before one of the guards said a word and they jumped out of their chairs, shuffling to the exit and handing their bowls and spoons to the next group. There was none of the dawdling or yawning that you would see at normal prisons. There was only fear and power, awesome power.

We were allowed to meander around the room and ask questions. It was another act of humiliation for the prisoners and, this time, for the journalists, too. Perhaps that's why it was done. The guards were never more than a few feet away, and there was no outdoor breeze to carry a prisoner's words out of snooping range. It was the sort of room in which the scraping of a spoon against a bowl was heard by everyone. Words bounced off the walls like those tiny, transparent "super balls" that I played with as a child. I bent over to a few prisoners and asked questions, but I never got a real response. They bowed their heads farther down, noses virtually in the bowls. This was a place where words, any words, could kill them.

"Please, don't ask me questions," one of them begged in a whisper.

I was playing the game according to the rules of the jailers. The visit of journalists was just another form of torture. I tried to turn the tables a bit, to interview one of the guards. I settled on a massive oaf who, like the other guards, was in need of a shave. His height seemed somewhere between six and seven feet. Dressed in a dark combat outfit, he had the physique of a steroid-pumped linebacker and was packing enough weapons to arm a platoon: a pistol on either hip, a compact AK-47 assault rifle hanging by a strap from his right shoulder and a foot-long bowie knife dangling from his belt. His hands were covered to the knuckles by black leather gloves. He wore reflector sunglasses. We were indoors.

I tipped my head toward the skies and tried to soften him up. The only thing we seemed to have in common is that we were sweating a lot.

"Hot in here, isn't it?" I suggested. He peered down at me for a second or two. He didn't respond. I tried again.

"How long have you worked here?" No response. The interview was going nowhere. Vlatka gave me a look that said, *Forget about it.* I gave it one last try.

"Is it true that you torture the prisoners?"

I had gotten his attention. He glanced down at me, and his lips arched into the kind of thin smile that fails to make you smile in return.

"Why would we want to beat them?" he said.

The show continued. We were led to a dormitory room filled with about forty bunk beds. It wasn't such a bad place, but of course it was created for our benefit. Until a few days earlier, the prisoners had been sleeping on the hard ground in an adjacent shed. A guard shadowed me all the time, so trying to talk to the prisoners was more fruitless than ever. I slipped my notebook and a pack of cigarettes to Vlatka and told her that I was going outside and hopefully the guard would follow me. As I headed for the exit, I passed the television crew. The reporter was interviewing a feverish inmate lying on a bunk bed. The television light was shining right on the poor guy, and several guards were hovering around the bed. The inmate was shaking, his blankets moving up and down under the furious heavings of his chest. "Are you being treated well?" the reporter asked. The prisoner's look of terror tightened a few notches more, and he glanced at one of the guards, not knowing how to respond. Obviously he could not speak honestly, but the guard might get mad if he was too fulsome in his praise. The truth would kill, and even the wrong lie would kill.

"*Dobro, dobro,*" he gasped. Good, good.

I left the room, feeling sad for the prisoner and angry at the TV crew, which seemed to have crossed a boundary by getting involved in this game. It was a sort of Russian roulette. Five empty chambers in the gun, one filled with a bullet. The reporter was handing the gun to the prisoner when he turned the camera on. *Speak*, the reporter asked. *Pull the trigger.* The prisoner was safe while we were around but what happens when we leave and the guards no longer need to put on a show? I suppose that my anger at the television guys was compounded by the fact that I had been doing much the same thing, although at least I didn't need to ask my victims to speak up because the sound level was too low. What were journalists supposed to do? Not go to the camps? Not try to talk to the prisoners? The answer might be this: Talk to the ones who are willing to talk, but for God's sake, when a prisoner is shaking in his bed, turn the camera off.

I didn't linger when Drljača, our tour guide, gave the signal to leave. We got into the van and headed out of the camp. We pulled into a coffee shop at the entrance because Drljača wanted to have a beer with us. We filed inside, and a few tables were lined up so that we could all sit together, like friends. Each of us was given a bottle of beer, and Drljača made a toast to peace, so we made toasts to peace. I was sitting next to him, and we got into some small talk. I asked what he thought of our escort from Banja Luka, the military officer whom Kovačević had cursed earlier.

"Oh, that guy," Drljača smiled. "After the war's finished, we'll take care of assholes like him."

The beers were nearly empty and Drljača loosened up. He wanted us to have a snack together. I was all for it, because there's nothing more talkative than a Serb after a few drinks. The television crew wanted to leave because they needed to race back to Banja Luka and then to Belgrade that evening in order to transmit their story about the camps, so it was time to go. Drljača walked us outside and stood at the side of the van to bid us each farewell. I shook his hand and thanked him for his time. I would have liked to say more, but there's only so much a prudent person should say in a situation like that. The French photographer who boarded the van behind me was accustomed to living closer to the edge. Snappers are genetically reckless. He thanked Drljača robustly and, turning away to board the van, added softly into the wind, "I hope you die in hell."

▶ *Two*

THE WHOLE TRUTH emerged as journalists and diplomats talked to Bosnians who had gotten out of the camps and reached safety in Croatia, where they could speak freely. I interviewed several dozen survivors in Croatia and read the written testimony of scores of others. The best overall picture was drawn, belatedly, by the State Department, with far greater resources than any single journalist, in a series of reports sent to the United Nations Security Council. The reports amount to a catalogue of the unimaginable and the unbearable. One of the most chilling passages is in an October 22, 1992, report under the heading of "Abuse of Civilians in Detention Centers." This is how it summarizes the experience of one ex-prisoner from Omarska:

"The witness stated that a young Muslim man from Kozarac who had owned a Suzuki motorcycle was tortured in front of the other prisoners. He was severely beaten all over his body and his teeth were knocked out. The guards then tied one end of a wire tightly around his testicles and tied the other end to the victim's motorcycle. A guard got on the motorcycle and sped off."

Do you believe that Europeans did this at the end of the twentieth century? Excuse me, the question should be rephrased. Europeans, as Bosnia reminds us, do not have an inside track on virtue. Ugandans, Europeans, Cambodians—there is no difference in the cruelty sweepstakes, it is a dead heat. Here's the question again: Do you believe humans can do this at the end of the twentieth century? I find it hard to believe that a man can get on a motorcycle and ride off with another man's testicles attached to the tailpipe. Yet the testimony from camp survivors is consistent. It gnaws away at me.

One survivor, Emin Jakubović, told journalists he was ordered by his Omarska jailers to castrate three prisoners. "They forced me to tear off their testicles, with my teeth, so I tore off their testicles with my teeth. They were screaming with pain." Impossible? At a refugee center in Croatia, I interviewed a man who said he witnessed the episode. It was wintertime, and we were sitting in a bare, unheated room littered with cigarette butts and trampled-on newspapers. My overcoat was buttoned up against the cold, and the ink in my pen was freezing up, as was my right hand, which became too stiff to write legibly. I had been interviewing prison survivors for several hours, and I was tired, fed up with it all. I looked at the man, whose name was Ibrahim, still half-emaciated from his ordeal, and shook my head. Even though I had heard of such things before, I could not believe it. No, I told him, I do not believe your story. *I do not believe it.* Even among torturers, there is a line beyond which they do not go, such as castration. I asked Ibrahim, Would you believe someone who said the things you have just said? He stared back at me.

"I know," he replied. "I wouldn't believe it unless I had seen it."

On February 13, 1995, in its first batch of indictments, the United Nations War Crimes Tribunal issued international arrest warrants for twenty-one Serbs on charges of committing war crimes and crimes against humanity. The indicted men included Dušan Tadić, who, according to the tribunal, forced a Muslim prisoner to bite off the testicles of another prisoner.

Bosnia makes you question basic assumptions about humanity, and one of the questions concerns torture. Why, after all, should there be any limit? For a person capable of torture, no form of it is out of bounds. The big moral leap backward has already been taken once the door marked Torture has been opened and the first cut made in the prisoner's skin, or the first butt-blow landed to the prisoner's face. Suddenly, the torturer realizes that he, or she, has entered a new universe of sadistic pleasures. The wild beast has been set free and taken up residence in his soul. What's the moral difference between slitting a man's throat or slicing off his balls? Please tell me, anyone. There is none. If you have the stomach to crush a man's head under your boots, then you probably have the stomach to cut off a woman's breasts. Will God treat you better because you killed but refrained from mutilating? No. You can do as you please and you have nothing to fear. You have entered a world that would sicken Edgar Allan Poe.

You can, for example, barge into a house and put a gun to a father's head and tell him that you will pull the trigger unless he rapes his daughter or at least simulates the rape. (I heard of such things in Bosnia.) The father will refuse and say, I will die before doing that. You shrug your shoulders and reply, Okay, old man, I won't shoot you, but I will shoot your daughter. What does the father do now, dear reader? He pleads, he begs, but then you, the man with the gun, put the gun to the daughter's head, you pull back the hammer, and you shout, *Now! Do it! Or I shoot!* The father starts weeping, yet slowly he unties his belt, moving like a dazed zombie, he can't believe what he must do. You laugh and say, That's right, old man, pull down those pants, pull up your daughter's dress, *and do it!*

You are the law, and you feel divine.

Prison survivors describe an odd enthusiasm on the part of their torturers, who laughed, sang and got drunk while inflicting their crimes. They weren't just doing a job, they were doing something they enjoyed. They felt liberated. They could smash every crystal glass in the shop and break every taboo in the book, and no law could touch these men. The only prying eyes belonged to foreign journalists, and we could be kept away from hot spots and lied to. Torture became entertainment. For kicks, guards even made prisoners assault one another.

"After beating us for a while one night, the guards got tired," Ibrahim told me. "They decided it would be a good idea to have the prisoners fight each other. A guard singled out me and another prisoner. He told the other prisoner to stand still and he told me to punch the prisoner as hard as possible in the face. I did it. But the guard said I wasn't doing it hard enough, and so he hit me in the back of my head with the butt of his gun. He kept hitting me until I was covered in blood. And then he took another prisoner out of the line and told him to hit me."

It was gladiator time. For the next two hours, the guards at Omarska ordered scores of prisoners to fight each other. It amused them no end, except when they spotted a prisoner pulling a punch, and then a guard would hit the laggard with a rifle butt. They drew particular pleasure from having members of the same family beat each other. Brothers would be ordered to hit each other. Hard. I talked to an American diplomat who debriefed prisoners freed from Omarska. "It was often a plaything between the guards," she said. "It was like [the] Roman Colosseum. You have to hit the other guy as hard as you can if you want to stay alive. If you don't hit hard enough, then you get shot."

The guards even opened the camp gates and allowed their friends to share in the fun. Civilians came from the outside and would spend a night beating or killing or raping. What's extraordinary is the reasons these Serbs entered the gates of hell for a night of twisted pleasure. They wanted to settle old scores. Survivors told me of hiding behind the backs of other prisoners when Serbs they knew suddenly showed up on the camp grounds. A poor Serb might search for the wealthy Muslim who refused to give him a job five years earlier; a farmer might try to find the Croat who, a decade before, refused to lend his tractor for a day; a middle-aged man might look around for the Muslim who, twenty-five years ago, stole away his high school sweetheart. Petty quarrels were settled with major crimes.

It sounds unbelievable, yet it happened. It makes me wonder what would happen if half the population of Peoria were put into a prison camp, and the other half was told it could go into the camp and do whatever it wanted to whomever it wanted, and that no punishment need be feared, because any violent or sexual act committed against a prisoner would be an act of patriotism. It is an official invitation for the wild beast to come out from its hiding place. How many citizens of Peoria would yield to the temptation? How many would resist?

The thousands of pages pumped out by the U.S. Government Printing Office on behalf of the State Department are a valuable addition to the annals of human sadism. A passage in one report outlines the fate of a high school girl from Kozarac who was interned at Trnopolje:

> Three days after her arrival at the prison, she went with a large number of women and other girls to fetch water from a well about 50 meters from the prison gates. Returning from the well, Trnopolje guards held back six girls, including the witness, and stopped them from reentering the prison gates. They were then joined by four more female prisoners. The guards took the 10 girls to a house across the meadow. They were taken to the side yard of the house, out of sight of the roadway. Thirty Serbian soldiers—including "some dressed like a tank crew"—were there and they taunted the girls, calling them "Turkish whores." The girls were ordered to undress or have their clothes pulled off. Three girls resisted or hesitated from their fear. Their clothes were cut off with knives.
>
> The Serbian soldiers told the naked girls to parade slowly in a circle. The men sat at the outside of the circle—smoking, drinking, calling out foul names. The witness estimates the "parade" lasted about 15 minutes.

Three soldiers took one girl—one to rape her while the two others held her down. The three men took turns. A soldier approached the witness and mocked her, saying he had seen her before. Though she did not recognize him, he pulled out a photo of the witness with her 19-year-old Muslim boyfriend, whom he cursed for being in the Bosnian Territorial Defense Forces. The man with the photograph raped her first. The witness said she fought and pulled his hair, but he bit her and hit her face. Her lips bled. He hit her hard with the butt of his gun on her cheek, causing extreme pain. Another rapist ran the blade of a knife across her breasts as if to slice the skin off, leaving bleeding scratches. After that, she was raped by eight more men before losing consciousness.

The reports become pornographic. It is the sort of pornography that repulses most people, but some are titillated by it. For a while, everyone in America and Western Europe was fascinated by it, for whatever reasons. The misery of Bosnia, it must be said, sold well in the summer and fall of 1992. Interest gradually tailed off, not because the atrocities were declining, but because America was growing tired of hearing about them. Even snuff films get boring after a while.

▶ *Three*

IT WAS DIFFICULT to listen to scores of hours of tales from the camps and be unaffected by it. My initial impulse was to be filled with anger and hatred against the Serbs. It's only natural. But then, as I listened closely to a Bosnian man crying as he described what hell was like, I heard him say that Serbs helped him; while one of his Serb neighbors was kicking him in the face with army boots, another Serb neighbor stepped in and demanded that the assault stop. Or a Bosnian would explain that after being thrown into a prison camp, one of the Serb guards whom he knew secretly supplied him with food and got word out to his family that he was alive. You hear about acts of decency, such as Serb soldiers who were ordered to rape girls and, after taking the girls away, did not touch them but told them to say they had been raped.

It is wrong to retreat into a blind rage against the Serbs. Few were camp guards, fewer still were torturers. Most were lemmings, a common affliction in all societies, and a handful were even heroes. Serbs are, like all humans, deeply flawed, and their actions in Bosnia are a reminder of that. It would be wrong to conclude that they are more flawed than anyone else. These years of war just happened to be the time when the wild beast that Andrić wrote about leapt from its hiding place in the grass and seized them by the throat. The Serbs do not have a monopoly on moral insanity. It is humans who have failed, once more.

Consider the following atrocity. In February 1993, a three-year-old Muslim boy was seized by two Serbs who proceeded to (1) strip him from the waist down, (2) batter him senseless with an iron bar and bricks, (3) stomp on his face with their boots, (4) place his dying body in the path of an oncoming train, which duly sliced the toddler in half. It is a shocking tale. I have misrepresented it slightly, because the three-year-old was not Muslim but British, and he was murdered in Liverpool. The murderers were British, and their ages were ten and eleven. Boys. All the other details of tiny James Bulger's murder are represented accurately—the iron bars, bricks, face-stompings and the denouement under the wheels of a British commuter train.

The telling of the My Lai story from Vietnam sounds like any of the village massacres that occurred in Bosnia. On March 16, 1968, American helicopters airlifted troops under the command of Lieutenant William L. Calley Jr. into the Quang Ngai province of South Vietnam, an area that had seen heavy fighting throughout the war. Lieutenant Calley's C Company entered the My Lai hamlet and shot everything that moved. Sadly, the things that moved were civilians, mostly women, children and old men. More than 300 were killed at My Lai, some thrown into ditches, screaming and crying, and then shot by young Americans who had grown up in places like Milwaukee, Dubuque and Fresno. Although My Lai got all the attention, another massacre was carried out at the same moment by a sister unit, B Company, in the adjacent hamlet of My Khe. It would be naïve to think that those were the only massacres involving American GI's.

Of all the soldiers brought up for court-martial, only Lieutenant Calley was convicted of murder. The other soldiers who were in My Lai, the colonels in Saigon who condoned the massacres, the generals in Washington who wanted to cover it up—they were untouched. America had a hard time digesting the fact that "our boys" were using their bayonets to slay women and children. Lieutenant

Calley got a twenty-year prison term, and America began the process of forgetting. Is it behind us? Somalia, Iraq, Panama, Grenada—they were short, clinical campaigns. What would happen if our boys are led back into a jungle to fight a hot war for more than a few months?

An answer of sorts came in 1982, when the British Army fought a brief war to liberate the Falkland Islands, a British possession off the coast of Argentina that had been invaded by Argentine troops. A British military flotilla steamed halfway around the planet to liberate the distant islands, a gallant mission that was accomplished in days. There was some fierce fighting, especially on June 11 and 12 at a place called Mount Longdon, where twenty-three British soldiers were killed. Afterward, a British soldier who served in the Falklands wrote a book in which he accused fellow soldiers of executing Argentineans who surrendered at Mount Longdon and cutting off their ears for war trophies. His commander later confirmed the account.

It doesn't sound very British. Thousands of British troops served in Bosnia to help deliver humanitarian aid. They were disciplined and well led, to the extent that on one occasion, when a British soldier agreed to provide me with twenty liters of gas for my jeep, he insisted that I sign a receipt so that the British Army could send a bill to the *Washington Post*. We were near the front line, listening to the sound of artillery with our knees deep in battlefield mud, and I suggested that he accept cash on the spot and dispense with the paperwork. "That's not the way we do it in the British Army," he said neatly. You had to be impressed, and slightly amused, by discipline like that. It works fairly well when troops are playing a neutral role under the U.N. flag, but it doesn't hold up very well in the heat of battle.

Elvin Kyle Brown, a private in the Canadian Army, wasn't in the heat of battle when he served in Somalia as part of the U.N. peacekeeping force. He was there to help Somalis stay alive. But after detaining a sixteen-year-old boy for allegedly trying to steal food from a warehouse, Private Brown and several other Canadian soldiers handed out an unusual punishment. The boy was kicked in the face and chest, beaten senseless with truncheons, and the soles of his feet were burned with a cigar. Soldiers posed for trophy pictures, one of which showed a truncheon stuck into the boy's bleeding mouth, while another showed one of the Canadians holding a cocked pistol to the boy's head. After three hours, the boy was dead.

Private Brown was sent home, court-martialed for torture and manslaughter and given a five-year prison term. (He was paroled after less than two years.) His commander got a ninety-day sentence for telling soldiers that they could do what they wanted with their captive, and advising them to beat the boy with a phone book, because it would not leave any marks. At least half a dozen Canadian soldiers, including some officers, heard the beatings and the boy's screams—"Canada . . . Canada . . . Canada"—but did nothing. The boy's family later got one hundred camels as compensation. Canada is still trying to figure out what went wrong, and why.

▶ *Four*

AS REPORTS of death camps trundled into American living rooms, the White House faced a dilemma. The election was a few months away, and candidate Bill Clinton was hammering away at President George Bush for ignoring the needs of ordinary Americans. President Bush would win few votes for talking about the need to protect Bosnians whose names were difficult to pronounce; he might even lose votes. For him, getting reelected was far more important than stopping the war. This raised a problem: How does the world's superpower ignore genocide in Europe?

In a marvelous confession, George Kenney spilled the beans: "The Bush administration pronouncements on the Yugoslav crisis between February and August exhibited the worst sort of hypocrisy. I know; I wrote them. For seven months, in addition to other duties, I was responsible for drafting most public statements on the crisis in Bosnia from the State Department's Yugoslavia desk in Washington. My job was to make it appear as though the U.S. was active and concerned about the situation and, at the same time, give no one the impression that the U.S. was actually going to do something significant about it. . . . The goal from the beginning was not good public policy, but good public relations, and from that perspective, the administration's approach was a smashing success. It managed to downplay the gravity of the crisis and obscure the real issues."

It was not an easy job. On August 3, 1992, the State Department reacted with honest indignation and condemnation to the first death camp reports by *Newsday*'s Roy Gutman, for which Gutman later won a Pulitzer Prize. But within a day the official line mysteriously softened, and instead of mobilizing public support for taking on the Serbs, the State Department was saying the evidence of torture and murder was inconclusive. As evidence of widespread torture and murder cascaded into its lap in the following weeks, the State Department refused to say "genocide" was occurring. Why the strange reluctance? An acknowledgment would have laid the groundwork for requiring the government to take action in line with its legal obligations under the 1949 United Nations Convention on the Prevention and Punishment of the Crime of Genocide, which defines genocide as "acts committed with intent to destroy, in whole or in part, a national, ethnical, racial or religious group." It fit Bosnia like a glove.

Kenney couldn't believe what was going on behind the scenes. "The danger . . . was that discovering additional horrifying details would multiply demands that the United States intervene," he wrote in the *Washington Monthly* after resigning from his job. "On the one hand, State officials were not prepared to consider journalists' accounts 'credible' or 'authoritative.' On the other, the State Department would not seek information on its own. There was no way for dissonant information to get through the door, making State Department brass look something like children who block out the world by covering their ears and humming loudly."

When Yugoslavia collapsed into war, Kenney was a faceless diplomat in the State Department working in an office that became the epicenter of hypocrisy. He lasted until August 1992, when he quit to protest the lies that his bosses told him to concoct. This was the first time since the Vietnam war that a U.S. diplomat quit in dissent, and within a year three more diplomats followed his lead out the door and into a blaze of publicity. Resignation on principle is an extraordinary act in any prestigious organization, especially at the State Department. It is like an exclusive club: you go through a strict application and initiation process, and once accepted as a member you stay forever, trading your loyalty for a lifetime of privilege, travel and financial security. In Kenney's case, membership was practically hereditary. His father was a retired diplomat, and Kenney joined up in the expectation that his offspring would take his place one day. At age thirty-six, after postings in Europe and Africa,

George Kenney was a company man, but he didn't figure on the company being so crooked.

When news of his resignation hit the front page of the *Washington Post*, lots of people began asking the same questions: Who is George Kenney, and why is he making such a stink? I got the answers when I checked into the Hotel Esplanade one evening in Zagreb, the capital of Croatia.

The Esplanade is the Balkans: old, stuffed to the rafters with history, tinged by scandals of every variety, home to royalty and mafia, surviving off its charm and guile. If you research Zagreb newspaper archives, you will find many stories about the Esplanade, with headlines that drip of intrigue, recounting tales of adultery, robbery, suicide and more. Now, the luxury hotel is like an aging chanteuse, perhaps unable to hold a note quite as well as in her past but compensating for it by broadening her repertoire to suit the needs of the day and performing for anyone who will pay, rather than a special few guests. The Esplanade caters to everyone's desires, a task that does not come easily during times of war in the Balkans.

The hotel, located next to the city's train station, the port of entry and departure for the high and mighty in the times of empire, was opened in 1925 to serve the wealthy passengers of the Orient Express, which stopped in Zagreb. The Esplanade is grand, like a Viennese palace, imposing rather than warm. The doorman is outfitted in tails like his ancestors, and his presence is welcome now not so much for the style that he lends but the strong shoulder he applies to budge the heavy iron doors at the entrance. Sliding electronic doors would go against the grain of the Esplanade. It was not built for the ease of its patrons; it was built to awe them.

Inside, the lobby is a lovely sight. The floor is made of several types and shades of marble, arranged in a delicate, circular pattern, shined to a mirror's finish. Above you, a wonderful chandelier is suspended from the high ceiling. Around you, the walls are covered with a unique Italian marble, white with black streaks, that cannot be replaced because the quarry it came from became exhausted long ago. It is priceless. The grand staircase, wide enough for a dozen people to ascend shoulder-to-shoulder, is at the rear of the lobby and makes a full, lazy turn before it disappears onto the first floor.

If you walk through the reception area, you pass into the Emerald Ballroom. There are few like it on earth. Its ceiling truly reaches to the heavens, more than sixty feet high, and its center is composed of a natural skylight. The walls are lined with impeccable mirrors and gold-trimmed neoclassical pillars that define the ballroom's oval shape. What I love most about the ballroom is its echo effect. You can sit at a table in one corner and, although you might have difficulty hearing the conversation at the table next to yours, the whispers from a table on the other side of the room, one hundred feet away, come through to you loud and clear. I always wondered whether this eavesdropping quirk was intended by the ballroom's designer, and I liked to think that, yes, it was, because this, after all, was the Balkans.

My suspicions were lent some credence when I visited the hotel's public relations director one day and learned a bit more of the hotel's history. During World War II, when Croatia was allied with Germany and had a pro-Nazi regime, the Esplanade was used as the headquarters for the Gestapo, which had a habit of requisitioning the finest hotel rooms in each of the capitals that Germany occupied or was allied with. Nine of the Esplanade's waiters were found to have been spying on the Germans for the underground Communist resistance, and were shot. I suspect that one of their spying tricks consisted of using the echo effect in the ballroom to listen to the conversations of unsuspecting Gestapo staff officers.

When the resistance, led by Tito, came to power after the war, a plaque was mounted in the hotel commemorating the sacrifice of the nine waiters. Forty years later, things changed when Yugoslavia fell apart and Croatia gained its independence under Franjo Tudjman, a onetime Communist general who evolved into a small-minded nationalist. Tudjman belittled the Holocaust in a book entitled *Wastelands of History*, and said, during a 1990 campaign rally, "Thank God, my wife is neither a Serb nor a Jew." (When Tudjman showed up for the 1993 opening of the Holocaust Memorial Museum in Washington, D.C., he was booed.) The Esplanade, a survivor at all times, sensed that new winds were blowing under Tudjman, and that it was no longer advisable to honor men who sacrificed their lives fighting Nazi Germany. The plaque was taken down.

Zagreb was the most elegant city in Yugoslavia, and the Esplanade was Zagreb's most elegant hotel, so any notable foreigner who visited Yugoslavia stayed there. It now has a wall, discreetly tucked away at the back of the lobby, with celebrity pictures and thank-you notes. I would have been willing to pay money to gaze at the wall. The pictures, dating back twenty, thirty and forty years, show a bizarre array of visitors, including Pele, Ella Fitzgerald, Orson Welles, Leonid Brezhnev, Mick Jagger, Woody Allen and Bob Guccione. Louis Armstrong visited in 1968 and left a polite note that said, "Had a great stay here. Thanks for everything," and he signed it, "Louis Armstrong (Satchmo)." There's also a picture, dating from the seventies, of Ike and Tina Turner in one of the hotel elevators; Ike looks steamed and seems on the verge of slugging the photographer.

The Hollywood jet set stopped visiting. The Esplanade became obliged to cater to the whims and needs of the wartime jet set. Every city that is caught up in a war has such a hotel. The Hyatt Hotel performed the function in Belgrade, and the Holiday Inn defied the odds in Sarajevo by not only staying open but serving three square meals a day to its patrons. In a single night at the Esplanade you could arrange to buy a multiple rocket launcher (ammunition included) over cocktails in the bar with an arms merchant, have a four-course dinner in one of the three restaurants with a government minister, spend several thousand dollars for a painting in an art gallery adjacent to the lobby, rub shoulders in the elevator with a foul-smelling warlord, have an after-dinner drink in the basement nightclub with a CIA spy and then retire to your room in the company of one of the club's nude dancers. The receptionists were regal and unruffled at all times, like statues that never flinch when pigeons land on their heads and relieve themselves.

Television reporters preferred to stay in Zagreb's Intercontinental Hotel, perhaps because it had a fitness club. The print and radio reporters, the slobs of the trade, stayed in the Esplanade. If you stayed often enough, the concierge got to know you, and this could be supremely useful. Whether you needed a tuxedo or a flak jacket, he could find one for you. The receptionists could also give you the best room in the house. Being an old hotel, the Esplanade does not have copycat rooms in which every item, from lamps to shower heads and electrical sockets, is in the same place. Instead, the hotel has double rooms no bigger than a closet—I got one the first time I stayed at the hotel—and double rooms bigger than a suite. My favorite was 249, a large corner room with high ceilings, flooded with sunlight. It is one of the best double rooms in the Balkans, and the receptionists did their best to save it for favored guests.

The first thing a journalist wants to know when he arrives in a

city is who else is there. The guest list of the Esplanade was always
a good place to start. The obliging receptionists knew what I desired
when I checked in and would discreetly slide the guest list over the
counter. It gave people's names and origin of passport. Aside from
finding out which journalists, friendly and competitive, were in
town, you could spot the arms dealers because they were the ones
registered with Swiss passports. If a lot of people with Swiss passports were staying at the Esplanade, a military offensive was probably being planned. You never knew what you would find. When I
arrived at the Esplanade on the evening of October 23, 1992, I
scanned the list and saw a surprising name: George Kenney.

I got to my room and called him. We had never met before, but
one of the advantages of working for the *Post* is that people want
to talk to you. We had dinner that evening. Kenney did not look
like a revolutionary. He had short brown hair, he was pudgy, his
clothes were bland and he seemed ideally suited to spend his life
sitting behind a desk. I learned that we had gone through similar
evolutions of discovery and dismay. Until walking through the gates
of Omarska and Trnopolje, I figured that the conflict in Bosnia was
just another scrap in the untidy mess that the world had become
after the end of the Cold War. The camps showed that something
far more hideous than a little civil war was happening in Bosnia.
Kenney tried to persuade the State Department to say that genocide
was occurring. He failed.

"The trick . . . was to ignore any facts—whether they pertained
to atrocities, rumors of concentration camps, or starvation—that
would complicate the policy goal of not getting involved," he wrote.
"Discussions about how to characterize the conflict without taking
sides often bordered on the absurd. Supported by others at the working level, I drafted press guidance—material for State Department
spokesmen—which consistently referred to and condemned Serbian
shelling of Bosnian civilians. The Serbs, after all, had more than one
hundred pieces of heavy artillery around Sarajevo, while the Bosnian
government defenders had fewer than a dozen. This was essentially
a Serbian siege in which the Bosnians were shooting back as much
as they could. But senior officers . . . pressed repeatedly to have
spokesmen say that 'all sides' were shelling each other, without fo-
cusing blame on Serbian forces."

It was this kind of policy that was chipping away at the desire of some journalists to report in Bosnia, myself among them. If the American government was capable of downplaying concentration camps, then there seemed little hope for Bosnia, and little reason to risk your life for the sake of excavating a truth that Washington knew but refused to acknowledge. In spare moments, I amused myself with a question: If journalists had found gas chambers next to the camps, would Washington have reacted differently in the pre-election summer of 1992? I gave my government the benefit of the doubt and decided it wasn't time to throw in the towel. I had it far easier than Kenney, whose duty was not to report the facts, but deny them.

"I just couldn't stand it anymore, writing stuff that was covering up our inability to deal with the problem, and by covering it up, we were letting things get worse," he said over dinner. "I got fed up. Every day, it was lies. You know, one time I even proposed that the department spokesman say, 'U.S. officials lied yesterday.' I suppose that I could have requested a transfer. That's usually what people do when they don't agree with a policy. If they have a family and a mortgage to pay, they can't afford to quit. Lots of people disagreed with policy in Central America during the Reagan years, but they just stayed away from postings in that area. I'm still fairly young and not married, so I didn't feel the financial constraints that other people have.

"I talked to my father about resigning, and he was against it. He couldn't believe that I was going to leave the Foreign Service. He was embarrassed. But he changed his mind a few weeks after I resigned. He listened to what I was saying and to what other people were saying about me. He finally came around after some of his friends called to say that they respected what I had done. I don't feel it was a courageous thing to do. I feel a bit embarrassed that people are praising me. I think most other people in the same position would have done the same thing. Look, the issue is genocide in Europe. How can you turn your back on it? The fact that other people are turning their backs made it even more important for me to stand up and shout."

A few hundred yards away from the Esplanade, the revelation of prison camps was fomenting a rebellion at the U.S. embassy.

On a story like Bosnia, an American journalist gets familiar with American diplomats stationed in the Balkans. They're usually happy to sit down for a "background" briefing, which means you can't use their names or even refer to them in your stories as an "American diplomat." They are "Western diplomats." As everyone in the foreign-policy world knows, the phrase "Western diplomat," when used by the *Washington Post* or *The New York Times*, invariably means "American diplomat." The drill is the same for these briefings. You go to the embassy, stride past the lumpen masses waiting for a visa, wave your blue American passport at the policemen with Uzis, walk through the front door, slip your passport under a section of bullet-proof glass for a very large Marine guard to inspect. He makes a phone call, then pushes a button, a buzzer goes off, he calls you "sir" and asks you to walk through another door that is made of three-inch-thick panels of bullet-proof glass. A secretary from Wichita named Mary-Ellen awaits you on the other side and leads you upstairs, through a steel bomb-proof door, this one opening after she punches in a series of code numbers, and then you enter the political department. You notice a large paper shredder in the corner. The walls are lined with steel filing cabinets marked "Classified." Reminders are painted in block letters on each drawer, such as "Always Lock After Use," or "Don't Leave Open." You glance longingly at the filing cabinets. You know what Eve felt like in the Garden of Eden.

The diplomat emerges from his office. He is not wearing a jacket but has a tie knotted firmly at the collar of his white shirt. He has an identification badge swinging at chest level from a metal strap. He shakes your hand. It is always the same kind of handshake—never too weak, never too long—regardless of whether this is your first meeting with him or the hundredth. You walk into his office, a cubicle with perhaps one window that has iron bars across it. His desk is littered with obscure journals. He asks whether you want a cup of coffee. Because you are about to begin an hour-long discussion about politics, you take up his offer. He asks his secretary to bring you a cup, and in a minute or two she appears with a Dallas Cowboys mug. The coffee is always the same, from Croatia to Korea, weak and rarely good to the last drop, but you don't mind, because it reminds you of home, and each sip is laced with nostalgia. Everything in the embassy reminds you of home—the American banter, the Yankees pennant on a wall, the pack of M&M's on the diplomat's desk.

The interview begins. It follows a pattern. If you are in a Third World country, the diplomat will talk quite frankly about corruption in the government and economic mismanagement. If the government happens to be a close U.S. ally, the diplomat is likely to talk about how the government is trying to eliminate corruption and turn the economy around. Ally or not, the diplomat will explain that U.S. policy toward the government is wise and successful, even if it isn't. The greatest sign of dissent he exhibits might be a lack of enthusiasm while discussing the policy or, if you're lucky, a shrug of the shoulders that pretty much means, "You've heard what I said, but I don't really believe it."

It wasn't like that in U.S. embassies in the Balkans. Diplomats were on the informational front line, passing on detailed reports to Washington about atrocities in Bosnia. They knew the facts because, in part, they had debriefed prison camp survivors and pored over the *Mein Kampf*–style speeches of Serbian politicians. They were shocked by what was happening, but their classified cables were being ignored by policymakers in Washington. And so, instead of giving a bland defense of U.S. policy, many diplomats in the Balkans would do the opposite and encourage visiting journalists to be as forceful as possible in their stories.

"You know, the jobs you and I have are very similar," one diplomat chuckled in the middle of an interview. "We're both filing reports about the same events. The only difference is that my boss in Washington doesn't read what I write, but he certainly reads what you write."

He paused. "That was off the record."

It was a bizarre form of mutiny. Few members of the State Department crew jumped ship, but they grabbed the collar of everyone who came on board and whispered intensely that the captain was a fool steering toward disaster. As I listened to a diplomat unburden himself, I noticed his hands were shaking when he touched on the U.S. government's refusal to bomb Serb targets. "The Serbs are not ten-foot-tall headhunters who would fight to the last drop of blood," he said. "Why don't we bomb targets in Bosnia and Serbia? My God, what are we paying $200 billion a year for—what is our military for? If you define our army as a force that won't risk taking casualties, then we don't have an army. We have Boy Scouts."

It was a splendid remark, and I used it in a story that evening, quoting a "Western diplomat." My phone rang an hour after I filed. It was him, sounding like a fugitive.

"Peter, listen, I was just thinking over the things I, ah, said to you, and, ah, you see, you can't use that quote about Boy Scouts. Please. If Colin Powell [then the chairman of the Joint Chiefs of Staff] reads it in tomorrow's *Post*, he'll hit the ceiling and want to find out who said it. He'll put on a manhunt until he gets to the bottom of it, and he'll know which embassy it came from because of your dateline. He'll have my ass. He'll think it's an insult to the military's manhood, which of course it is. So please, don't use it."

I agreed. I sent a message to my editors telling them to delete the quote. I really had no choice, unless I was willing to pay the diplomat's mortgage while he looked for a new job.

The diplomats were useful because they realized that domestic politics was only one of the busted pistons of American policy. "It's not just the elections," Kenney explained over dinner. "If the situation was reversed in Bosnia, and a fanatical Muslim regime in Belgrade was slaughtering thousands of innocent Christians in Sarajevo, then America would have reacted by now. We would not watch Christians get killed by Muslims in Europe. Period. But we can watch Muslims get killed by Christians." The problem for Bosnia was larger than the fact that George Bush was getting clobbered by Bill Clinton in the polls. Bosnia was Islam.

The media and politicians referred to Bosnia's government as "Muslim-led," which was technically correct, or simply as "Muslim," which was wrong. For journalists, it was a result of sloppy shorthand. We are always trying to simplify things, even at the expense of distorting them. We didn't have the time or space to explain in every story that Bosnia's government included a large minority of Serbs, Croats and "mixed" people who refused to support nationalist rebels on the other side of the front lines. We rarely mentioned that Bosnia's Muslims were secular and westernized, that they believed in the same things Americans believed in, such as the goodness of diversity, the importance of freedom. There was a joke that summed them up very well:

QUESTION: How do you define a Bosnian Muslim?

ANSWER: A Bosnian Muslim is someone who drinks liquor, eats pork and doesn't pray to Mecca five times a day.

Particularly at the start of the war, it would have been more relevant, and more revealing, to call Bosnia's government "pluralistic" instead of "Muslim-led" or "Muslim." Perhaps, in journalistic fairness, we should have noted the dominance of Christians in the American government (which was *very* relevant to its reaction to the war) and referred to it as "Christian-led." I'll make a start now. One of the better jokes created during the war touched on the Christian-led American government's reluctance to stick its neck out for Muslims and featured a Bosnian soldier who never stopped digging his trench:

ONLOOKER: Why are you digging so deep? Seven feet is plenty.

SOLDIER: I know. But if I dig really deep, maybe I'll strike oil, and then America will decide that us Bosnians are worth saving.

President Bush was voted out of office in November 1992. The transition period began the day after the election and continued well past Clinton's inauguration in January 1993. The gap gave the outgoing Bush administration, and the incoming Clinton administration, an opportunity to forget about Bosnia. Cables from embassies in the Balkans piled up in Washington and were ignored, perhaps filed alongside stacks of ignored newspaper stories. Everything was on hold until Clinton became president and carried out a policy review. Then, perhaps, things might change. In the meantime, the carnage in Bosnia would continue.

COUNTRY OF

HEROES

AY I ASK you a favor?" Muharem Kržić said.

"Of course," I replied.

"There is something I would like to have smuggled out of Banja Luka."

He paused. I must have frowned or made some gesture that tipped him off. I didn't know what he had in mind, but no matter how innocuous the object might be, I knew I wouldn't be comfortable with it. Anything that must be smuggled is, by definition, not innocuous, and I'm a terribly bad smuggler.

I had to hear Muharem out. We had just spent two hours in his backyard talking about the troubles, the second or third time we had spoken at such length. Muharem was the Muslim leader in Banja Luka, the largest Bosnian city controlled by Serbs, and the darkest of places in the darkest of worlds. To be a Muslim or Croat in Banja Luka in 1992 was nearly as frightening as being a Jew in Berlin in 1942. Out of sympathy or respect or pity, I don't know which, I considered Muharem a friend, a doomed friend. A death sentence had not been passed in any court, such things not being necessary in a place like Banja Luka, but it was there, hovering over his head like a bee buzzing around a succulent flower. As we talked, I wrote in my notebook, "How long will he live?" I underlined it.

Muharem was well aware of his likely fate; once, after an outspoken press conference, he whispered to some of the reporters, "I've probably just written my own obituary." We sat in his underattended garden with tomato plants and spring onions. I looked into the hills and heard gunfire, a soldier having fun. The shots were being fired rhythmically, in sync with a disco beat. I thought of that soldier, or any bored soldier, sitting on his hillside perch with a telescopic lens, lining Muharem or myself up in the crosshairs and mouthing the words, "Bang, you're dead," through rotten teeth. He could pull the trigger anytime.

Perhaps I couldn't grant Muharem's last wish, but at least I should listen to it.

"My wife and daughter are in Zagreb, you know. When they left they took only a few clothes with them. We all thought the troubles wouldn't last. I was wondering, could you take their diplomas out with you?"

Diplomas. Not coded messages, not money or pictures or people. Diplomas. It was a reminder of the type of people Muharem and his Bosnian brethren were. "Muslim" is a horrible word in America because it dredges up racist images. The images are of unshaven rug merchants with a hand on your shoulder and another in your pocket; of billionaire sheiks in white gowns who ooze piety and hypocrisy at the same time; of Koran-waving fanatics chanting "Allah is great" as they try to blow up the World Trade Center or plow through a Marine barricade in a truck laden with dynamite; and of toothless nomads in the desert who sleep under the stars with their camels.

In Bosnia, the caricature didn't fit. Bosnia's Muslims are Slavic, not Arab. As I said earlier, they are not descendants of Turks or Saudis; they are native Slavs who converted to Islam when Bosnia was under Turkish rule. A man with blond hair and blue eyes in Bosnia is just as likely to be a Muslim as a Serb or Croat. The American media always referred to "ethnic rivalries" in Bosnia, but the truth of the matter is that all the combatants were the same ethnic group—Slavic. "Ethnic rivalry" was an erroneous term for things that had nothing to do with the complexities of ethnicity and everything to do with the simplicity of aggression. It was a mistake for journalists to use "ethnic" to describe the things that happened in Bosnia, but we fell into a habit and became addicted to it, which is unfortunate, for the words "Balkan" and "ethnic" are like a mountain of explosives and a match; you put them together and people in the West retreat as though facing a volcanic eruption.

Because Bosnia was under Turkish domination from the four-teenth century until the nineteenth century, its Muslims were the privileged class, the landowners and mayors and professionals. When the Turkish empire fell apart, most Muslims in Bosnia man-aged to hang onto their positions of prominence during a spell of Austro-Hungarian rule, and the pattern continued when after World War I Bosnia became part of a country that was first called the Kingdom of Serbs, Croats and Slovenes and later called Yugoslavia. The Muslims continued to live primarily in the cities, which is where a society's elite usually sets up camp and, generally speaking, Serbs and Croats were the country bumpkins. In the 1990s, most Muslims were nonreligious and lived like other city dwellers in Europe: Fa-thers went to work wearing ties and swallowed a shot of brandy after dinner (and often at breakfast), while their daughters had post-ers of Andre Agassi on their bedroom walls and their sons listened to Guns N' Roses.

The best way to understand Muslims in Bosnia is to think of Jews in America. Mecca was distant and unimportant to most Bosnian Muslims, just as Israel is distant and unimportant to most American Jews. Bosnia's Muslims have lived with people of other faiths for centuries and have been diluted by it, to the extent that most thought of themselves not as Muslims but as Bosnians or Yugoslavs or Eur-opeans. Same for the Jews in America, who call themselves Ameri-cans first, perhaps New Yorkers second and Jews third (if at all). Many Muslims married Christians in Bosnia, just as many Jews did in America. Equating a Bosnian Muslim with an Arab fundamen-talist is about as accurate as equating an American Jew with an ultraorthodox Hasidic Jew living in Israel.

Muharem felt shocked when all of a sudden he was told at gun-point by the Christians he had grown up with that they didn't want his kind around anymore. A second shock hit him when Americans and Europeans, too, identified him as nothing but a "Muslim" who, sad to say, should probably do as the Serbs wanted and leave his hometown and live, from now on, in a little Muslim state that would be created for his kind in central Bosnia. Muharem heard the phrases coming from the gatekeepers of civilization—"Pity that those people

in Bosnia just want to kill one another"—and he replied, "Wait, I
don't want to kill anyone! We don't want to kill anyone! But these
nationalist Serbs, they want to kill us!" It was no good. Serbs told
him to pack his bags, and American and West European politicians
counseled him to go along with it.

If I sympathized with Muharem and his brethren it was because
I had an inkling of what they probably felt like. My sympathy did
not come from my conversations in Bosnia. Talking is a limited form
of communication. A dozen psychiatrists can explain to you the
emotion of fear or love, but you cannot feel it yourself until you are
afraid or in love. Words are stored in the brain, not in the heart,
which is where emotions reside. Besides, in the Balkans words are
tools of manipulation, not instruments of meaning. I tried to understand what Muharem felt like by imagining myself in a similar
position. What if someone told me that I am only a Jew, not an
American or a Californian, and that I must live with other Jews on
a kosher reservation in Oklahoma, and that, in all probability, the
reservation would be run by Hasidim who would forbid me, for the
rest of my life, from watching movies on the Sabbath or wearing
shorts on a hot day?

I would feel like Muharem. I could have nothing but sympathy
for him when he asked me to take his family's diplomas to safety.
But I hesitated.

"I don't know," I said. "Journalists' cars get searched. You know
Chuck, the *New York Times* correspondent?"

Muharem nodded. They had met a few days earlier.

"He returned to Belgrade on a bus. He was taken off the bus at
a roadblock and searched. Everything."

"It might not work?" Muharem said.

"I don't know. Let me think about it."

I was stalling. I would not have been disturbed if Muharem withdrew the request. What would happen if I was stopped at a roadblock and a soldier found the diplomas? The name of Kržić was well
known in the region. Perhaps I gave Muharem the impression that
I was concerned about the safety of his diplomas, which I was, and
that I would be an unsafe courier. That was only the partial truth.
I was worried about my safety, too, and worried about breaking a
professional rule about "taking sides," as though outside rules had
any relevance to what was going on in Bosnia.

"The diplomas are important, more important than the house," he said.

"I know. You would be running a risk of losing them if I took them out."

Silence.

The obsession with diplomas was intriguing. A few months earlier, I interviewed some Bosnians who had been forced to flee from the town of Bosanski Novi, which Serbs were cleansing. The Serbs had managed to trick the United Nations into doing some of the dirty work. The U.N. High Commissioner for Refugees (UNHCR) was told that about a thousand or two people wanted to leave Bosanski Novi to join their families in Western Europe. The UNHCR agreed to send some trucks and buses to fetch them. The Serbs, meanwhile, stepped up their campaign of terror and announced on local radio and television that all non-Serbs had to leave on the UNHCR convoy. Soldiers roamed around the town firing their guns into the air. Everyone got the point. The buses and trucks were swamped by more than 8,000 Bosnians. The United Nations had been duped, not for the first time, nor for the last.

The refugees were dropped off in the Croatian city of Karlovac. They slept in the municipal sports hall and, because it was summer, some of them slept outside, like livestock. A day after the exodus, I sat in a bit of shade under a tree and talked with Ibrahim Velkić, an economist who had worked for the city government and was fired when Serb nationalists staged a coup. It was a carbon copy of Banja Luka. All non-Serbs were fired. The terror came swiftly, and Ibrahim realized he needed to get out of town to survive. The authorities insisted that he, like other property-owning Muslims, sign away his land and house and refrigerator and everything else that would not fit into the single suitcase that he was allowed to leave town with. The program was so successful that the line to sign away a life's possessions was two days long. When Ibrahim finally entered the stuffy little room where a Serb clerk was stamping the documents, he had to go through the final humiliation, which was to be the official witness for the Muslim in front of him. Ibrahim signed his name at a line marked "Witness." Then, when it was Ibrahim's turn to sign away his own possessions, the Muslim behind him signed on the line marked "Witness."

Ibrahim still had his document. It was a photocopied form presided over by the words "Serbian Republic of Bosnia and Herze-govina," which must have seemed as alien to Ibrahim as the words "Mexican Republic of California" would look to me. The date and Ibrahim's name were typed in blue ink at the appropriate places. At the bottom was a dotted line where Ibrahim signed, where the wit-ness signed, and then, next to those squiggles, there was a fat, blue seal of the Socialist Federal Republic of Yugoslavia. The "Serbian Republic of Bosnia and Herzegovina" had not yet produced its own seals, so the old ones had to suffice. I could almost hear the sound —*thump!*—that the heavy seal made as the Serb clerk stamped it onto Ibrahim's papers, and then the clerk, without looking up at Ibrahim, probably barked out, "Next!" Another filthy Muslim gone. The line of Bosnians that stretched out of the building and around the block inched forward a bit more.

Ibrahim was left with the following statement in his hands:

I, Velkić Ibrahim from Bosanski Novi, by my own will came to this office after I was informed of the order of the War Crisis Committee of the Bosanski Novi district about the criteria for the possibility to emi-grate, and I hereby give the following statement. I state that in the dis-trict of Bosanski Novi I do not own any property and that I permanently leave the district of Bosanski Novi with my wife and two sons and two daughters-in-law. I give this statement with complete responsibility, without any pressure, and in the aim of obtaining documents for per-manent emigration and departure from the district of Bosanski Novi. This statement has the authority of an executive document.

Ibrahim sat, cross-legged, on the grass.

"If I hadn't signed that paper, I wouldn't be alive today," he said. "Please, keep it. It is worth nothing to me now. Tell the world about it."

"But you should keep it. When the war is over you might be able to get your property back."

Ibrahim smiled. "Look at the document. I don't have any prop-erty anymore."

A man sitting a few feet away from Ibrahim started to sob.

"Do you know him?" I whispered.

"Yes. He is my brother."

An open suitcase lay between the two men. It was carry-on size, and it contained a change of clothes for Ibrahim's family. His wife was rummaging through it. Ibrahim had a green leather tube across his legs. I nodded at it.

"What is it?"

"It is my only property now."

"What's in it?"

"My diplomas."

These Bosnians had sniffed the historical winds and sensed that something more lasting than a short quarrel had broken out. Perhaps it was the brutality that tipped them off. Perhaps it was the fact that Serbs were destroying ancient mosques. Perhaps it was the forms they had to sign in which they pledged never to return. They knew that the people who had seized power would not, as long as they held power, let them return, and this could be a long time indeed. And so, as they fled their hometowns, Bosnians brought the pieces of paper that they would need to start building new lives in strange countries. Surgeons brought their diplomas. Economists brought their diplomas. High school graduates brought their diplomas. They needed those documents to prove to their new masters in Germany or Britain or America or whatever country would accept them that they possessed useful skills. They were not camel herders or religious fanatics. They were Europeans whose names were preceded by professional titles like "Doctor" or "Professor" or "Engineer" or "Editor" or "Artist."

In the garden, Muharem was having second thoughts about surrendering his family's diplomas. One of them was his own, the one that certified he was a veterinarian. Before he made the terrible mistake of getting involved in politics, he was a vet. He loved two things, he said, animals and music. Earlier in the day, he had put his hand on the piano that dominated the living room like an altar and said the house felt empty without his daughter filling it with music. His fingers stroked soundlessly along the keyboard, as though he was playing an imaginary piece of music. He wasn't. He was trying to touch his daughter by touching the keys that she had touched. If only he could see his family before dying. Just once, for a minute or two, that's all he wanted.

"You must excuse me," Muharem said. "I need a strong drink."

He returned to the garden a minute later with a bottle of brandy and two glasses.

"I don't usually drink during the day, but these are very difficult times," he apologized.

Muharem was dressed casually in jeans. He was a handsome man and a precise thinker, and it was enjoyable to listen to him talk. He unpacked ideas in the same way that he would diagnose an animal's medical illness. Probing here, pushing there, reflecting for a few seconds and probing again. It's easier to be a doctor than a vet because your patient can tell you what's wrong, where it hurts, how long it has hurt. Veterinarians have to be more intuitive, more imaginative, yet always analytical. They have good minds, and usually good natures.

Muharem had brought out some papers. They were photocopies of a handwritten testimony by a Bosnian who had been held at the Keraterm prison camp. The statement explained a few nights of brutality in a locked storage shed with no ventilation for the 150 prisoners detained inside. The guards refused to give the prisoners water for nearly two days, and finally the prisoners began to die of heat exhaustion. Some of them pleaded for water, screaming and crying, and so the guards silenced them by firing through the doors. About 20 prisoners died immediately; at least as many were wounded and lay on the ground, bleeding, crying for help, and when the doors were finally opened a day later, just a few men crawled out alive.

"It was worse than a gas chamber," Muharem said. "I cannot read these documents a second time. In a gas chamber, the people died within minutes, but can you imagine, they were pleading for hours at Keraterm. For hours. We wouldn't do that to animals. Maybe if the Bosnians were whales instead of people the world would do something to stop these slaughters."

It was time to refill the glasses. He didn't bother with the slight nod that would symbolize another toast. Muharem explained making periodic visits to the mosque, where occasionally the bodies of torture victims would be washed before burial. The bodies had to be stolen from the mortuary in the middle of the night. This was baffling; these people were willing to risk their lives to save a corpse. Muharem recalled viewing the body of a prominent Muslim from a neighboring town. His skin was blue like the sky, Muharem said, "His sexual organs, too.

"My conclusion is that I am in great danger every night when I go to bed. I am not sure whether I shall wake up when the sun rises. But we are all in danger here. We are in the center of mass crimes, pogroms and genocide. We didn't believe that this would happen. This is the twentieth century. We are in Europe. We have satellite television here. Even today, when there is electricity, we can watch CNN. We can watch reports about our own genocide! What's really sad is that we are alone, and we don't have any guns. The Western countries will not defend us and will not allow us to defend ourselves. This embargo is killing us, and the West is responsible for it. Our only weapon is the truth, but it is of no use.

"When this war started, we couldn't believe the things we were hearing. The authorities announced that for every dead Serb soldier they would kill five Muslims. We couldn't help but laugh at this. You know, the majority of Serbs who have lived here for years are completely polite and we are used to living together. But they cannot help us. There is really only one answer. We must leave. If we don't, we will die. You know, if the mayor announced that the road to Zagreb was open, but that we could only go on foot, everyone would go. Muslims, Croats, women, children, grandmothers. I don't think that I can escape by running over that hill. If I thought I could, I would do it at once. Everybody would. At least I have been able to move my family."

But not the diplomas. The subject floated above us, like a kite struggling to stay aloft in a weak breeze. It was time to leave. I wanted to return to the hotel before dark, and it would be a long walk back from the edge of town where Muharem lived. Neither of us mentioned the diplomas as we walked out of the garden and through his darkening house to the front door. Muharem had been poking and probing me like one of his veterinary subjects. He had sensed my reluctance and the danger of losing the diplomas. They were just pieces of paper. They were all he cared about.

I left his home without his diplomas. When I drove back to Belgrade, I was not searched.

▶ *Two*

FIGHTING had prevented Serb farmers from tending their crops in the summer of 1992, but they were reaping a bumper harvest of loot. I was traveling through Serb-controlled northern Bosnia in a bus, and the driver tooted his horn as we passed farmers atop tractors and horse carts weighed down by rugs, sofas and kitchen pots stolen from ransacked homes. The farmers waved as the bus roared by, belching diesel fumes in their cheerful faces, and their wives laughed from the rear of the carts, sprawled amid the belongings of the dead. Their smiles were toothless, their minds, apparently, empty.

This was the second wave of looting, the main activity in territory "liberated" by Serbs. Soldiers made up the first wave, and they got the best stuff, value-added things like stereos and televisions and, when they got real lucky, wads of cash hidden under floorboards or buried in a garden. You could tell which soldiers had been searching for money by the black earth lodged in abundance under their fingernails. In the Balkans, a soldier doesn't earn money, he digs for it. Once the soldiers moved out in their trucks and vans, with Japanese VCRs heaped on top of ammunition boxes, the farmers plodded in behind them to grab the bulky leftovers. I shouldn't have been surprised. Conquerors have done it for centuries.

The bus was heading to Banja Luka, to my first rendezvous with Muharem and his darkness, and the land I traveled through was getting the final touches of an ethnic cleansing. The result was anything but clean. Towns and fields looked half dead, and sometimes, when the wind blew straight from a freshly cleansed village, there was the real stench of death, too. The bus had left Belgrade early in the morning on what was supposed to be an eight-hour journey. It took more than twenty-four hours. In these early months of the war, it was better to travel in a bus, wedged among soldiers heading to the front and civilians returning home after the fighting, than to drive a private car and get searched or robbed at roadblocks. Hold-ups were a simple affair: an unshaven soldier would point his gun at a desired item and grunt.

So I traveled with the boys on the bus, and the girls and the old women and their chickens, too. The stereo system blared out an odd medley of Western pop and nationalist jingles. "Serbia Forever" trailed off into "Like a Virgin" by Madonna. The soldiers, most of whom claimed to have a cousin or brother living in Chicago or Cleveland, moved their lips in unison with the strangely appropriate lyrics of a Paul McCartney song, "Band on the run, band on the run." They had looped their AK-47s onto the little hooks above their heads intended for sweaters and jackets. If you felt something roll to a stop at your feet, it could be an apple that fell from a peasant's food bag or a grenade from a soldier's pocket. Either way, you scooped it up and sought its rightful owner.

"Excuse me, soldier, is this your grenade?"

Pause. "Why, yes, it is."

He nudges the snoring soldier next to him.

"Heh, Radomir, look what happened to my grenade. The motherfucker fell out of my pocket and rolled to the back of the bus!"

They snicker like schoolboys sharing a dirty joke.

"Hah!" Radomir laughs. "It's a Serbian grenade. Only explodes when it hits Turks!"

A peasant would hear the joke—"Turks" is a derogative word for Bosnia's Muslims—and laugh along, perhaps handing a bottle of slivovitz across the aisle. "Here, hero, have some of this."

The bus bumped its way through a twilight zone of mortar craters and nuked houses, taking a roundabout route to skirt mop-up zones. Most road signs were destroyed in the fighting, so arrows were painted on the side of houses to indicate which way to turn, and they pointed the bus through cornfields and back alleys. A few signs remained intact, and everybody got a good laugh when we passed one indicating the way to Sarajevo. Timbuktu was more accessible. The bus had the road pretty much to itself, or the cornfields to itself, because civilian traffic consisted mainly of farmers and their carts. Occasionally a military convoy loomed in front or behind, or a gas tanker roared past with fuel from Belgrade for the thirsty machines of war.

The dust stuck to my skin like thick makeup grandmothers cake on. I wiped it off the window so that I could get a better look at the wartime graffiti. Houses were interesting. The untouched ones had the word "Serbian" painted by the door, which meant it was owned by a Serb and should not be looted or dynamited. The words "Muslim" or "Croat" were invitations to rob and bomb, and those houses were, indeed, wiped out. It was rare to see more than two or three letters of the original word, "Mus—." The rest was blown away by bullets or grenades. Nationalist slogans were everywhere, always the same insipid sort, "Glory to Greater Serbia." There were funny variations, and a British colleague stumbled upon the best of them all. "This is Serbia!" blared a dumb slogan painted on a building, and underneath it a subversive soul wrote, "Wrong, dummy. This is a post office."

The bus stopped coughing and broke down in front of a village called Kotorsko. It was a Muslim village, or had been. A few houses still smoldered, and the place was deserted. Night was coming, a time when only drunks and bandits ventured outside, so we had no hope of finding a mechanic or hitching a lift to the nearest town. We would sleep in the bus. Before settling into a chilly night of intermittent sleep, the soldiers on board went into a field and returned with a few dozen ears of corn. A bonfire was lit, the corn was toasted up and the drinking began. It's times like that when soldiers drop their guard. A major named Branko, handsome in a Bruce Willis style, started talking about a roundup in his hometown.

"We were arresting all the men. I grabbed one guy and threw him to the ground. I looked at his face and realized we had gone to high school together. I was on top of him. 'Do you know who I am?' I asked. He looked straight at my eyes and said, 'Yes, I know you. You are a Chetnik. Fuck you.' "

Branko paused and shrugged his shoulders, giving his listeners a moment to realize that such insolence merited only one kind of response.

The sky was black. Tracer bullets rose to the heavens in staccato red beams that were like a laser show and so pretty you could forget they were deadly. I turned my head in the direction of a burst of machine-gun fire, and Branko patted me confidently on the shoulder and said everything was okay. *"Naš,"* he nodded. Ours. It meant we were safe, but it carried a different meaning for any Bosnians out there in the darkness. My attention drifted back to the soldiers as they swapped tales about their war against "fundamentalist" Muslims and "fascist" Croats. Theirs was the boasting of conquerors, the kind of talk that has taken place around military campfires throughout the ages. The chatter even had a soundtrack, because the bus stereo played a war ballad that everyone knew by heart:

> *Sing Serbia,*
> *You country of heroes,*
> *Sing stronger and louder,*
> *So everyone will fear you.*

After twenty-four hours, the bus arrived in Banja Luka. The Hotel Bosna, located off the city's main square, was open for business although its only clients were journalists and soldiers. It was an apartheid hotel in which the journalists paid and the soldiers did not, even though the soldiers made all the noise, wrecked their rooms and fired drunken shots into the air from their balconies.

Everyone came together in the morning for a breakfast buffet of stale bread and cheese, the journalists whispering about the crimes that the gunmen at the surrounding tables were committing. The city's infrequent supply of electricity meant the hotel rarely had hot water or coffee in the mornings, so the soldiers were never in a good mood, and neither were the journalists, and this was all we had in common.

In this city, the victors had delusions of grandeur. It was visual. Across the street from the hotel stood City Hall, sporting an over-sized Serb flag that hung from the roof to the ground, a hundred feet tall, fifty feet wide, three horizontal stripes of blue, white and red, so large that only a strong breeze could make it flap. The flag, hanging over a building where, fifty years earlier, Kurt Waldheim worked as a lieutenant in the Wehrmacht, was meant as a projection of Serb nationalism, as though size was all that mattered, rather than content. I had never thought of flags as weapons, but in Bosnia, and in the rest of Europe, they were becoming the deadliest weapons of all. As though to remind me of their effect, trucks rumbled past with soldiers who shouted to no one in particular, "Serbia!," a slogan full of meaning to goons with guns. They wore black leather gloves, like Hell's Angels, except these ones were the real thing.

About 195,000 people lived in Banja Luka when the war broke out, and nearly half of them were Muslim, Croat or of mixed parentage. The rest were Serbs. What do you do with such a large number of undesirable minorities? It is easy to bomb and cleanse isolated villages or towns, tossing the survivors into a camp, but it's something else to do this to nearly 100,000 people in a major city that you already control and don't want to destroy. Serbs had gone crazy, but not that crazy. The solution was simple: Squeeze them out slowly, like dishwater from a towel. A few killings here, a rape or two there, job dismissals everywhere, confiscations of apartments. Scare them enough, and they will want to leave, they will even pay for the privilege of leaving. It was a Balkan water torture, and it worked wonders.

Things were so bleak that Muslims and Croats in Banja Luka wanted the U.S. Air Force to bomb *them* so that they would be taken out of their misery. It's not a joke. People who had the misfortune not to be Serb, and be trapped in Banja Luka, pleaded for America to perform mass euthanasia with F-16s. They were in the position of a torture victim on a rack who has tried futilely to persuade a hesitant onlooker to shoot the torturer. No, the onlooker says, violence is never good, it just begets more violence. Besides, if I miss, the torturer might try to take a shot at me! You must settle the problem among yourselves.

The torture victim makes a final, desperate plea.

"Then shoot me, damnit!"

Of course the onlooker refuses that request, too. The torture continues.

An old Muslim woman was walking down a street at twilight. It was an ordinary street that she had probably been walking down for scores of years, starting way back in the times when the oak trees were waist-high saplings. She would stop off to say hello to her neighbors as they watered their tomato plants or grilled *čevapčići*, a tasty Bosnian meat specialty, for dinner. She might pause to scold a child who ran out of a gate and nearly tipped her over. But the street was silent when I approached her. Children were staying indoors. The knife etchings in the trees that said things like "Bogdan Loves Senada" were joined now by new ones that said "Death to Muslims." Old people are usually the most talkative ones in perilous times because they have the least to lose. They are old, they're going to die soon, and they are stubborn enough to believe that the thugs do not kill grandmothers. But the old lady didn't want to talk. No, she said, everything is fine, I'm sorry, I don't have time to talk. A few slices of bread were stashed in her bag. I asked if she had enough to eat. She broke down in dry tears, too old or too upset to weep properly.

"We live in fear," she cried. "We wait every night for Serbs to come slaughter us. If only the Americans would just bomb us with their planes and get it over with."

More than eighteen months after the old woman pleaded for America to drop a bomb on her head, the Bosnian enclave of Goražde was attacked by Serb forces. It was a classic operation in which howitzers and tanks smashed the city center and its hospital, which was singled out for particularly rough treatment. The attack went on for more than a week without any Western response, aside from two ineffectual F-16 air strikes that the Serbs laughed off, hardly bothering to tone down their assault. Goražde's outlet to foreign journalists was a ham radio linkup, and as the Serbs closed in, Goražde's mayor made a special plea over the radio link.

"Gather the courage to bomb us," Ismet Briga said in a message to President Clinton. "Stop the agony of the people of Goražde. We beg for air strikes against the citizens of Goražde!"

A doctor who had survived the attack on Goražde's hospital, and who apparently had seen *Apocalypse Now*, requested over the radio link that America attach loudspeakers to the wings of its F-16s and have them fly over the city blaring out the "Death March." Perhaps, the doctor thought, if America could not be begged into action, it could be shamed into action. He was wrong.

You didn't need to talk to a soul in Banja Luka to learn how bad things were. Trees talked. Along the main boulevard, trees were festooned with scraps of paper, a bit like Christmas ornaments, and the papers contained handwritten notices that said, "Wanted: Apartment in Sarajevo." The notices did not predate the war. They were put up well into the siege of Sarajevo, when the Bosnian capital was a worldwide symbol of misery. Yet the Muslims of Banja Luka looked on Sarajevo, hellish as it was, as a paradise compared to their hometown, and they wanted to move there as quickly as possible. And so they scrawled their ads in nervous script, hoping that Serbs who had left Sarajevo for Banja Luka would agree to an apartment swap. Sarajevo or bust. Imagine that.

I even met a man who wanted to escape to Somalia. Mogadishu or bust. Imagine that.

The time was a few minutes past five in the afternoon, and prayers had just ended at Banja Luka's main mosque. After putting their shoes back on, a handful of middle-aged men lingered at the entrance, leaning against ancient pillars, conversing in whispers. I approached them. Could any of them talk about the situation in town? None responded. Some vanished quicker than the smoke from their cigarettes. I want to find out what's happening to Muslims in Banja Luka, I said. I need your help. There were a few seconds of silence. A black man came forward and spoke in African-accented English. He said his name was Ismail. "I will talk to you. But please, we must leave this place now."

"This place" was the Ferhad Pasha mosque, built from white stones in the early days of the Ottoman empire. In walking distance, the mosque was half a mile from the Hotel Bosna, but the chronological distance was nearly half a millennium. Finished in 1583, the mosque was modest in design, perhaps a fifth the size of Notre-

Dame Cathedral, built neither to awe nor to dominate, but to impress and endure. It aged over the centuries with a waterfall's grace, staying in place while the surrounding landscape was reshaped by man and nature. Survivors of history don't cling to existence; immortality comes naturally to them, and it seemed to come naturally to the Ferhad Pasha mosque. It certainly deserved its spot on the list of world historical monuments drawn up by the U.N. Educational, Scientific and Cultural Organization.

You can literally feel the magic of such a building when you press a hand against one of its ancient stones. What has happened since a workman dressed in feudal rags put this stone in place four centuries ago? The Reformation, the Renaissance, the founding of the United States of America, Napoleon, the Industrial Revolution, the two World Wars, the Cold War. And the mosque was still alive, serving the purpose for which it was built, a place of worship and the heart of the Muslim community. It was the opposite of so many of the monuments or historical buildings that are worshiped in textbooks and worshiped by tourists but are dead to the touch because they exist only to be looked at (and often you must pay a fee to look). Those places—the Colosseums and Towers of London and Forbidden Cities—are lifeless, like the embalmed corpse of Lenin. The form still exists, but it does not have a heart that beats, because the heart was torn out long ago. The Ferhad Pasha mosque was different, just touch one of its stones, listen to the muezzin in the minaret call the faithful to prayer, hear the men shed their shoes at the entrance and feel the 400-year-old heart beating with steady strength.

We went across the street to an ice cream parlor and climbed to its second-floor terrace, where we ordered coffee in the lengthening shadow of the mosque. The coffee was prepared in the classic Turkish manner, a social and culinary rite grafted onto Bosnian culture during Ottoman rule. Muslims, Serbs and Croats drank the same kind of peculiar coffee in the same peculiar ritual in Bosnia. Hot water was poured into a small copper goblet, called a *džezva*, that had a long, thin handle and contained two spoonfuls of ground coffee. The potion was put over a flame and brought to a frothing boil, then carried in the goblet to the table, where it was given a break to cool off before being poured into the handleless cups, the *fildžan*. The grounds rushed into the cup with the coffee, half of them resting like a thick cream at the surface, the rest falling to the bottom. No matter how dainty you were, the first sip would leave you with a small mustache of coffee grounds. A few more sips would bring you close to the murky bottom of the *fildžan*. Only drunks and tourists took the last sip, which left them spitting up coffee grounds.

It was one of the ironic aspects of wartime Bosnia that a Serb warlord would interrupt an anti-Muslim tirade to take a sip of his beloved Turkish coffee. The coffee recalled a truism that too many Serbs forgot when they began waging war on their neighbors, and the truism is this: A Serb in Bosnia has quite a bit in common with a Muslim in Bosnia. Banja Luka's Serbs and Muslims adored the same Oriental-sounding music, shared the same regional accent, and their jargon was the same, too. They drank the same potent coffee and loved *čevapčići*, which always lost a crucial bit of taste when it was prepared in a Belgrade or Zagreb restaurant. A Serb farmer in Bosnia would get no relief from drought if a rainstorm hit Belgrade. His problems might lie in Bosnia, but so did the answers.

Ismail wiped the coffee grounds from his upper lip. He was from Somalia, and he had come to Yugoslavia twenty years earlier as a medical student, back in the days of fraternity between socialist regimes. After graduation he married a Muslim girl in Banja Luka and settled down. His wife became a journalist, and they built a cozy middle-class life together. Color television in the living room, five-speed sedan in the garage, money in the bank. When Somalia fell into civil war and then famine, Ismail was thankful for the good fortune of living in Yugoslavia. His attitude changed when the war broke out. He and his wife were fired from their jobs, his friends vanished after being nabbed off the street or pulled out of bed by Serb soldiers. Ismail lived in terror and had the same wish as every other non-Serb in Banja Luka. He wanted out.

"I know what is happening in Somalia," Ismail said. "But honestly, I would rather be in Mogadishu right now."

I am writing this passage more than a year after I finished that cup of coffee and said good-bye to Ismail. I hope he found a way out. I hope, at least, he fared better than the Ferhad Pasha mosque. At three a.m. on May 7, 1993, light sleepers in Banja Luka were woken up by the sound of two huge explosions, much louder than anything they had heard before, and many of the woken Muslims thought, Praise to God, the Americans have finally done it, they've started bombing! Not true. Serb soldiers or thugs—nobody knows which, and the difference is hard to tell—had detonated several thousand pounds of dynamite under Ferhad Pasha and its sister mosque, Arnaudiya, built in 1587. After four centuries, all that remained of them was rubble.

Serb authorities pretended to be shocked by the act, saying it was perhaps done by outlaws who would be punished. They also floated the theory that Muslims had destroyed the mosques in the hope of blaming Serbs and stirring global outrage. Such lies, like the acts they attempt to cover up, are beneath contempt. If you want to find the truth in Bosnia, you must ignore words and examine actions, and even then, you must be careful of the conclusions you draw. After the explosions, Muslim notables begged the Serb authorities for permission to preserve the rubble. Perhaps it could be used in better times as cornerstones for rebuilding the mosques, a symbolic tie to the past. No, the authorities said, you can't keep the rubble. They later detained U.N. officials who tried to salvage bits of it. The rubble was trucked away to a secret dump site.

Bosnia's war had its visual hallmarks. Parks that were turned into cemeteries, refugee families piled onto horse-drawn carts, stop-or-die checkpoints with mines across the road. The most hideous hallmark of all was the blackened patch of ground in the center of town. It always meant the same thing, a destroyed mosque. The goal of ethnic cleansing was not simply to get rid of Muslims; it was to destroy all traces that they had ever lived in Bosnia. The goal was to kill history. If you want to do that, then you must rip out history's heart, which in the case of Bosnia's Muslim community meant the destruction of its mosques. Once that was done, you could reinvent the past in whatever distorted form you wanted, like Frankenstein.

▶ *Three*

BANJA LUKA is blessed with a refreshing river, the Vrbas, which kids swam in during previous summers, but in the summer of 1992 it carried the occasional corpse in its cool waters. I walked across a bridge over the Vrbas, a step quicker than usual, as though traversing a flowing graveyard, and headed toward a crowd of people gathered in front of a cement, two-floor building. A plastic sign hanging next to the entrance said, "Bureau for the Removal of Populations and Exchange of Material Goods." It was, of course, the bureau for ethnic cleansing.

The people gathered outside were Bosnians trying to get out of Banja Luka. They came with all the proper papers, including ones that said they had signed the deed of their home over to a Serb (assuming the home had not already been confiscated when they were fired from their jobs) and that they had forfeited their savings account at the bank. There was even a slip of paper from the library saying they did not possess any overdue books. With these white slips of surrender in their hands, the cleansees lined up to get their names put onto a list of infrequent and perilous bus convoys across the front lines. They had to pay for the tickets with German marks.

I politely pushed my way inside, up a dark staircase lined with the eyes of the fearful, and went to the office where Miloš Bojinović, the bureau's director, held court. Bojinović was a skinny man in his forties with a wispy goatee that looked straggly, perhaps in sympathy with the pale face it was attached to. The only sturdy thing about him was the pistol strapped to his waist. He was the man, I had been told, who decided who got out and who didn't. In the universe of Banja Luka, he was a god of sorts, playing with people's lives. This one stays, that one goes, this one lives, that one dies. I didn't quite know what to expect out of an ethnic cleanser, but surely it wasn't a nervous, underweight man who could be wrestled to the ground by a fish. His was the face of evil that I had been seeking out, yet I felt a bit like Dorothy when she finally reaches the palace of Oz and pulls back the curtain to reveal the "mighty" wizard as nothing but a quivering little man.

A classic bureaucrat, Bojinović spent the first fifteen minutes demanding identification and then asking questions. What was my mother's maiden name? My father's occupation? He asked similar questions of my interpreter, a Serb from Belgrade. Why, Bojinović asked the interpreter, are you working for a foreigner? How much are you being paid? Bojinović must have heard the slogan about the best defense being a good offense, because he portrayed his bureau's activity as being for the sake of goodness. No, this is not ethnic cleansing, he explained. The non-Serbs want to leave, and I am aiding them do that. It's a very hard job, you know, I am here from dawn until dusk.

"But why do these people want to leave?" I asked.

"It's a fashion," he said.

"A fashion?"

"Yes. You must understand that this agency helps people for humanitarian reasons. You cannot use words like ethnic cleansing to describe the voluntary movement of people."

Bojinović stretched the word "voluntary" to the limit. He was reminiscent of Adolf Eichmann, who was in charge of deporting Europe's Jews to death camps, arranging the paperwork and making sure the cattle cars arrived and departed on time with their human cargo. Eichmann's deeds were incomparably worse than Bojinović's, but the striking thing is that both men portrayed their actions as aimed at benefiting their victims. Eichmann, while on trial, pleaded that he made deportation more humane and orderly for Jews who, without his efforts, would have been brutally shot in their apartments or forced to walk to the death camps. Bojinović's explanation was similar—without his efforts, these poor souls would have no way of following the latest fashion and leaving their hometown. He was helping them.

Hannah Arendt wrote the following lines about one of the Holocaust's architects, but she could have been writing about Bojinović and most other human cogs in the Serb machine: "The trouble with Eichmann was precisely that so many were like him, and that the many were neither perverted nor sadistic, that they were, and still are, terribly and terrifyingly normal. From the viewpoint of our legal institutions and of our moral standards of judgment, this normality was much more terrifying than all the atrocities put together."

▶ *Four*

THE MAGNETIC center of Banja Luka was the desk occupied by Major Milovan Milutinović. Every journalist who visited the city was drawn to it, ineluctably. Major Milutinović was the spokesman and press attaché of the regional military command, the "Doctor No" who explained the thousand-and-one reasons why you could not visit the places you wanted to visit, but could visit the places *he* wanted you to visit. You could not get out of Banja Luka without a pass from Major Milutinović, so you had to see him, talk to him, plead and argue. He was a friendly man who would give you a hearty handshake each time you met, as though he was glad to see you, or glad to see that you were not in Omarska or Kozarac. His army fatigues were cinched tightly around his waist, and for a man in his forties, he was in trim physical shape. He had thick dark hair, and his office was brightened by several female assistants who typed out the passes with polished fingernails. Their work was occasional.

A visit to his office entailed the same rituals. Handshake. Turkish coffee served by one of the girls. Refusal to issue passes for the places you wanted. When things seemed at a dead end, Major Milutinović would suggest that you read one of his brochures, perhaps the one which says that "Serb skulls have been halved, brains have been split, bowels have been torn out," and adds that Islamic warriors made necklaces out of the eyes and ears of dead Serbs. He might also propose that you watch one of his movies. You would say, Okay, but how about giving me a pass to, uhm, Bosanska Gradiška, and he would smile and say, Yes, perhaps we can work that out, but first you should see my movie. You agreed and sat down in front of a Sony television set. An office girl, shuffling through the stack of videos, might ask you for guidance.

"This is a new one, *Genocide Against Serbs in Krajina*. Have you seen it? Or the one about the Afghan mujahadeen killing Serb babies?" There was no irony in their sweet voices.

You lobbied for the shortest one. If there was an Academy Award for the Crudest, Goriest Propaganda Film, then the Serbs would win, hands down. Their desire to fight in Bosnia was stoked by the kinds of horrifying images displayed in the films screened in Milutinović's office. Most of the movies were not about atrocities against Serbs in Bosnia in 1992, but about atrocities committed during World War II, during World War I, and before then. No matter. Serbs had been killed, Serbs were being killed—what was the difference? Some footage was even of Dachau, as a reminder of what happens to people who fail to defend themselves. The message was Reaganesque in its simplicity: The cruelties of the past awaited Serbs unless they went on the offensive and committed preemptive genocide. Twisted and sharp, the blade of history was lobotomizing them.

The best propaganda contains some truth. The truth behind Serb propaganda is that Serbs never had it easy in the past 600 years. History has tormented the Serbs, trapping them in a tomb of oppression that became more hellish with each attempt they made to escape it. Serbs never pretended to like their oppressors, and when an opportunity arose to rebel, they seized it, always with disastrous consequences, because the conquerors usually were stronger, and when they were not, another conqueror was waiting nearby. These troubles spawned countless myths, yet Serbia has no need for them, because its reality was more mythic than any myth.

The Turks held sway for five centuries, starting in 1389, when, at Kosovo Polje, the Field of Blackbirds, a huge army led by Tsar Lazar was demolished by the Turks. One of Lazar's supporters, a nobleman named Miloš Obilić, tried to delay defeat by defecting to the Turks and, when brought before the sultan, pulled out a hidden dagger and murdered him. This had no effect whatsoever on the outcome of things. The Serbs were defeated in due course, and the event is remembered with a famous poem in which the tsar builds a splendid church at the Field of Blackbirds before sending his doomed troops into battle. The poem ends with these lines:

> *And the Tsar Lazar was destroyed,*
> *And his army was destroyed with him,*
> *Of seven and seventy thousand soldiers,*
> *All was holy, all was honorable,*
> *And the goodness of God was fulfilled.*

The poem does not tell the whole truth, for the defeat of the Serbs was due in part to their lack of unity, an Achilles' heel for all time, continuing to this day. No sooner do Serbs score a victory than they start fighting over the spoils, and it is no surprise that their main slogan is "Only Unity Saves the Serbs." At Terazije Square in Belgrade, there is a large bronze statue of Prince Miloš Obrenović, who is on horseback. Through bravery and guile, Obrenović gained autonomy from the Turks in the early nineteenth century, a process that began with him arranging the murder of his rival and then outsmarting the Turks on the battlefield and at the negotiating table. In a loose way, he was a Serbian George Washington. However, Obrenović turned into a dictator soon after getting the better of the Turks and was tossed into exile in 1842 by his fed-up subjects, who learned that being ruled by one of their own could be just as horrible as being ruled by their enemy. A century later, Obrenović's statue at Terazije reminds Serbs only that they live in a bad neighborhood and must survive through cleverness and ruthlessness.

After the Turks were thrown out, the Austrians and Hungarians and Germans took turns invading Serbia. Things got particularly bad in 1914, when Austria declared war following the assassination of Archduke Franz Ferdinand. This, of course, was the beginning of World War I, a moment when, as Rebecca West wrote in her classic book *Black Lamb and Grey Falcon*, "Millions of people were delivered over to the powers of darkness, and nowhere were those powers more cruel than in Serbia."

The Serbs initially fought off the Austrians, but the Austrians increased the size of their forces, struck an alliance with Serbia's neighbors, and as a result the Serbian Army was forced to retreat from Belgrade and, inevitably, from the country. This is where myth met reality. Serb monks joined the retreat and brought from their crypts the bones of previous Serb kings. The living monarch, King Peter, was an old man, and he fell sick, so his soldiers had to carry him on a stretcher as they withdrew from the capital. The king's son, Prince Alexander, had also fallen sick with a painful internal disease, and he too was carried on a litter. I cannot hope to describe the meaning of the retreat in better words than Rebecca West's, so I must quote again from her book: "It is like some fantastic detail in a Byzantine fresco, improbable, nearly impossible, yet a valid symbol of a truth, that a country which was about to die should bear with it on its journey to death, its kings, living and dead, all prostrate, immobile."

As the Serbian Army withdrew farther south, the Austrians stopped pursuing and let the Bulgarians step in, hounding a quarter million Serb soldiers to the foot of a mountain range that blocked their escape to the Adriatic Sea. The defeated Serbs had their backs to a huge wall, and there was only one thing for them to do, climb the wall, which they did, crawling in a tortuous march over the snowy mountain peaks. They had run out of food, so they ate the flesh of animals that fell dead along the way, and they even ate leather from their own boots. Nearly half of the retreating Serbs died before reaching the Adriatic. There, the survivors rested, and in 1918, as the Austrian empire collapsed, they returned to Belgrade. At great cost, the invaders had been repulsed, but as usual other invaders waited in the wings, the Germans and Hungarians, and they didn't have to wait long, just until 1939, when the powers of darkness could once more inflict their brutality on Europe and, of course, on Serbia. In World War II, the Serbs would be conquered from the outside, torn apart by their own civil war and then, on the eve of World War II's conclusion, bombed by their Allied liberators, who were chasing out the last of the German occupiers.

All of this was as familiar as mother's milk to Major Milutinović, who wandered over to the corner of the room as I watched the movie. There was footage of people with holes in their faces, or what remained of their faces, because most of what you saw was their brains dribbling over their nose or chin. Faces with cigarette holes, corpses with maggots burrowing in the eyes, heads without torsos, torsos without heads. Major Milutinović tapped me on the shoulder, like a teacher getting the attention of a distracted pupil, and whispered, "Pay close attention to this. It is very important." And so I peered intently at the screen as the narrator said that Islamic holy warriors were burning Serbs alive. It was accompanied by a black-and-white picture of what seemed to be a singed corpse on a spit. "They were roasted like pigs," the narrator said.

The films failed to impress. Were the scenes from Bosnia at all? The out-of-focus picture of a soldier smiling as he held two severed heads in either hand could have come from any conflict over the past few decades, from Lebanon to El Salvador. You might see the picture in a Belgrade newspaper, with a caption that said it showed a Croat soldier with Serb heads. You might, a week later, see it in a Zagreb newspaper, with a caption that said it showed a Serb soldier with Croat heads. If you are a well-traveled war correspondent, you might have even seen it a few years earlier in a Kabul newspaper that said it was an Afghan mujahadeen with Soviet heads.

Some people might envy my privilege to see real snuff films, but I have always disliked horror movies and scenes of graphic violence. This may stem from the time when I was on summer vacation during my elementary school years and went to see a matinee film about a child's pet mouse that went wild and recruited thousands of rats to invade the house. They ate the parents. What drove me over the edge was the ride home afterward. I felt something inside one of my sneakers and screamed when I realized that a large insect was crawling around my toes. No more horror films for me. I've always wondered why, with all the fear and violence in the real world, people pay money to see more of it. This is fun?

The pornography of war remains in the back of my mind, and

always will be, and perhaps that's what I dislike the most, mental pollution. You go to Bali for vacation and have pleasant memories for the rest of your life about pristine beaches and turquoise waters. You go to Bosnia and return home with images of an armless corpse that had a bloody hole where the genitals used to be. It doesn't help to say to yourself, It's only a movie, it's only a movie. It wasn't. It stays with you, like a pebble in your shoe. It is irritating and perhaps a bit painful at first, but eventually the tissue it rubs against becomes hard and unfeeling, so you can walk without a limp, and nobody knows the pebble is there, unless you talk about it. I haven't forgotten the images from Bosnia, but they no longer disturb me as before, and I don't know whether this is good or bad. All I know is that a part of me is no longer as soft as it used to be.

The film ended. The office girl pushed the button for rewinding the video, and she shook her head in disgust. "Those Muslims, you see what they are doing to my people?" I gave a shrug. She was so attractive but her thoughts were so warped. She returned to her desk and typed up the pass for Bosanska Gradiška. The typewriter keys went *bang-bang-bang*, like shots from an old revolver. Finished, she pulled the pass out of the typewriter and put it on Major Miluti-nović's magnetic desk.

"You must wait for your escort," he said, "and you must be back before dark." I could not protest; at least I was getting the pass. A half hour later a paunchy guy who looked like a double for Ringo Starr came into the office, dressed in a short-sleeved floral shirt, the kind seen on *Hawaii Five-O*. My escort had arrived.

As evil as this place was, it had an endearing slapstick side to it. At times, the Serbs seemed to be the gang that couldn't shoot straight; a colleague who wrote a book about Bosnia called them the "Keystone Gestapo." An often told incident in the press corps concerns a Serb roadblock where a carload of journalists was stopped, searched, and then one of them was hauled away for "questioning." The quivering journalist, from a Dallas newspaper, was taken to the commander, who demanded to know who shot J.R. This tale might be apocryphal. A similar episode is described in Thomas Friedman's book *From Beirut to Jerusalem*, regarding a checkpoint in Lebanon. I suspect that both episodes occurred.

I once visited the front-line town of Rogatica, held by Serbs. I drove there with two British colleagues, and the burly commander greeted us with an anti-Western tirade and threatened to shoot us because we did not have authorization to be in his sector. He calmed down and led us to his office, through a corridor that was lined with fifty-pound sacks of flour stamped with the message, "U.S. Government Aid. For Civilian Consumption." We pretended not to notice. He answered a few questions and blew up once more, tearing the notebook from my hands, ripping out some pages and vowing to kill us. He kicked over the ashtray, an empty casing of a 155-millimeter shell.

"I should shoot you right now. I know you will write lies. So listen to me. If you write lies, I will find you wherever you are, and I will kill you!"

He calmed down again, returned my notebook, apologized for tearing it up, answered some more questions and then invited us to a lunch of bean soup in his canteen. Then, midslurp, he asked when was the last time we had sex.

"Three days ago," offered our interpreter, grinning. "With my girlfriend in Belgrade."

"Oh," the commander moaned. "It's been so long for me, here on the front line."

Major Milutinović could not spare a soldier—it was Saturday, and nonessential soldiers were on weekend furlough—so he ordered a local journalist to be my escort. This was Ringo. He had a pistol in a waist holster, probably posing a greater danger to himself than anyone else. As soon as Ringo plopped into the backseat of my car he began cursing Milutinović, who had ruined what was supposed to be Ringo's quiet Saturday at home with his wife. "Oh, she has breasts this big," Ringo said, his hands splayed out as though holding a huge bowl of fruit. He would get even. "When we arrive in Gradiška, just drop me off at a coffee shop. You can go wherever you like. I don't care. Milutinović, what a bastard."

Bosanska Gradiška was in midpogrom. The main newspaper in Banja Luka, about thirty miles away, had felt obliged to mention, in a brief story, that "renegade" Serb soldiers went on a weekend rampage and killed eight Muslim residents while setting off sixty-three "explosions." This was the official version, presumably sanitized. Bosanska Gradiška was a city of nearly 70,000 people, about 30,000 of them Muslims and Croats, and it straddled a key border crossing into Croatia. It was marked for cleansing.

After depositing Ringo at a coffee shop and promising to pick up his tab, I set off with Bogdan, my interpreter. It doesn't take long to attract attention in a town like that when you are an American journalist and your interpreter is six foot six. In a place where divining nationality was an obsession, people could spot differences in an instant. Did you cross yourself with two fingers? A Catholic Croat. Two fingers and thumb? Orthodox Serb. You don't drink? Obviously a Muslim. Even handwriting could give you away. Did you write with Cyrillic letters? Ah, a Serb. Latin script? Croat. You have a dark complexion? Gypsy. The notebook sticking out of my back pocket was a giveaway, which is what I counted on.

"Hey, mister, what are you doing here?"

The voice was that of a teenager who had followed us into a park. Through Bogdan, I explained what I was after.

"Follow me," the boy said.

He led us to his house, a single-story job with a chest-high stucco wall in front, and we went to a small patio in back rather than inside. The boy disappeared. I stared at Bogdan. Where are we? He shrugged his shoulders. Wait. After a few minutes, the boy reappeared with a man, his father. An old woman in baggy, Turkish-style trousers came from the house with two glasses of water. His mother. The boy told us to speak quietly. More men arrived, and they talked among themselves in whispers, a few feet from us. I looked at Bogdan again, and then back at the whispering men, who had disappeared.

An armored personnel carrier had just rolled onto the street. The soldier in the gun turret was high enough to look behind the fences, which was the point. It was too late to make a move. You don't need any time to figure out what could happen. You know it in your gut, and it doesn't feel good. The soldier atop the APC would spot you, stop the vehicle, soldiers would rush into the patio, push you against a wall, order everyone out of the house. Once they learn you are a journalist, the family is doomed. They will be shot on the spot or, if they are lucky, they will be taken away, and perhaps only the men will be shot. The mother will beg on her knees for mercy, howling and clasping her hands together, imitating a Christian in prayer, desperate to score brownie points. "Please, sir," she will cry to a soldier who possesses the power of God and is perhaps nineteen years old. "Spare my husband and sons. They are good people, they have never done anything wrong. We have money in the house, please take it. It's yours. Please, sir, please."

The father will stand against the wall, stunned, and he will shoot a withering glance at you. It says, "This is because of you."

You'll never forget that glance. You'll get out of this alive, and you'll be able to impress your friends back home with fearsome tales of the dangers you braved in Bosnia. Your friends won't be able to see the inadvertent blood on your hands. But you'll see it, no matter how many times you try to wash away the memory, and it will remind you that you were another do-gooding American who made foolish mistakes that other people paid for. This was one of the curses of working in Bosnia. You had the monstrous power to lead people to their deaths.

Luckily the APC passed us by without stopping. It served as a ten-ton reminder of the ill fortune you can bring to others. When you talked to inmates at prison camps, you exposed them to danger. When you took colleagues or interpreters to the front line, you exposed them to danger. One of my interpreters in Sarajevo was a mother of two boys. She needed the money, $100 a day, and she knew the risks of the job, but what if she got killed? When I knocked on her husband's door and had that look on my face that said it all, would he grab my neck, pour all his energy into his fingers and shout, "You killed my wife"?

One of my good friends, a reporter for the British Broadcasting Corporation, led his cameraman to his death. I was with them at the time.

▶ *Five*

ALLAN AND I have spoken very little about the death of his cameraman, a Croat whose nickname was Tuna. I felt miserable about it, and Allan felt a thousand times worse than that. Tuna was twenty-five years old, lanky and handsome in an androgynous way that made men and women envy his looks. I remember meeting him for the first time in Travnik and thinking, Damn, I bet he gets all the women he wants. A bullet-proof vest made him look like a knight in armor, which didn't seem fair, him being just a camera-man. Tuna happened to be one of the best cameramen in the war,

and he had made a tips-for-survival video for neophyte war reporters. It probably saved some lives, but not his. Irony knows no limits
in Bosnia.

Allan, a working-class Scot, and I were covering the fall of Jajce,
a city in central Bosnia that the Serbs bombed into submission in
October 1992. It was a famous city, the place where modern Yugoslavia was proclaimed by Tito on November 29, 1943. After
showering it with howitzer shells during the summer, the Serbs
promised at a London peace conference in late August to withdraw
the big guns. They didn't do it. By October, the city's defenses collapsed and everyone fled—a wave of 30,000 refugees whose exodus
looked like an event from Tolstoy's times. Some walked, some rode
donkeys and some died of exhaustion during the forty-mile trek to
safety over mountain paths that they called the Ho Chi Minh Trail.
Young men pushed their grandmothers in wheelbarrows. Everyone
walked in silence, like the living dead who had nothing to say or no
energy to speak. They died in silence, too, falling by the side of the
road, a war's human litter.

Allan and I were the first journalists on the scene when the survivors began trickling into Travnik, a few miles behind the new
front line. We wanted to go into the forty-mile no-man's-land that
stretched between Travnik and Jajce. It was in this free-fire zone
that the exodus was most visible, most horrendous and most dangerous. We did it on a Thursday morning, driving in a BBC armored
Land Rover. This was early in the war, a time when journalists felt
secure within $50,000 armor cocoons. The Land Rover had slabs
of steel underneath the cab to protect against land mines, its sides
were plated with more steel, and the windows and windshield were
composed of two panes of bullet-proof Plexiglas. We drove through
the stream of refugees to a midway village called Karaula, did some
interviews and returned to Travnik. The stories we filed got high-
profile play.

Allan had asked his bosses to send a cameraman, and Tuna arrived after we returned from Karaula. The next morning, Tuna took
the Land Rover and headed out alone to shoot some footage of the
refugees as they crawled through no-man's-land. They were still
coming. He drove on the same road we had traveled, in the same
vehicle, at the same time—but a day later. Somewhere in the hills,
a Serb with an anti-aircraft gun took aim at the white BBC Land
Rover and pulled the trigger. The bullets were six inches long and

tipped with explosives. The windshield shattered like a pane of glass. One bullet hit Tuna in the shoulder and ripped his arm off. Another bullet hit him clean in the chest. We were told that he didn't feel a thing.

I was in Travnik when this happened and heard the news within an hour. A Bosnian soldier, Josip, whom I had befriended, and who had befriended Tuna, wanted to retrieve Tuna's body immediately. It was the soldierly thing to do, honorable and impulsive, though not reasonable or necessary, given the danger. I demurred. I remember my words to Josip as we stood outside Travnik's military headquarters: "He's not from my company." It was the first thing that came to mind. I would not risk my life to retrieve the corpse of a journalist who had not worked for the *Post*. This was an excuse, not a reason. Even if Tuna worked for the *Post*, I would have been reluctant to tear down that road, in full view of a sniper who was having a good day, and drag his mutilated body out of the shattered Land Rover, which had skidded off the road, tumbled down a ravine and landed on its side.

I had been in Bosnia long enough to establish a private rule: Don't take risks that you don't need to take. Reporting on the war required me to take many more risks than I felt comfortable with, so I did my best to avoid unnecessary ones. Everyone has to make his own private rule, draw his own private line. Mine might be more conservative than others, less heroic, and it might mean I would miss out on stories or experiences that other journalists would get, because they were willing to do things I would not. I could live with that. I remember a moonless winter evening in Sarajevo when two colleagues finished dinner at the Holiday Inn and decided to go for a walk down Sniper Alley under the cover of total darkness; they wanted to get some fresh air, and maybe they counted on learning deep philosophical truths as they strolled down what was, at the time, the most dangerous road in the world. I laughed within myself at their silliness. I had decided that fate was a fickle animal, and I preferred to not taunt it. I stayed at the hotel. I had my own rules. And so when Josip asked me to retrieve Tuna's corpse, I begged off. One dead journalist in a day was enough.

The death of a colleague causes two emotions, sadness and relief. The reasons for sadness are obvious. The reasons for relief are multiple, and all of them are perverse.

A colleague's death can enhance your own sense of being invulnerable. Other people die and you don't, so you are special. Destiny is on your side. You feel smarter because there's always a mistake the dead colleague made, a mistake you would never make, of course. Slowing down to take a look when a mortar explodes nearby instead of speeding up to avoid the inevitable second round; driving through a tense area without knowing for sure where the confrontation lines are; trusting a soldier who says "trust me," instead of trusting your own gut. There's a faint notion that the death of a colleague shows everyone else the dangers you are running, and increases the respect you receive when you return to America on home leave. It's primal.

In his book *Liar's Poker*, Michael Lewis coined a phrase to describe the high-rolling bond traders on Wall Street who earned annual multimillion-dollar bonuses during the wild 1980s. He called them "big swinging dicks." The journalistic world has an equivalent animal, the war correspondent who has seen battle, known death and returns home with the been-there-seen-it-all swagger of a victorious general. These are our big swinging dicks. The category would not exist if other correspondents did not die. Danger is defined by one thing—death. No death, no danger, no glory. Only a minority of war correspondents are full-fledged big swinging dicks, but there's a bit of it in most of us.

Allan was an exception. He had a real heart. I learned this two days before Tuna was killed. We were interviewing refugees from Jajce as they stumbled to the first Bosnian Army checkpoint outside Travnik. It was the finish line of their ordeal. An old man limped toward us, dried blood on his forehead, his pants covered to the thighs in mud. His name was Radovan Micko. He hardly knew where he was, whether he was alive or dead. We could have told him he was dead and in hell, and he would have nodded his head, slowly, perhaps saying, "I knew it." He moved in slow motion, covering the last fifty yards in ten minutes. He carried a briefcase in one hand. A woman's purse was strapped across his chest. That's all he had. From a distance, he looked like one of "them," the anonymous mass of refugees whom we see on our television screens and consider a race apart. We cannot, for a moment, imagine ourselves in their shoes, assuming they have shoes, which the old man was lucky to still have.

Radovan stood in the road and answered our questions. He was so dazed, so tired, that he might have thought we were soldiers and that he could not pass until responding to our queries. He probably didn't hear the younger man who walked by and said out loud, "Let the foreigners look at what's happening to us. Let them see. We have been betrayed by the world." Radovan was eighty years old, a retired music teacher. He had fallen down many times since leaving Jajce; how many times, and why, he could not say. I asked about the purse hanging below his neck. He looked at it in a glimmer of amazement, as though he hadn't noticed it. It took a few seconds for the words of explanation to come out of his dried mouth, and when they did, the words sounded so weak, so tired, that they seemed like refugees themselves.

"The purse belongs to my wife," he whispered. "My wife, my wife . . . I . . . I . . . don't know where she is. We were together in a truck. I fell down. I . . . I . . . I . . ."

I asked what was in the briefcase. The papers, he said, were his favorite music scores.

"I left my instruments in Jajce. I had a violin, it was from 1907. I had, I had . . . a piano, a Steinway. I . . . I . . . I . . ."

It was too much. Old people are the saddest ones of all because they are helpless and without hope. It is worse to talk with them than to look at a corpse. Dead bodies don't talk, they can't tell you of their woes, of their losses and the terror they have faced, and still face. But old people can talk. They can break into sobs as you ask them about the purse hanging from their neck. They can look at the corpses at the side of the road and whimper, "Oh God, I wish I were dead. I wish I were dead." It's true, they envy the corpses. Their past has been obliterated, their future consists of a grim spell in a refugee camp, where they will die in poverty, among strangers, in a strange land. They know it. The misery has ended for the corpses. It goes on for the living.

Radovan would never find his wife, I knew it. He would die soon. His body was broken, and his heart was, too. Allan took a few bills from his wallet and put them into Radovan's pocket, as we had been doing for the past hour, talking to one devastated refugee after another and stuffing a few bills into their pockets. It was the saddest of rituals. After Radovan, Allan turned away, took a step to the side and cried. So did our translator, Vera, a legendary woman known in the press corps as Checkpoint Vera because she could talk her way through any roadblock.

I did not join Allan and Vera in their tears for Radovan. I never cried in Bosnia. I had not seen sadder things in my life, or felt greater sadness in my heart, but tears do not come easily to me. It is a family trait. I have four brothers and one sister, a set of divorced parents, and we have our dysfunctionalities, as most families do, but we are close to one another and our gatherings are boisterous, full of jokes and storytelling. We get many of our laughs by needling one another, and our years of friendly barbs have sharpened our tongues and toughened our skin and taught us how to cover up our feelings when, perhaps, a word cuts too deeply.

When Tuna was killed, Allan came undone. Tuna was a friend of his, but what devastated Allan most was the fact that he had brought Tuna to Travnik, brought him to the place where he would be killed. On the day Allan and I went to Karaula, the Serbs had agreed to a brief cease-fire to exchange prisoners. That's why we survived our journey. When we passed the checkpoint at Turbe, we barreled straight ahead into no-man's-land, knowing only that the shelling was at a thankful lull. We even took a wrong turn at the first fork in the road and drove straight toward the Serb front line. Without the cease-fire, we would not have had the opportunity to turn around. I'm sure of that, because a day later, when the cease-fire was over, the shooting resumed and Tuna drove straight into it. He didn't even make the mistake of going the wrong way at the fork in the road.

As Tuna headed out to his death, Allan was driving in another BBC car to Split, eight hours away. Allan and I didn't meet up until I reached Split several days later, after Tuna's body had been retrieved. In his room at the Hotel Split, Allan was quiet, and his eyes said he had not slept or had been crying, or perhaps both. He had not done any work since Tuna died. He couldn't. We talked but, as people might do in a situation like that, we didn't really talk. In two days' time, he would have to attend the funeral and give his condolences to Tuna's family.

"I don't think I'll go to the funeral," Allan said. "I can't."

"You must," I replied.

It was the night of elections in America, so I wandered off to another room where some friends were having a party while watching the returns.

The funeral was in Zagreb, and Allan attended it, as did much of the BBC's top brass, flying down from London. I remained in Split and called Allan at his hotel in Zagreb.

"There were a thousand people at the funeral," he said, "a thousand people."

I don't know what he was thinking. How many of those thousand pairs of eyes were fixed on him? Hopefully few. Tuna's family was aware of the risks he had chosen to run, and the journalists who mourned his death were aware of it, too. Tuna killed himself. It did not happen in an armored Land Rover near the Bosnian village of Karaula. It happened months earlier when Tuna made the decision to work in Bosnia for the BBC. Covering a war is like playing Russian roulette. If you pull the trigger and blow your head off, your friends and family should not blame anyone else. They should blame you for playing that stupid game.

It was like that in Bosnia. If you drive into a no-man's-land between an advancing army and a retreating one, you know that anything can happen. The fact that everything was quiet yesterday is no guarantee that everything will be quiet today. There are no guarantees anywhere in a war zone; you can be a veteran correspondent, and you can chuckle at a novice who rushes off after breakfast to visit an active front line, but the truth is that a few hours later the novice might return from his escapade without a scratch, and you might have been shot by a sniper as you napped at your hotel. Allan did not tell Tuna that the road to Karaula was safe. Allan knew better than to say a road was safe in Bosnia, and Tuna knew better than to ask. You could tell the novices in the game, because they were the ones who asked if a road was safe, or told someone that a road was safe. The word was not in our vocabulary.

Allan left for London the day after the funeral. I guessed that he would not return to Bosnia. It was an unforgiving country in which good people like Tuna got killed for no reason at all, and nobody noticed or cared. What was the point? But Allan returned. Again and again. He established himself as one of the most incisive and sensitive journalists covering the war. Over the next months, when I listened to his Scottish accent on the BBC's shortwave broadcasts, I heard more than words. I heard anger, and I thought I heard obsession.

Six months after the funeral, Allan and I met up at the Esplanade in Zagreb. We always got along well. The bar was empty by the time we finished our work. The arms dealers had gone upstairs with the prostitutes, and the other journalists had gone to bed, some, as usual, with each other. We had a few drinks as the bartender emptied the ashtrays. Like everyone else who covered Bosnia, including myself, Allan looked horrible. His hair was going gray. I wanted to know why he was still at it. I was on the verge of deciding to stop covering Bosnia when my contract expired. Why didn't he get out? He responded after a pause, never mentioning Tuna.

"You're American," he said. "Bosnia is not as important to you as it is to me. It shouldn't be. In America, you're far away from it. But I live in Europe. What happens to my country and my generation is affected by this. If Europe goes back to the past, this is the moment it started, here in the Balkans. I want to be here."

Midnight came, and the bar closed down, not a minute too soon. I could not keep up with Allan's Scottish drinking pace for much longer. We walked up the grand staircase to the second floor. Allan reached his door before I reached mine.

"Tell me something," he asked. "Do you ever dream about Bosnia?"

"Every night," I replied.

"Yes, so do I."

▶ *Six*

THE DIFFERENCE between dreams and nightmares is the difference between night and day. The dreams come at night, when eyes are closed. The nightmares come during the day, when eyes are open, and what they see are the hollow faces of refugees, or the different shades of blood on display in Bosnia (the three main categories are fresh, dried and frozen). When you start working in a war zone, you might look forward to the dreams. They are an escape, an entertainment. The reality of war is mutated into new, intriguing forms. A dream might take you to a familiar battlefield, but a tank in the distance has turned into an object that looks like—no, it couldn't be—Noah's Ark! The soldier at your side, instead of wearing a helmet, has a diving mask and snorkel. You dreamily think that the war is the flood, and so you return to your hotel room and build a canoe. You *must* have a canoe.

A dream took me to the office of Radovan Karadžić, leader of Bosnia's Serbs. The wall, instead of being decorated with an Orthodox cross and Serb flag, had been turned into a bank of televisions showing different images of the war. Bodies on one screen, hands on another, tanks on a third. Video jockeys appeared from time to time to narrate the sequences. Camera angles were tilted and jittery. It was WTV, War Television. Karadžić's words were vintage Karadžić, blaming the Muslims for bombing themselves, the usual trash. I don't remember him having a body; there was just a face, *that* face, big and fleshy and obscene in its deceptive, polite innocence. A bowl of fruit sat on the table between the two of us, so I grabbed a tangerine and threw it at Karadžić's face. Bingo—a direct hit! Every American journalist who interviewed Karadžić had wanted to do at least that, but I was the only one to manage it. My laughter carried me out of the room, upward, through the ceiling and roof. I hovered above the building and threw tangerines at the soldiers who guarded it. They ran for cover. I had the high ground, and I had all the tangerines. What a scream.

The sanctuary of dreams turned into a prison as soon as the novelty wore off, which was after a few months. The dreams became less fanciful, converging with reality so that what I saw with closed eyes at night was similar to what I saw with open eyes during the day. Tangerine dreams evolved into grimmer stuff of villages going up in flames—*whoosh*—as I drove through them, or me sheltering behind a rock from howitzer shells, watching women dash for safety through a valley, screaming, dropping babies from their arms so they could run faster. I also had logistical nightmares. It's a sign of the nature of journalists today that I dreamed about being stuck in a remote part of Bosnia without a special computer cable to transmit my stories through a satellite telephone linkup. Refugees shrieked at night because of murder; I was more likely to shriek because of modems.

The brain torments those who abuse it. Refugees who saw friends or family members killed or raped—they exposed their brains to the radiation of tragedy. Same for the soldiers who saw their commander's head explode from the impact of a sniper's bullet, who hid like rats in shallow trenches as mortars blew dirt and hot metal onto their backs for days on end, who listened to the moans of comrades lying mortally wounded in no-man's-land. The result was predictable. They would wake up at night screaming and shaking, or they would not wake up at all, because they could not sleep. These people were haunted by a war that was inside of them, lodged somewhere

in their brains in a spot that a knife could not get to, nor the soothing words of a best friend.

There was no need for friends to look at me warily, wondering
whether, because of the war, the cheese was slipping off my cracker.
Journalists rarely overdose on tragedy. It's one thing to see a man
get shot, and it's something else when that man is your father. Journalists observe other people's tragedies; we rarely experience them.
The difference is immense. Sensible journalists try to keep a respectful distance between themselves and danger. Even so, we all had
brushes with the graveyard, sometimes at the graveyard, which, in
the case of Sarajevo, was one of the most dangerous places. But any
shell shock we suffered was temporary. We were visiting hell, not
living in it.

It was the repetition of dreams that was most worrying. At first,
when I retreated to Budapest or London for a break, I needed just
a few days to clear my head. But after the first few months of covering Bosnia, the dreams never cleared out. I could spend two weeks
in London and still, every night, I would dream of Bosnia. It was
inescapable. Bosnia was on the tube, and I usually had an unwritten
story or two in my notebook, so the breaks ended up being contin-
uations of the war, at day, at night. This bugged me. How long
would it go on for? Would I need a year to clear my head of Bosnia?
A decade? A lifetime? What was it doing to me?

The answer came from an unusual source, Colonel Bob Stewart,
the commander of the first British troops in Bosnia. He was a jovial
guy, hale and hearty as British officers are. He wore a checkered
scarf around his neck and never slouched. It was easy to imagine
him chasing Rommel around Africa, bellowing from the turret
of an advancing tank, "Forward men! Forward for the Queen and
for England!" One of his officers said that no matter what happened
while the Brits were in Bosnia, "We shall be smart, we shall clean
our boots and we shall salute the ladies." Colonel Stewart began
and ended his commands with the same word, using it like
parentheses.

"*Right!*" he bellowed to his executive officer while inspecting his
regiment's new base at Vitez. "I want a perimeter fence with barbed
wire staked out here. Get some wood, get some posts, and get it
done. By tonight. *Right!*"

He looked at a field that was being used as a motor pool.

"*Right!* What's that bloody cow doing inside the perimeter? There's a cow inside my perimeter! I want it moved out within the hour. *Right!*"

Because of Vietnam, the U.S. military brass views the press as an adversary. The British military has no such complex. During the Falklands war, the British press was as jingoistic as they come, cheering on their boys. When an Argentine warship, the *Belgrano*, was sunk by the British armada, a London tabloid splashed a huge headline across its front page: "GOTCHA!" The British military has been repaying the favor ever since.

In Bosnia, Colonel Stewart was happy to have the press around and made sure we never had trouble getting a good meal at his canteen. In a pinch, he would make room for a visiting correspondent in his living quarters. He was known, affectionately, as Colonel Bob. We were his boys. He gave us rides in his armored fighting vehicles, which were called Warriors, and he confided to a British journalist, "I love Warrior." He tried to sell me on them. "Right," he said during an interview. "You Americans really should buy our Warriors. Here's a photo. Keep it. They're the best machines that money can buy. Right!"

He had a standard answer for the question of what effect the war was having on him. It wasn't half bad.

"All I know is that I am a middle-aged man and this is the most fundamental experience that I have ever undergone. I know that this war is changing me, but I don't yet know in which ways."

And then, as always, he had one more thing to say.

"Right!"

So Colonel Bob was dreaming about Bosnia, too.

▶ *Seven*

WHATEVER question you might have about men and war, the answer could probably be found in Banja Luka. Such as, why do some people resist, and why do others obey?

An acquaintance, Slavko, offered to help me find the answer. "Come with me," he said, taking me by the arm one afternoon. "I know a brave Serb."

The Serb's name was Spasoje Knežević. In his younger years,

Spasoje was a star water polo player, a sport equal in status in Yugoslavia to basketball in America. Before Yugoslavia became synonymous with war, most Americans would only hear about the country once every four years, when the Yugoslav water polo team would wallop the Americans or Soviets at the Olympic Games. Back at home, water polo players got the best-looking girls and never paid for a meal. Spasoje did not make it to the Olympics, but he scored enough goals on the local team in the 1970s to make a name for himself, a good name.

Spasoje had the unfortunate burden of being blessed with a conscience. A lawyer, he chose to defend Muslims and Croats when the war broke out. He told anyone who would listen that the war was a violent hoax. He was rewarded with death threats through the mail, by the telephone, and to his face, when the bearers of hate would slide a finger across their throats and tell him that his body would float down the Vrbas River some day.

His small office was cluttered and noisy. The phone rang, clients stopped by, nonclients pleaded for his help, the walls were infested with bugs (mechanical). We decided to talk at a nearby tennis club, and sat on the patio of its coffee shop, run by a friend of Spasoje's. He was still welcome there. It was morning, and the sun was beginning its patient trek across the Balkan horizon. The Vrbas flowed quietly in front of us, and behind us early-bird tennis players swatted balls back and forth. In such a setting, surrounded by the sweet sounds and smells of summer, it was hard to imagine a war was going on, and sad to acknowledge that, yes, this was the case. Serbs were playing tennis in Banja Luka, and Muslims were being terrorized in Banja Luka. Parallel universes.

"In history, progress is possible only with the mixing of nationalities," Spasoje said, as though speaking to a jury. "I'm not only mad and embarrassed about this stupid war but disappointed. What is being done here is not in the favor of Serbs. We are losers too. Look at the number of Serbs who have died or been forced out of their homes. Look at the destruction. We used to go to Italy for vacation. Now we can't afford gasoline to drive our cars across town. After this war is finished, it will be a shame for someone to be a Serb."

Spasoje defended Muslims and Croats who were lucky enough to have their fates decided by a judge in a municipal court rather than by a guard in a prison camp. Most of his cases concerned young men who refused to join the Serb Army, because doing so would require them to take up arms against their brethren on the other side of the front line. It was a horrible choice: Dodge the draft and get thrown in jail or join the army and fire mortars at your cousins. Either way, as Captain Yossarian, the hero of *Catch-22*, would recognize in an instant, you're getting screwed.

I asked Spasoje how many cases he had won.

He laughed.

"How can I win cases when I don't even know what the laws are? I'm not joking. They change all the time. We have something in this city called the War Crisis Committee. It issues decrees that have the force of law. But I don't know who is on this committee or how it got the power to issue decrees. Nobody knows. All I know is that this committee is illegal and its decrees are illegal and I must obey them. There is nothing I can do about it."

His batting average was abysmal in the courtroom and worse in the streets. Just before the war broke out, Spasoje tried to organize an antiwar protest. He got permits from the police and city administration. When the protest was about to get under way, a gang of thugs barged onto the scene and threw tear-gas grenades at the small crowd. Those who didn't run away fast enough got punched in the gut or the groin. The police watched from a distance.

"I am a lawyer, and for me it is very sad to say that there is no law here. There are weapons rather than law. What did Mao say? Power comes out of the barrel of a gun. It's very true. The situation is decadent. A lot of Serbs think this is leading us nowhere but they feel powerless. How many disagree? I don't know. Perhaps thirty percent disagree, but most of them are frightened and quiet. Perhaps sixty percent agree or are confused enough to go along. They are led by the ten percent who have the guns and who have control of the television towers. That's all they need."

It was time for another soft drink. Coffee was unavailable because, at the moment, electricity was unavailable. The waiter brought the drinks. We stopped talking while he emptied the ashtray, which had filled up quickly, thanks to my interpreter's generosity with his Marlboros. If you want to make friends in Bosnia, offer a Marlboro. I always carried a few packs with me even though I don't smoke, and sometimes I gave them to kids who helped me out, for even kids were dying for a smoke. Cigarettes were the lucky charms of war, more useful than a flak jacket.

The waiter moved away and the silence at our table was broken by two Serb warplanes that roared over the city's rooftops before tilting their wings to the side and returning to their base outside town. They flew so low you could see the empty bomb racks under the wings, and your ears hurt from the sound of their engines. Spasoje looked to the sky, like a defeated boxer sitting in misery in his corner of the ring, watching his rival raise his arms into the air. Spasoje explained that the pilots like to buzz Banja Luka when they return from a raid.

"It is a sign of victory."

Spasoje slouched deeper into his chair. He would keep fighting, for he was a stubborn man in a nation famed for stubbornness, but he knew he would not win. He could not use words to shoot down warplanes, and his affidavits would not stop tanks. He had failed to rouse much support among fellow Serbs, the greatest pity of all, because a few more brave souls might have made a difference. Edmund Burke died two centuries before the first shots were fired in Bosnia, but his famous words could be the country's epitaph: "The only thing necessary for the triumph of evil is for good men to do nothing."

I was surprised in Bosnia to see how much evil a good person could be persuaded to tolerate or commit, and how little persuasion it took. A day after talking with Spasoje, I cruised through an apartment complex looking for Serbs who had moved into cleansed apartments. Bogdan, my interpreter, spotted a teenager wearing cut-off shorts as he took out the trash. Bogdan was a magazine journalist, so he had a sharp eye for talkers. We pulled alongside the kid and Bogdan asked, in a roundabout way, whether he knew of any Serbs who recently moved into the neighborhood. He did not.

The youth wore round, John Lennon–style glasses that gave him an intellectual look, so I asked if he spoke English. Yes. He had just graduated from high school, and his name was Boris, a good Serb name, and his English was quite good. The day had been long and hot, so I was too tired to go through the usual routine of friendly chatter. I asked a sensitive question in a lazy, how's-the-weather tone of voice.

"What do you think of the war?"

He shrugged his shoulders, as though I had asked a question that anybody with a double-digit IQ knew the answer to.

"The Serb people are being seduced. They don't know what is happening. They see what they want to see, or what others want them to see. I think it's pretty sick."

He was eighteen years old, which meant he would be drafted soon.

"What will you do when the army calls?" I asked.

He shrugged his shoulders again. Another dumb question.

"I will go to the army. It's better than jail."

Simple as that. The killing is wrong, but I'd rather do it than go to jail.

He was not a monster. He seemed to be a good kid. His hair was long and knotted into a ponytail. He was not, I thought, unlike a lot of young Americans who had been persuaded to cut their hair and fight in the Vietnam war. Particularly at the later stages of that war, when its wrongs became apparent, many GIs kept on killing Vietnamese even though they knew they had no business doing so. A journalist might slide into a trench with a twenty-year-old grunt from Detroit, ask what he thought of the war and get a salvo of laughter in return. "No fuckin' idea, man," the soldier would say. "S'pose I'm just waiting to get the hell outta here. What the fuck are you doin' here? You ain't gonna tell me you wanted to come to this shithole of a jungle?"

So what's Boris supposed to do? Conscientious objection did not exist. Medical excuses were tossed out; if your trigger finger worked, you could fight. There was no Canada to flee to—almost every country in Europe was shutting its doors to Serbs. Just getting to the border was difficult enough; the checkpoints on roads to Serbia were designed, in part, to keep fighting-age men from sneaking away. Some managed to get out while others failed or dared not try, fearing retribution against their families. And so Boris, like many of his peers, would choose a combat trench over a prison cell. In a few months, when he got the call from Banja Luka's recruitment center, he would turn into a soldier and do what he was told. Kill. Kill Muslims. Kill Croats. In his spare time, he would watch MTV. He would become a deadly lemming.

In Bosnia, I found many members of the species. A few weeks after talking to Boris, I visited one of the Serb gun sites above Sarajevo. The four soldiers posted to the position were sitting on empty ammunition boxes and drinking cheap wine when I arrived with two British colleagues. The soldiers were bored. Only two exciting things ever happened in their besieging lives—they got an order to fire, or they got new porno magazines. They seemed desperate for any form of amusement on the day I visited, so they settled for a chat with three foreign journalists.

Dragiša, a middle-aged Serb with a receding hairline and advancing paunch, was in charge of the detachment, which had set up shop in the parking lot next to a wrecked restaurant. Until a few months earlier, tourists visited the restaurant for a bite to eat while enjoying its lovely view of Sarajevo. Dragiša's men had built a bunker a few feet away from the restaurant's remains and surrounded it with mortars, bazookas and rifles. Dragisa gave a friendly tour of the bunker, like an eager-to-please real estate agent showing off a model home. I pretended to be in the market.

His prize attraction was a well-oiled 12.7-millimeter Browning heavy machine gun. It's not one of those tinny Kalashnikovs that go *rat-tat-tat-tat* when fired. The Browning goes *boom-boom-boom-boom*. It's about six feet long, weighs nearly a hundred pounds without ammunition and must be anchored to the ground before firing. Its muzzle, which is as thick as a man's forearm, fires oversized bullets strong enough to pierce the metal of an airplane fuselage. Dragiša and his men were not shooting at planes, they were shooting at people. Judging by the hundreds of empty bullet casings littered like peanut shells under the gun, they had shot lots of people. The Browning had a direct line of fire at the Sarajevo Holiday Inn. I declined an offer to fire off a few rounds at the hotel.

Other visitors had not been so reluctant. A well-known Russian writer who strongly supported the Serbs made a pilgrimage to one of the perches above Sarajevo and, in front of a film crew that tagged along, and in the name of Orthodox unity, fired a few anti-aircraft rounds at the city below, grinning like a kid with a squirt gun. It had become a tradition for visitors, especially ones from Serbia and Montenegro, to squeeze off a few shots, and this spawned a new class of soldiers, the "weekend warriors" who visited the front line on Saturdays and Sundays, when they had time off from their nine-to-five jobs. Down in Sarajevo, the weekends became known as the most dangerous time of all.

The soldiers at the perch I was visiting were not weekend warriors. One of them, Želja, a midtwenties sniper with the looks of
George Michael, used to live in Sarajevo, where he had a small ex-
port-import business. He left as the fighting began and became a
conscript in the Serb Army. Želja reminded me of ponytailed Boris
from Banja Luka. He seemed unexcited about participating in the
destruction of his hometown, yet he followed orders. It had become
a job, and he tried to avoid thinking about it. The people at the
receiving end of his gunfire were abstractions, and they had to be,
because some were his friends or fellow Serbs who stayed behind in
Sarajevo. Two of them were his mother and father. Serb propaganda
told Želja that Bosnia's Muslims were Koran-waving fanatics trying
to set up an Islamic state in which Serb women would be forced to
wear chadors. At any moment, the "Turks" could storm up the
mountains that Želja and his colleagues were "defending." Sarajevo
had to be liberated from these Turks, and that meant destroying it
or forcing the Turks to surrender and accept partition of the prized
capital (as well as the country). Želja seemed too smart to swallow
the party line whole, but it gave him a plausible excuse that made
his job easier to stomach. Just fire, don't think.

There are plenty of Serbs who enjoyed killing civilians and eagerly
sought the opportunities to do so. Želja was not among them, and
I'm sure that Boris would not join their ranks either. Those killers
never had so much fun. They wore black jumpsuits, Rambo-style
headbands, coils of bullets were wrapped over their shoulders and
grenades hung from their belts. They even smelled of gunpowder.
Journalists paid a lot of attention to them, not to slugs like Želja,
because the Rambos were more quotable and picturesque. They
puffed up their chests and played stupid games with their bayonets,
tossing them into the air and catching them by the handle. As I
waited for clearance at a checkpoint one day, a Rambo pulled the
pin from a grenade and juggled it from one hand to another. After
a few tosses of the live grenade and a couple of macho laughs, he
slipped the pin back in, and even his buddies seemed relieved.

Želja and many other soldiers were different. They did not wear
trendy combat outfits and did not get the opportunity to loot, pillage
or rape. Perhaps they didn't want to. They got hot meals occasionally and showed little lust as they carried out the dirty work assigned
to them. The high point of their day, aside from killing their bore-

dom by killing civilians in Sarajevo, was wandering off into the forest for a private look at the girlie mags. When Želja learned that one of the visiting journalists was from the BBC, he wrote a short letter and asked that it be delivered to a Serb friend who worked in London. I took a peek at it once we bade farewell. (I'm a journalist, okay?) The letter included these lines: "I am shooting from the front line. I have become as stupid as an empty bottle of cognac." He was a deadly lemming.

Gaining the support of ordinary people like Želja and Boris is a crucial element of any successful reign of terror. The wavering masses, the silent majority, the good men, they must feel stained by the same blood as the Visigoths who fired the first shots. They must be made into accomplices to the crime. Once this is done, once their moral backs are broken, they will do virtually anything. Like Želja, they will even fire shots that might kill their own parents.

▶ *Eight*

VERA AND STANA Milanović had no idea that their minds had been poisoned. They were Serbs who had been forced out of their homes by fighting in central Bosnia. They made their way to Banja Luka, where a relative lived, and took over a vacant apartment. It happened like this: A few days after a family had been cleansed out of Banja Luka, Stana borrowed a crowbar and broke into the apartment. She was Serb, and her three children needed a decent roof over their heads. The toys that they found in the apartment were an unexpected bonus.

At least the flat was uninhabited when she moved in. Serbs occasionally barged into houses before the Bosnian owners had moved out. A Serb who wanted a better apartment, or a Serb family whose house was destroyed in fighting, would bang on the front door and tell the owners that the living room and kitchen no longer belonged to them. The Serbs would troop in, armed, and a week later suggest that the owners move out of the rest of the house, or else. It had a legal veneer because an old and forgotten municipal code in Banja Luka limited the apartment space that a family could have. The limit was minuscule by modern standards, which made it perfect for use against non-Serbs. This trick was known as the "rationalization of living space."

Stana opened the door a crack when I knocked, afraid that I might be an angry relative of the cleansed owners. Warily, she let me in and showed the way to the living room. The door shut behind me and, because the lock had been busted by her crowbar, she secured the door with a padlock. The sofa was covered in what seemed to be the same white shag carpeting that was on the floor. The wallpaper was pimpled with rectangular spots, reminders of the family pictures that used to hang there. The electricity was out, so Stana served water in small coffee cups, explaining that the previous occupants must have sold off the large glasses before leaving.

Her mother, Vera, a peasant woman as big as a haystack, sat next to me. It was a hot day, so she wiped the sweat from her brow with a handkerchief and then blew her nose into the same handkerchief. I sensed that, if I stayed long enough, I would likely see the same performance in reverse order.

Bogdan pulled out the Marlboros. Mother and daughter beamed.

Stana had been the first to hit the road. After her village was caught up in the war, she fled to her mother's village on Vlašić Mountain, overlooking Travnik. But the fighting branched out and threatened the mother's village, too, so Vera joined her daughter in an exodus to Banja Luka. Vera said it was a pity they had to leave. Her village, after all, had been cleansed of its Muslims in the first days of the war.

I asked, out of politeness, whether the fighting in the village was heavy.

"Why, no, there was no fighting between Muslims and Serbs in the village," she said.

"Then why were the Muslims arrested?"

"Because they were planning to take over the village. They had already drawn up lists. The names of the Serb women had been split into harems for the Muslim men."

"Harems?"

"Yes, harems. Their Bible says men can have harems, and that's what they were planning to do once they had killed our men. Thank God they were arrested first." She wiped her brow.

"How do you know they were planning to kill the Serb men and create harems for themselves?"

"It was on the radio. Our military had uncovered their plans. It was announced on the radio."

I glanced at Bogdan. Harems? Over the past few months I had

heard that the Muslims would make Serb women wear chadors, the black ankle-to-head gown. I had heard that the Bosnians bombed themselves and blamed it on the Serbs. I had heard that an Islamic-Vatican-Croatian-Germanic conspiracy had been hatched to kill off the Serbs. But I had not, to date, heard anything about harems.

The look in Bogdan's eyes said, Please don't grin, because if you grin, then I'll grin, and then you'll start chuckling, and that will make me start chuckling. Bogdan knew how to keep a straight face; he learned it a few years earlier as a conscript in the Yugoslav National Army.

"How do you know the radio was telling the truth?" I asked.

Stana and Vera stared at me as though I wore no clothes. God, these Americans are dumber than cows. Vera's kindness evaporated as she flashed the kind of scowl that, I imagined, was deployed against grandchildren who wore farm boots indoors.

"Why," she demanded to know, "would the radio lie?"

I had to give up. It was the polite thing to do, even though Vera translated my silence as confirming the verity of the harem report. She took a triumphant puff on her Marlboro.

"Did any of the Muslims in your village harm you?" I asked, softly.

"No."

"Did any Muslim *ever* do anything bad to you?"

"No."

She seemed offended.

"My relations with Muslims in the village were always very good. They were very nice people."

▶ *Nine*

I CAUGHT the bug of spiritual sickness in Banja Luka. Everyone did. I don't know a journalist or aid worker who emerged from that city without thinking it was the most pitiful, heartbreaking place in Bosnia. It was infinitely cheerier to be with Bosnians in Sarajevo. Though under siege, Sarajevans could go to sleep without worrying that Serb soldiers would barge into their homes to rob or kill them. The sound of incoming mortars in Sarajevo was less scary than a knock on the door in Banja Luka. Even Bosnians cleansed out of their homes who ended up in barren refugee camps as far away as Jordan or Norway were in better shape than their friends in Banja Luka.

In a place like Banja Luka, it is difficult to understand the rule that says a journalist must not become "involved" in a story. I used to think it meant you should not show agreement or disagreement with the person you are interviewing. When, for example, you are asking a Serb soldier about the burning house at the end of the street, you are not supposed to show disbelief when he says the flames were started by a short circuit. You are not supposed to show disapproval when he shrugs his shoulders and says, Well, it was a Muslim house anyway, and the Muslims are scum, so what's the big deal? When Radovan Karadžić would tell another one of his whopping lies—always proportionate to his bearlike size—you just smile and nod your head, as though you agree with his suggestion that the Muslims are dynamiting their own mosques and shelling their own kindergartens. You refrain from throwing tangerines at him. Don't get involved, don't take sides.

The situation becomes difficult to bear when you are in a town that makes you think of Berlin during Nazi times. What do you say to the Bosnian who lives with the same kind of fear in his gut as the Jews who were rounded up in Germany fifty years earlier? When the Bosnian looks at you, with anger and fear and incomprehension in his eyes, and asks why America, the America that loves democracy and human rights and just built a Holocaust Museum that receives millions of visitors every year, won't stop genocide in Europe at the end of the twentieth century, what do you do? Shrug your shoulders in neutrality, pretend like you don't know? What would you say to the Jew in Berlin? "Sorry, I can't take sides."

This is when you start to feel the spiritual sickness. It can be held at tolerable levels if you convince yourself that your efforts as a journalist or aid worker or diplomat might make a difference. You soldier on. But the sickness takes over if you sense futility, if you can no longer look a Bosnian in the eye and say, in honesty, that the reason the world doesn't react is because it doesn't know what's happening or doesn't understand. When you conclude that the world does know, and does understand, and still doesn't react, your time is up. When that happens, you do unusual things. Canadian diplomat Louis Gentile, who worked in Banja Luka for the U.N. High

Commissioner for Refugees, wrote an unusual letter to *The New York Times* on January 14, 1994. It was a diplomat's primal scream:

> The terror continues, terror of attacks by armed men at night, rape and murder, children unable to sleep, huddling in fear behind boarded up doors and windows. The latest victims were three Muslim residents of the Banja Luka suburb of Vrbanja on December 29. In broad daylight, four armed men (two in uniform) entered the home of a couple 58 and 54 years old. The man was shot in the head and killed, his wife was shot in the hand and then beaten to death with a blunt instrument. A Muslim neighbor, who had the courage and misfortune to inquire what was happening when the murderers left carrying a television set, was shot in the heart at point-blank range. . . .
>
> To those who said to themselves after seeing *Schindler's List*, "Never again": It is happening again. The so-called leaders of the western world have known what is happening here for the last year and a half. They receive play-by-play reports. They talk of prosecuting war criminals, but do nothing to stop the crimes. May God forgive them. May God forgive us all.

MERRY CHRISTMAS, SARAJEVO

SARAJEVO was a temptress, and it was hard to know which was more seductive, the half-mad look in her dark eyes, or the scarlet drops of blood on her extended hand. Temptresses have different allures with which they entice their victims, and the oddest thing about Sarajevo's allure was that the more ghastly she appeared to the outside world, the more her buildings were destroyed and the more starved her residents looked, the more seductive she was. Sarajevo was violence and passion, which, for journalists, is the ultimate temptation. She also frightened me—any sensible person would be wary of entering a city from which some colleagues were being carried out on stretchers and in boxes, victims of anonymous assailants.

There were two ways to enter Sarajevo. You could try to get a seat on a U.N. cargo plane bringing relief supplies to the city, as I had done for my daylong visit a few months earlier, or you could drive into the city on one of the two roads that Serbs allowed the United Nations and foreign press to travel on. The airport option was quicker and safer but the runway was often shut down because of fighting or weather. This was the case when I needed to enter the city during Sarajevo's first Christmas under siege, so I pursued the overland option, and got the ride of my life.

The jumping-off point for driving into Sarajevo was a town about twenty-five miles away called Kiseljak, controlled by a Croat militia allied at the time with Bosnia's government. Kiseljak was separated from Sarajevo by a thin strip of Serb soldiers who formed part of the siege ring around the capital. A mile or so outside of Kiseljak was the front line with the Serbs. The term "front line" implies a certain amount of tension and, presumably, shots being fired from time to time, but it had been a long time since shots were fired outside Kiseljak. The town had turned itself into a commercial hub supplying the Serbs and the Bosnians whom the Serbs were besieging. The double-crossing was completely in the open. The Bosnians in Sarajevo knew that their Croat allies in Kiseljak were providing the Serbs with food and drink and gas, but looked the other way at this treachery because the Serbs, in turn, looked the other way as food and gas from Kiseljak filtered into Sarajevo.

The bounty of material goods in Kiseljak attracted the foreign press and United Nations, which turned the place into a boomtown. The United Nations requisitioned the best hotel, on a hilltop overlooking the town, while journalists got the second-best accommodations. Inevitably, Kiseljak earned the spite of millions of Bosnians who were suffering from the war rather than profiting from it. At checkpoints leading to Kiseljak, Bosnian soldiers who hadn't eaten a hot meal in weeks would chuckle in bitterness when they heard the town's name. "So you are going to our El Dorado? Bring us back a steak dinner when you return."

Foreign journalists made frequent trips from Sarajevo to Kiseljak to get gasoline and food. The Serbs permitted this traffic because it was part of the overall deal, and because there was usually a bottle of brandy on hand to smooth the way at touchy moments. Even so, the journey was risky because the blighted no-man's-land around Sarajevo was infested with mines, snipers and robbers. If you had to make the journey, it was best taken care of in the morning or middle of the day, when the players were shaking off the previous night's brandy. Shooting and thieving picked up after two in the afternoon. You could set your watch by it.

It was preferable to make the journey in an armored car. The *Washington Post* had not yet bought one, so I had no choice but to loiter around the Kontinental Pension, where the day-trippers from Sarajevo usually had lunch, and try to hitch a ride in someone's vehicle. The BBC had an office and satellite phone at the Kontinental, which meant you could get a cup of English tea for free and call your girlfriend for $25 a minute. You could wait for days at the Kontinental, because space was hard to come by and, when fighting got heavy, the traffic ceased entirely. I got lucky. Two hours after arriving at the Kontinental on December 23, I was on the road to Sarajevo.

I put my life into the hands of one of those veteran correspondents who can no longer remember the number of wars he has covered. David was a producer for an American television network, and, as I later found out, he volunteered before anyone else to make supply missions to Kiseljak. Maybe he liked the thrill of the drive, maybe he was tired of working behind a camera or maybe he just wanted a steak and salad at the Kontinental. I cornered him at lunch and he offered me the spare seat in the cab of his Land Rover. I felt lucky until I noticed that the back of the jeep was filled with jerricans of gasoline. He was on a fuel run. He was a madman.

We were waved through the last Croat checkpoint outside Kiseljak and followed a narrow road through a forest that was absolutely peaceful and, with the exception of mines planted on the shoulder to prevent a tank blitz, unaffected by the war. We soon rolled up to the Serb checkpoint. The Serbs knew David, and after a light inspection of our cargo, they accepted his offer of a bottle of cognac and waved us through. We began an uneventful drive through the band of Serb territory surrounding Sarajevo. Soon we were in Ilidža, a suburb controlled by the Serbs. The buildings were run-down and had sandbags or stacks of wood covering windows facing toward the city, from where the Bosnian Army occasionally fired mortars. It was a futile effort, because every shell fired at the Serbs was answered with ten fired back at the Bosnians. Ilidža had suffered slight damage; the same could not be said for Sarajevo.

After Ilidža, the landscape underwent a metamorphosis, turning into a wasteland. The place felt dead, as though buildings, not just people, had been killed, reduced to disfigured corpses of concrete and steel. Everything was gray, the ruined buildings, the asphalt, the sky. The farther we went, the worse things became, because we were nearing Sarajevo. Serb soldiers patrolled the area, but they moved quickly, in twos and threes, like fugitives. No one could feel safe, not even the men with guns.

We accelerated. Speed serves two functions that oppose each other. The faster you go, the harder it is for a sniper to shoot you. That's the reason you go fast, as fast as possible. But speed means loss of control, because armored cars weigh several thousand pounds more than they should, and as a result, they are much more difficult to turn or brake. Many journalists dodged sniper bullets by going fast, but others were injured in crashes. Even so, a weighing of speed's risks and benefits was not necessary, because inside every one of us is an instinct that tells us danger can be overcome by speed. Drive fast, run fast, crawl fast. *Go.*

We entered a hairpin turn. The asphalt had turned to packed dirt covered by a thin sheet of ice, and the road was marked only by faint tracks from vehicles that had gone before us. I had heard of this turn, because a few weeks earlier a U.N. armored personnel carrier strayed off it and hit a mine, killing the Ukrainian soldiers inside. You had to slow down to avoid skidding, but if you went too slow the snipers could get you. David downshifted to first gear and stayed off the brake as he wound his way through the turn. As the jeep straightened out, he accelerated fast, first gear to second gear to third gear, the engine performing perfectly, obediently, never coughing or sputtering, as though it, too, sensed the danger and wanted to get away, far away.

The road turned into a lane alongside houses that were used by soldiers resting up between patrols. Front-line soldiers were the most dangerous of all, because they were tired, angry, poor and, often in this war, drunk. They hated everyone, not just the enemy but their commanders and even the civilians they were protecting, because all those people were living so much better and taking fewer risks. When a $50,000 armored car, painted a cheery white, came down the road, bearing a couple of foreign journalists protected by $1,500 flak jackets, carrying several thousand dollars of cash each, wearing down-filled parkas and L.L. Bean hiking boots with fur linings, it's easy to understand why the soldiers became testy.

This particular lane was the place where robberies occasionally happened. It was very simple. The soldiers waved you to a halt with their assault rifles and found an excuse for confiscating your belongings. The money, they would say, could not be taken into Sarajevo because it might be used to buy weapons for Bosnians; the flak jackets might be given to Bosnian soldiers; cars were stolen on the excuse that registration papers were out of order, or, again, that they might be given to Bosnians. Carjackings were the worst of all, because you would have to walk the rest of the way into Sarajevo. On this day, we got through without any trouble. So far so good.

We turned onto a deserted boulevard. This was Sniper Alley, a classic stretch of wartime blight, its streetlights shot out and asphalt pimpled with bomb craters. On the north side of the boulevard, twenty-five yards to the right, were apartment buildings hiding Serb snipers. The south side was held by the Bosnian Army, which had its own snipers stationed there, close enough to curse the Serbs. Back-and-forth shooting was constant but you could have a hard time telling if it was directed at you until you heard the impact on your car's armor and felt the shock wave. Then you knew, and then you really hit the gas.

As bad as Sniper Alley was, it was the homestretch and a better place than the no-man's-land we had just traversed. I was surprised when David pushed the car faster and faster along the Alley, and he must have sensed my concern, because he spoke up as he shifted into high gear for the first time that day, shouting over the whining sound of the hardworking engine. "I hope you don't mind this, but I'm practicing for the New Year's Day rally. We're having a race for the armored cars. Two laps around Sarajevo." David was not pulling my leg. Out of the corner of my eye, I noticed a slogan painted on a bullet-pimpled wall, "Welcome to Hell."

We pulled into the Holiday Inn, the last thing you would expect to find in a war zone. For me, Holiday Inns represent suburban quiet and comfort, everything that is ordinary and unexciting about the world. They are reassuring, because you know what you will get, including an ice machine at the end of the corridor, a Bible in the top desk drawer and a toilet that, according to the white paper strip across it, has been sanitized for your protection. During times of peace, Sarajevo must have been a relatively exotic location for a Holiday Inn, and American tourists must have been surprised, and relieved, to find one there.

They would have been particularly surprised if they had been staying at the hotel on April 6, 1992. At the time, the Holiday Inn was being used as an unofficial headquarters for Radovan Karadžić's Serbian Democratic Party, and, when peace demonstrators gathered in an adjacent park, a few of Karadžić's goons opened fire from the rooftop and upper floors. For Sarajevo, those shots marked the start of the war. From then on, it was all downhill for the Holiday Inn. Once fighting began, executives at corporate headquarters in America must have been floored by the things happening at and to their Sarajevo franchise.

The Holiday Inn is a twelve-floor rectangular box painted an unappealing yellow. It would be hard to imagine an uglier building. I am not being unduly harsh. The prewar tourist brochure for the hotel features a dozen color pictures of its restaurants, sauna, swimming pool, atrium and assorted other attractions. The only picture of the hotel's exterior is a nighttime view in which you can hardly see the building. From an architectural standpoint, it's quite a pity that so many ancient monuments were shelled to their foundations in Sarajevo while the Holiday Inn survived.

The hotel was located along Sniper Alley, and its south side, squarely facing the Serbs, was shot up beyond habitation. It had sustained dozens of direct mortar hits and was exposed to constant sniper fire; living in a southern room was out of the question. The northern side was the safest of all. The other sides, western and eastern, were habitable even though snipers could angle their shots inside the rooms; thankfully, they had easier targets to go after. You could stay at the hotel for $62 a night, including breakfast, lunch and dinner. The hotel had its own generator, so during the long spells when the city had no electricity or heating, the Holiday Inn might have some for a few hours a day, depending on the amount of fuel the manager had procured on the black market.

It was surprising that the Serbs hadn't shelled the hotel to the ground, but there was a reason for their oversight. War causes inconveniences for both sides, but some can be overcome with mutually beneficial consequences. It goes like this: the Serbs have a building that they want to preserve, perhaps an old church, and the Bosnians have a building they want to preserve, perhaps the Holiday Inn. The two sides cut a deal on shortwave radio in which the Serbs agree to not wreck the Holiday Inn, and the Bosnians agree to not wreck the church. It can be simpler than that, too: the Bosnians simply pay the Serbs not to shell the Holiday Inn. A time is set to meet at a quiet part of no-man's-land, and a sack of Deutsche marks is handed from Bosnian to Serb. That, and the presence of the foreign press, helps explain the hotel's survival.

The main entrance, facing Sniper Alley, had not been used since the war began, so I entered through a rear door. The interior consisted of a large atrium that was a pleasant place for relaxing and sipping coffee during the old days, but during a winter siege, it was pretty much the coldest place in the world. I dragged my backpack and computer bag across the atrium to the reception desk, where a shivering woman was to be found under a half dozen sweaters and jackets. She gave me the keys to a fourth-floor room and apologized for an absence of towels. I walked up a stairwell (the elevators had not worked for months) and was surprised when I entered the room. Aside from the missing towels and a cracked window, it had the look of a Holiday Inn room, a bit more run-down than usual, but the sheets seemed clean and the toilet did, indeed, have a strip of paper across it that said, "Sanitized for Your Protection." The toilet, however, was not functioning, because the generator was out of service, and therefore the hotel had no running water, nor electricity or heat. My inspection was carried out with a flashlight.

I knew no one in Sarajevo. No matter how confident a journalist might seem on the surface, inside we are neurotic wrecks, worrying about getting the story first, obsessing about our deadlines, fearful of our competition, dismissive of our editors, cursing our salary rates and lamenting the absence of a normal social life. The neurosis reaches a high point when you find yourself amid a big or dangerous story and you realize you don't have a clue about how to cover it. Those are the times when you must lean on fellow journalists, hoping that at least one of them is a friend of yours or is willing to act like one.

My *Washington Post* colleague, who had spent substantial time in Sarajevo, had given me the name of an amiable British reporter and his interpreter, both of whom lived at the hotel, but neither was present when I arrived. I walked upstairs to the fifth-floor office of the Reuters news agency, which had its own noisy generator and a satellite telephone that could be used for $40 a minute. I called Washington, let the foreign editor know I had arrived safely, and he of course asked whether I would be filing a story. I made a joke about my fingers being too cold to type, and told him I would not be sending anything until the next day. End of call. It had cost several hundred dollars.

I went downstairs for dinner. I noticed a journalist chatting in

French and taking large sips of red wine. What grabbed my attention was his parka. Everyone was wearing a parka or overcoat because the dining room was, like the rest of the hotel, without heat. A large "B+" was stenciled above one of his chest pockets, and "Medical Aid" was stenciled above another. When I realized what it meant, I knew I was among the lunatic fringe. His blood type was B-positive. Sterile bandages were in the other pocket. Writing your blood type on your clothes was a battlefield precaution, as was the practice of carrying a few sterile bandages, because it would quicken transfusions and first aid in the event that you suddenly needed them.

Dinner, served between six and nine, was a communal affair in which everyone sat together at large tables and ate the same food, like at boarding school. The only thing unchanged from peacetime was the attire of the waiters, who still wore white shirts, bow ties and dark green jackets with name tags bearing the Holiday Inn logo. Within a minute or two of sitting down, a waiter would bring the first course of soup, followed by a main course of greasy meat and vegetables and finally a small dessert, usually rice pudding or cake. You could order wine for $40 a bottle, a fortune by siege standards, but for journalists on expense accounts, this was no problem. In Sarajevo, it was very easy to convince yourself that you deserved any luxury that came your way.

I asked the diner next to me if he knew Kevin Sullivan, whose name I had been given. Yes, he said, Kevin is sitting three feet away on the other side of the table. I looked across the table and saw a guy with Brillo-pad hair, a brown goatee and eyes brimming with mischief.

"Kevin?"

"Yes."

"I'm Peter Maass. Blaine Harden told me to look you up."

"Ahh, yes," he smiled. "Peter Maass. Of course. Welcome to Sarajevo. Have you met Džemal yet?"

Džemal was the interpreter. Kevin didn't wait for an answer.

"This is Džemal," he announced, nudging a man who was mopping up the last drops of his soup with a piece of bread. Džemal, in his thirties, had short brown hair and, looking up, inspected my face with the same keenness he had been applying to his appetizer. He smiled broadly and nodded hello.

The conversation could have ended with that. When journalists get together, they quickly sniff each other out and, if they smell a rivalry or an aroma of arrogance, they will back away without turning their backs. The degree of warmth between friendly journalists in a place like Sarajevo can be matched in intensity only by the coldness you feel from others. I had no idea which way things would turn out with Kevin and Džemal, no way of knowing that these two men with strange looks in their eyes were in fact Balkan angels who would shepherd me through heaven and hell.

Kevin was a Scotsman from Glasgow who had been working in Singapore for United Press International when the war started. UPI had gone through a dozen or so owners in recent years, never leaving the brink of bankruptcy. This created opportunities for people like Kevin, a "stringer" who was paid a day rate with no job security. Even though UPI paid miserable wages, and often failed to pay at all, Kevin volunteered for duty in Bosnia. I was not mistaken when I saw a bit of mischief in his eyes.

Džemal was a classic Bosnian. A Muslim, he had been to many more bars in his lifetime than mosques, and his girlfriend was a Catholic from Croatia. He was a businessman before the war, importing and exporting anything that would sell, including shot-sized bottles of liquor, the kind you get on airplanes. He had a significant stockpile when the war broke out, which was fortunate, because whenever we got into a tight spot, or when we got bored, Džemal would pull a miniature bottle of cognac out of a pocket, wink at me like a magician and say, "Artillery," and then down half the bottle, handing me the rest. In a siege, Džemal was precisely the kind of interpreter you wanted, because he was a dealmaker at heart. No matter what we needed or whom we needed, Džemal could take care of it. Cars, gas, coffee, ministers, he could arrange it all. And like Kevin, he had a profoundly ridiculous sense of humor.

▶ *Two*

FOR AS LONG as I can remember, my family has celebrated Christmas. It was a social rather than religious event that we always looked forward to, especially as children. A few days before Christmas, my mother would have a big party, inviting her friends over and serving eggnog and shortbread cookies. On Christmas Eve, we would read " 'Twas the Night Before Christmas" and, before going to sleep, hang empty socks next to the fireplace and leave, for Santa, a plate of cookies and a glass of milk. The next morning we got up early and opened stockings full of trinkets that our mother-turned-Santa had substituted for the empty socks. The glass of milk would be depleted, and most of the cookies would be gone, proof that Santa had come and nourished himself in our home. Our mother would remind us during breakfast to save room for the big turkey lunch we would eat in a few hours, and after rushing upstairs to, brush our teeth and wash our faces, we opened the presents piled under the Christmas tree. We made a few concessions to the fact that we were Jews celebrating a Christian holiday; the tree was topped with a nondenominational star rather than a replica of Jesus, and we did not go to any church services. Otherwise, it was a typical American Christmas, down to the three-log fire in the fireplace even if the weather was warm, as it usually was in Los Angeles. If necessary, we would turn on the air conditioner.

I think of my Christmases past, and of my Christmas in Sarajevo, and I am tempted to classify them as poles apart. In one, there is abundance and peace and love, and in the other, hunger and warfare and hatred. But the more I think about it, the more I find that the Christmases are similar, and that if I had to select one in which the spirit of the occasion reached its fullest expression, I would select my Christmas in Sarajevo, because that's where I found miracles.

The parishioners of Saint Anthony's Cathedral were deprived of the right to attend midnight mass on Christmas Eve, because the wartime curfew meant they had to be home before ten o'clock, and at any time of day a packed cathedral would be an inviting target for the Serbs in the hills, like a red cape waved in front of a bull. So they made do. At four in the afternoon, they crammed into the cathedral's basement chapel, winter coat to winter coat, standing because there was no room for sitting, and as the temperature quickly rose, and the room took on the heavy smell of damp wool, everyone started to perspire, but nobody cared, for this was far preferable to the cold outside. A choir sang hymns from the back of the basement, and everyone joined in when it was time, creating a harmony beyond music.

The main defense mechanism of the people of Sarajevo was to stand together, helping one another out, because no one else would.

Suffering does much to bring people together and coax out the good in them, making a hero out of an office worker who, in normal times, would not help an old woman cross a street, but in wartime runs into a street at the risk of his own life to save her from sniper fire. The man might be a Muslim, the woman a Croat. It no longer mattered, for they were in it together, just as they were in the basement chapel together, Muslims, Croats, Serbs, Jews. If you wanted to find the Christmas spirit on Christmas Eve 1992, you could do no better than visit Saint Anthony's Cathedral in Sarajevo.

The priest's name was Ljubo Lučić. He had no altar to stand on, so only a lucky few in the front rows could see him and the sickly Christmas tree behind him; it had been scavenged from the forests at the front line, and it looked every bit as malnourished as the parishioners to whom it was supposed to deliver good cheer. Father Lučić told his flock that they were getting an insight into Jesus that few others had; the terror in their lives was like the terror of Jesus' life; their poverty was no different from Jesus'; and Jesus was a refugee, cast from one town to another. I could see people wiping tears from their eyes, out of sadness or happiness. Perhaps Father Lučić heard the soft sobs and worried about them, for he suddenly said, almost in desperation, "The Christmas message in our situation is that life is worth living, no matter what."

I visited Father Lučić after the service. He had a small office above the chapel, and he poured glasses of cherry brandy to the half dozen people who crowded around him, and somebody asked about the artillery shell on a corner table. Father Lučić smiled broadly and explained that it failed to explode when it hit his cathedral, so he kept it as proof that God watched over him. Father Lučić was thrilled by the service, and refilled our glasses as soon as we had taken a sip. He said the service was beautiful because there had been so many people and no bombs. It was far better than the last Christmas service he attended under fire. "I am sixty-two years old," he said. "This is the second war for me."

Just before midnight, I went for a drive in an armored Land Rover with two British correspondents who had been drinking heavily at the Holiday Inn and claiming that they preferred to be in Sarajevo at Christmas rather than London because they were relieved of the burden of fighting the crowds of shoppers on Oxford Street. We had heard of a secret midnight mass, and we tried to find it. We failed, but the drive itself was worth the effort, because I had never felt such desolation.

There was no light at midnight, thanks to the absence of electricity in the town, and thanks to the fact that no one stayed up by candlelight, because it was easier to stay warm under the blankets of your bed rather than huddling around a wood-burning stove, for which you had to collect the precious fuel on your own outdoors, under the crosshairs. We drove around aimlessly. All that we could see were parts of buildings illuminated by our dimmed headlights. More than 350,000 people were living in Sarajevo at that moment, but there was not the slightest clue of any of them. Everywhere we looked, we saw only darkness and emptiness and destruction, and we felt a coldness that was more chilling than the subfreezing temperatures outside our car. I was reminded of newsreel footage of cities destroyed during World War II, scratchy black-and-white films of Berlin or Dresden, in which the buildings were hollow and gray, windows filled with a blackness deeper than the earth itself. It was Christmas Eve in Sarajevo, and the only sound was of gunfire.

One of the rules of Bosnia was that whenever things were going well, something terrible would happen soon. Another rule was that whenever things were going terribly, something good would happen soon. The rules are not contradictory but complementary. Continuity was the exception in Bosnia, and this was the case on Christmas Eve. The hotel was a postmodern cave. The radiator in my room was still stone cold; I had worn thin wool gloves as I typed out my story earlier in the evening, relying on a flashlight for illumination. Before going to sleep, I hauled several gallons of icy water up to my room for washing my face and flushing the toilet. I slept fully clothed, in my sleeping bag, under as many blankets as I could find. The first thing I saw when I woke up in the morning was my own breath. I went downstairs for breakfast, which consisted of a slice of Spam, a muffin hardened by coldness or staleness or both and weak tea. Conversation was minimal among the journalists, limited to groggy, ironic exchanges of "Merry Christmas" in half a dozen languages. This was the worst Christmas any of us had experienced.

A few hours later, I was sitting in a warm apartment, snacking on the sweetest baklava I have ever tasted, and thinking I could not have dreamed up a finer Christmas.

Kevin and I wanted to write a story about a Catholic family's Christmas in Sarajevo, so Džemal, ever resourceful, found the Pelzl family and got us invited to their home. Karlo and Janja Pelzl were Croats, members of the Catholic strand of Sarajevo's complex fabric of nationalities and religions, which even included a vibrant Jewish community that settled in the city in the fifteenth century after being expelled from Spain by the Inquisition. If you were a troublemaker who wanted to destroy a city that, more than any other in Europe, was a symbol of integration and tolerance, you would do well to pick Sarajevo. You could find, on virtually the same block, a Muslim mosque, Roman Catholic cathedral, Christian Orthodox church and Jewish synagogue. The people of Sarajevo—Muslims, Serbs, Croats, Jews, Albanians, Gypsies and a kaleidoscope of mixtures therein—lived in Europe's truest melting pot.

There is a tradition in Sarajevo that people of different religions visit one another on religious holidays. On Christmas, the Pelzls' Muslim and Serb friends would come by for a visit. In turn, the Pelzls would visit their Muslim friends on the first day of Ramadan, the Muslim holy month, and visit their Serb friends on Orthodox Christmas, which falls in January. Kevin, Džemal and I were part of the parade of visitors who stopped by the Pelzl household on Christmas Day. After shedding our flak jackets at their doorstep, we sat down at their dining table and were served a platter of sweets, which were unimaginable delicacies under the circumstances.

The Pelzls lived in a building not far from the Holiday Inn, within shouting distance of the front line, and they kept count of the number of direct mortar hits on their building, which was nine, if I recall correctly. Several people had been injured. The Pelzls were untouched, although bits of shrapnel and a sniper bullet or two had crashed through their windows and struck the living room, leaving the sort of holes you get when you try to drive a nail into a wall and succeed only in making a mess of chipped plaster. A small statue of the Virgin Mary stood on a table in a corner, presided over by one such shrapnel hole, an ironic halo of sorts. Mary's serene smile seemed a bit mischievous.

Karlo was the director of Sarajevo's Croatian Cultural Center, and he had the physical appearance of a classic bureaucrat, a short, rotund man in his early fifties who dressed conservatively. He was a devout Catholic who went to church every Sunday, even during the war, when he had to dodge sniper fire and fret about being blown up as he received communion. He was a strict man, this was clear, an unlikely candidate for having a Koran parked next to his Bible, to be tolerant of others who didn't agree with his way of life, or his religion. In another city or another country, Karlo might have been a different kind of fellow, but we were in Sarajevo, and the city had a tendency to infect its inhabitants with mutual respect.

Karlo and Janja were a Bosnian Ozzie and Harriet, with three kids, a tidy apartment, a parquet floor polished to a shine, a piano in a corner. Their home's only aesthetic blemish, aside from shrapnel holes, was a makeshift stove built into a hallway connecting the living room to the bedrooms. This was the apartment's source of heat, and it was fueled by wood that Karlo and his oldest son cut down from Sarajevo's few remaining trees, or scavenged from ruined buildings. Almost every apartment in Sarajevo had one of these contraptions, as necessary for survival as air. The design was rudimentary, a tin or iron box of any size, propped up on four legs, with a chimney attachment that funneled smoke out of the apartment, through a flap cut into a wall. The Pelzls had a deluxe model with an interior shelf that permitted them to bake bread and other foods, including their Christmas cookies. When we entered, the apartment was as warm and fragrant as a bakery.

The Christmas preparations had been under way for three months, with military precision, as though the family was planning an ambush rather than a meal. Food had been salted away since August, when they collected nuts for the baklava. Smoked ham that a friend gave them in November had been put aside in a kitchen cabinet, the only meat in the house, delectable and untouchable. Wood was stocked up to ensure that there would be enough fuel for baking, and money was saved so that, a few days before Christmas, Janja could buy eggs on the black market for her sweets. She had been able to buy four. Traditionally, the family's big Christmas Eve dinner was centered around fresh fish from Janja's hometown of Bosanski Brod, along the Sava River, but it had been captured by Serbs early in the war, and in any event fresh fish was a laughable impossibility in Sarajevo, so the family made do with canned tuna fish.

On Christmas morning, Karlo and Janja went to mass at separate churches. It had nothing to do with a marital spat or preferences for different priests. They were afraid that if they went to the same church, and if it was bombed, their children would be left without parents. They lessened the odds of this happening by splitting up; one of them might get killed but probably not both. This passed as normal behavior in Sarajevo. Parents rarely went outdoors together. If, by chance, they had to leave home at the same time but for different destinations, perhaps one going to work, the other searching for food, they would not step outside at the same time. One would stay behind and wait until the other was far enough ahead so that a single shell could not kill both of them.

Karlo and Janja returned home safely after mass and spent the rest of the day receiving visitors. After an hour of friendly discussion over glasses of plum brandy, Kevin and I unveiled the gifts we had brought, causing the family's jaws to drop, almost as one. There was a gaping silence, so long and obvious that Kevin and I looked at each other, worried that we might have done something wrong, broken some sort of etiquette, perhaps an unspoken rule that guests are not supposed to offer gifts on Christmas, or that the gifts we offered were inappropriate. The silence was broken by a giggle from the Pelzls' daughter, and then Karlo spoke up, motioning to the gifts we had placed on the table and explaining that his well-bred family had not seen such items since the war began. We needn't have worried about offending them, for in fact the Pelzls were delighted to be presented with a banana and four tangerines.

The discussion turned to faith. Times of tragedy test a believer's faith in God, and the worst tragedy of all was being inflicted on Bosnia, so I put a blunt question to my hosts. How can you believe in a God who permits such things to happen? Karlo and Janja smiled with self-confidence, as though they expected the question and knew it was not rhetorical but came from my heart. I was not interested in starting a theological debate, for that ground had been plowed many times before by people far more learned than any of us in that apartment, and no one had yet come up with a bullet-proof answer, and never would. But I wanted to know *their* answer.

Janja, who had been quiet, spoke up, and as she did so, she looked at the statue of the Virgin Mary.

"I believe more strongly than before," she said. "I can't explain why, but I have more faith now. I pray more, I believe more, and I believe that this is all God's will."

Even now, after a long time has passed, I can't decide whether her answer was touching or insane.

▶ *Three*

THE CLASSIC war book of my generation is Michael Herr's *Dispatches*, about the Vietnam war. It contains a passage in which Herr recounts riding in a helicopter that carried several corpses, one of them covered with a poncho that flew off in midflight, revealing a dead soldier's face. It made Herr think back to when he was a child. "You know how it is, you want to look and you don't want to look. I can remember the strange feelings I had when I was a kid looking at war photographs in *Life*, the ones that showed dead people or a lot of dead people lying close together in a field or a street, often touching, seeming to hold each other. . . . I remember now the shame I felt, like looking at first porn, all the porn in the world."

A month after the Bosnian war started, I was in a town, Slavonski Brod, where thousands of Bosnians had sought refuge after being cleansed by Serb forces. The refugees were staying in a sports stadium, and at midday the Serbs fired several shells that landed smack in the middle of the stadium, killing more than a dozen people. I went to the local hospital with a Canadian colleague, because that's where you go to interview survivors and count bodies. I did okay at the interviewing part, but the counting was a different matter. My colleague, who had more experience in affairs of that sort, asked one of the doctors how many had been killed, and the doctor said she did not know, because the staff was too busy treating the injured to count the dead, and most of the dead had been blown into bits and pieces; feet were no longer connected to legs, legs were no longer connected to torsos, torsos were no longer connected to heads and so on. My colleague asked to see the pieces, from which, he explained, he could deduce the number of dead. The doctor resisted, saying it would be improper, but my colleague pressed on, explaining that he needed to report the number killed, and there was, apparently, only one way to get that information.

The doctor reluctantly agreed, and led us down a corridor. She stopped in front of a door, pulled a key chain from her pocket, chose one of the keys, put it into the lock and then opened the door halfway. The room seemed no larger than a closet, and it might have been a closet, but for the moment it was the temporary resting place of the human debris collected from the stadium infield. Later, when the injured had been taken care of, someone would take care of the dead, or what was left of them. My colleague stood beside the doctor and looked inside. I stood behind them and looked over their shoulders, but not in a focused way. I noticed, on the ground, objects that were flesh colored and shaped like the unassembled parts of department store mannequins. I did not focus on them, and I was glad that I was not presented with a greater opportunity to do so. My colleague quickly nodded his head, and the doctor shut the door again. We left the hospital in silence. I had just seen my first war porn.

The richest lode of war porn was found in Sarajevo, at Koševo Hospital. Visiting Koševo was like walking into a nightmare, and I developed defense mechanisms to deal with it. I trained myself to resist the temptation to look where I should not look, to not glance into open rooms where, I sensed, someone was dying, or having shrapnel removed from the abdomen, or losing an arm to amputation. When I interviewed patients, I tried not to let my eyes focus on the soiled bandages sticking onto their wounds, or the blood-stained sheets tossed under their bed, or the rows of metal rods poking out from their shattered limbs. I controlled my breathing, too, trying not to inhale deeply, taking shallow, even breaths, thinking that this would prevent the diseased air from reaching the core of my body. I could last for no more than half an hour, and at the expiration of that time, I would go outside, inhale fresh air, breathing deeply, purifying myself, and then, if my work was not done, go back inside. Without the outdoor break, I might have started screaming.

Koševo Hospital consisted of more than a dozen modern buildings, spread across a hillside, like a college campus. It had a maternity building, an infectious disease building, a psychiatric building and so on. It also had a morgue, adjacent to the emergency room. I never went there. If I had to, I would have, but other journalists were willing to go inside and make the body counts, so I steered clear and got statistics from them. I was not scared of throwing up or screaming or, in some way, making a fool of myself. I assumed that if I could take the horrors of the emergency ward, I could take the horrors of the morgue. Of course I would be repulsed by the bodies, yet what I feared was not the disgust of seeing a boy without a head, but the memory I would have of it for the rest of my life.

Others didn't mind filling their minds with as much porn as possible. I saw a multitude of facial expressions in Bosnia, expressions of horror or sadness or joy that were of an intensity I had not encountered before, and one of those memorable expressions was on the face of an American colleague as he sat in his room at the Holiday Inn and watched Sarajevo television news display, for the umpteenth time, one of the most gruesome scenes of carnage that the war bestowed upon the global village. It was the aftermath of the Breadline Massacre. The footage, which I have already mentioned, showed pensioners cradling their shredded limbs, lying in pools of their own blood. You cannot imagine a scene more ghastly. It was occasionally broadcast on CNN or other American networks, but only in fleeting bits, so that viewers did not have enough time to realize that the object dangling at the end of an old man's leg was his severed foot, connected to his ankle by a thin strand of blood-covered tendon. The scene was broadcast over and over again on Sarajevo television, uncut, a reminder to Bosnians, as though they needed one, of the suffering inflicted upon them.

I have not forgotten the expression on my colleague's face. He was sitting on the edge of his chair, leaning forward, his chin resting on his fist, like Rodin's *Thinker*, and his nose was not more than two feet from the television screen. His eyes stared dead ahead, fixed on the television, as though he was in a deep, loving conversation with it. The images on the screen were classic war porn, some of the world's best war porn, in fact, and, when I think back on his obvious fascination with it, my first instinct is to ask what kind of a person stares at scenes like that, with such obvious interest and—yes, I will use the word—*delight*?

The more I think about it, the more I sense that my colleague's fascination was natural. War porn holds a strange attraction; most people want to look and don't want to look, but, in the end, there's a bit of the voyeur in most of us. When an anchorman warns that the footage in the next report contains "disturbing pictures," how many people change the channel? I suspect the answer is, very few. If the viewer feels disturbed, the cause is likely to be the fact that someone has walked into the room and noticed his fascination with the disturbing pictures on the screen.

I was born and raised in Los Angeles, and one of my summer jobs was as a delivery boy for a magazine. I became profoundly knowledgeable about L.A.'s freeways, about the habits of drivers, the flow of traffic, the design of overpasses, the desirability of cruising in the diamond lane, and I became intimately familiar with the phenomenon of rubbernecking. I realized, in my hundreds of hours on the freeways, that it wasn't just the drivers on the same side of the freeway slowing down. People driving in the opposite direction, facing no impediment whatsoever on their accident-free side of the road, also slowed down for a closer look, creating, in the process, a wholly unnecessary traffic jam.

I spent dozens of hours in these rubbernecking traffic jams, bumper to bumper, as everyone stretched their heads around, hoping to soak up more of the accident, to see more broken glass, more twisted metal, and perhaps—if the accident had just happened, or if the paramedics were slow in arriving—a titillating glimpse of blood and guts on the San Diego Freeway. Yes, I would look.

What I know for sure is that my colleague in Sarajevo was one of the best journalists in Bosnia, employed by a prominent wire service. He was honest and hardworking, and he was repulsed by the appeasement of Serbia. Yes, he liked to watch war porn on television, and he had no problems making body counts at the morgue. The same could be said about many, many people. Perhaps I should respect him for not covering up his tastes. At least he was not the kind of hypocrite who would condemn pornography in public and then, in the privacy of his home, slip a triple-X video into his VCR.

I have a confession to make. In the period that I covered the Bosnian war, approximately 100,000 human beings were turned into corpses. I saw precisely one of them. It was not easy to miss the 99,999 other ones, but I did. I stayed away from morgues, steered clear of battlefields when possible and, when all else failed, averted my eyes as I drove or walked past an object that had the form or smell of death. And so, of course, I have a strikingly good memory of the one corpse that I did see. In a war that killed many more civilians than soldiers, it is fitting that the corpse was that of a civilian; and in a war that killed primarily the weakest of civilians, it is fitting that the corpse was that of an old woman who had suffered the most agonizing of deaths.

The Old People's Home was located in Nedžarići, a neighborhood marooned between the city center and the airport, in a dangerous area controlled by Serbs who had a small military unit there. Because of constant shooting, few civilians remained in Nedžarići, aside from the nursing home's residents and five heroic workers. The last doctor at the home had been killed by a sniper. (Serb soldiers sniped at Bosnians from the four-story nursing home, the tallest structure in the neighborhood, so Bosnian soldiers sniped back.) The home had not been evacuated because no one could figure out what to do with the old people, and until the weather turned fatally cold, they did not want to leave, despite the fact that two dozen among them had been killed by mortars or sniper fire. Where would they go? To another nursing home, to die among strangers? Better to stay put and die with your friends.

I first heard of it on January 5, when a few journalists returned to the Holiday Inn with news that 10 people had frozen to death at the home in the previous three days, 45 in the past month, and corpses were stacked in utility closets. The home, which had 115 residents, counted precisely three stoves, one for the staff, two for the residents in sitting rooms. Bedridden residents could not reach the sitting rooms, so they stayed in their unheated rooms around the clock, occasionally moaning a single word, over and over again: "Cold, cold, cold." The temperature inside was often below freezing, and ice collected on the few windows that had not been shattered by bullets. No one had a sleeping bag, no one had enough blankets or clothes, no one had heating, and no one was younger than sixty-five years old.

On January 6, a dozen journalists convoyed to the nursing home, myself included. We had to drive on the airport road, always dangerous, and then veer off it, into Nedžarići, to the front line. I had failed to get a lift in an armored car, so I drove with Kevin in our Renault hatchback, a vehicle of the apocalypse that still had a windshield but four of its five windows, including the rear one, had been shot out and covered with plastic sheeting. It wasn't even rainproof. Shots were fired around us, perhaps at us, but we did our best to ignore the unignorable, which is what you must do, because if you dwelled on it and on the risks you were taking, you would skip Nedžarići and head straight for the airport and bribe your way onto the first plane leaving town. I hated making that drive in that car but I had no choice. If one journalist in Sarajevo was crazy enough to play Russian roulette, others felt obliged to join the game, which is why a dozen of us were going to Nedžarići.

We arrived just ahead of José-Maria Mendiluce, who was in charge of U.N. relief operations in Bosnia. Mendiluce was an impeccably dressed, handsome Spaniard who was hopelessly out of context in the nursing home, surrounded by such filth and despair. An old man cornered Mendiluce in a frigid hallway and begged for deliverance, bending to his knees in supplication, clinging onto the U.N. envoy's warm hands. "Help us or we will all die," the old man cried. "We will freeze. You must help us." Mist formed from his breath. Mendiluce almost wept on the spot but held together and promised, in a voice full of good intentions, to make sure that the old man would not freeze to death in bed. That evening, Mendiluce slept at the U.N. residence, which was toasty warm and had a kitchen that served good steaks and fine wines. The old man slept, once more, in frozen squalor at the nursing home.

U.N. troops soon installed stoves at the home and, on January 10, evacuated the sickest residents. I returned to watch the evacuation. An old woman sat outside, wrapped in blankets, waiting her turn to be lifted into one of the armored ambulances, and she started to cry and whimper at the same time, making everyone who was near her, journalists and soldiers and aid workers, turn silent in shame and embarrassment. A nurse embraced her, whispering into her ear, "Don't cry, don't cry," and stroked her hair. The old woman's withered head rested on the nurse's shoulder, and then slipped toward the nurse's soft breast, like a child seeking nourishment. Her weeping continued.

Mileva Šuka, who was eighty-five years old, watched this scene from the stairs of a fire escape, perched up there like a dying sparrow. She leaned on her wood cane, and a slight wind played a bit with the untamed whiskers on her chin. Her friends were leaving, one by one, never to be seen again, and dying, one by one. Did she want to leave with them? "I don't feel well," she replied, overwhelmed by the horrible implications of the question. After a few seconds, she added, "My luggage isn't packed." She then broke down and said, "I expect to die any night." She, too, began to whimper. A photographer nudged me aside so that he could get a better shot.

On my first visit to the home, before the United Nations got around to helping out, I walked into a room and found three old women on their beds. One of them was in a coma, her toothless mouth wide open, barely breathing. She was so fragile it seemed her bones were no firmer than toothpicks. A weary nurse entered the room, felt the woman's cheek and said to me, as though addressing a vulture, "No, not yet. But soon." The other women shivered under their blankets, watching their friend die. They were curled up into corners of their beds, sitting, and the fearful look of their childlike eyes seemed to say that they knew they were seeing their own bleak futures.

I was joined in the room by a British journalist, Janine di Giovanni, and she did what I could not imagine doing, sitting on one of the beds, holding the hand of one of the women who was not in a coma, stroking the woman's wrinkled forehead, speaking softly into her ear, words of sympathy in a language the woman could not understand, but did. The old woman smiled in amazement, hoping, I am sure, that this unexpected moment of kindness would not pass, that it would endure until her death. I, as usual, watched. This was much easier than sitting down and taking the other woman's cold hand into mine and telling her, in soothing words, that everything would be fine, don't worry, the United Nations is coming to help. I would feel awkward when the time came to leave, and I would feel foolish if other colleagues saw me doling out tenderness.

I soon went to another room, down a corridor that the winter wind whistled through, because the windows had been blown out. There, in the other room, another three women. One of them, curled into a fetal ball, was nearly in a coma, and I noticed that her urine had seeped through the thin mattress and collected in a small puddle under her bed. Her lips were moving but no sound came out. One of the journalists in the room bent close to her head and heard the word "water." Someone fetched a cup of water and poured it into her mouth. The second woman was sitting on the edge of her bed, washing her bony face with water from a bedpan, moving in slow motion, repeating over and over the same word, perhaps for our benefit, although I am not sure she realized we were in the room. "Cold," she cried, "Cold . . . cold . . . cold."

The third woman, Milena Topalović, in the middle bed, was lying on her back, and she was dead. The cold had taken her away during the night. Her tiny blue eyes were still open, staring at the ceiling, toward the heavens. A knitted brown cap was on her head. She seemed quite peaceful, and I must say that, among the things I saw at the nursing home, and in that room, her corpse was among the least disturbing. Corpses do not sob or whimper, they do not bleed or moan. I found it much more disturbing to look at the women who occupied the beds on either side of Milena's corpse; their misery would continue. Milena might have been the lucky one.

Three journalists were in the room, and we looked at one another for direction. Who was going to close the corpse's eyelids? Who was going to pull a sheet over the corpse's face? Who was going to wrap the corpse in a blanket and put it somewhere else, so that these two godforsaken women in the adjacent beds would not, quite literally, be forced to stare death in the face? Who was going to find blankets to keep these women warm? I hadn't a clue. Nobody had a clue. We were like aliens in that room, dressed in our high-tech clothing, wearing Gore-Tex gloves, our wallets stuffed with money and passports that meant we could leave this hell at any moment we wished and fly, for example, to Paris, where we could stay at the Ritz and impress our friends with tales of adventure from Bosnia.

Our questions were answered by a Serb soldier who, noticing the press vehicles outside the home, came inside to see what was happening and then pointed his assault rifle at every journalist he found, ordering us out. We left in a hurry, and I would be lying if I didn't admit I was relieved. I returned to the Holiday Inn, wrote a thousand-word story and, later on, drank several glasses of wine with dinner. I could not put the nursing home out of my mind, and I could not erase the thought that Milena Topalović could not possibly have done anything in her life that merited the kind of cruelty she endured in her final days at Sarajevo's Old People's Home.

▶ *Four*

I HAVE the good fortune to live in Budapest, a city at the core of Central Europe, and on virtually any evening I can listen to the heirs of Mozart and Bartók perform miracles in concert halls that are nearly as exquisite as the music echoing within their walls. There is, a mile from my apartment, the Academy of Music, on Ferenc Liszt Square, home to a dreamlike concert hall that has nourished my interest in classical music. Its interior is decorated with an extraordinary assemblage of turn-of-the-century frescoes, statues, chandeliers and stained glass. The best way to convey its complex beauty is to say that the men who designed it must have been trying to create an architectural companion to Beethoven's Fifth Symphony.

I have brought up the subject of classical music because I am trying to figure out a way to introduce a man whom I met in Sarajevo. His name is Tajib Saltagić, and he makes me think of classical music. I cannot listen to a symphony without feeling, at certain moments, joy, and at other moments, despair; this is the intent of the music. It is the same with Tajib; he makes me feel those things. All I can say, at this point in the story, is that he made it possible for me to leave Bosnia with the idea that there is at least as much dignity and generosity in the human race as venality and cruelty.

The Serbs had a habit of bombing Koševo Hospital. The busiest bombing time was midday, during visiting hours, and this created one of Sarajevo's ironies: you could be injured while visiting an injured friend at the hospital. I wanted to write about these attacks, and my starting point was Dr. Faruk Kulenović, the emergency room director, a man of patience who always found a few minutes to inform journalists of the day's casualty toll or whatever subject we were interested in. He told me that a few days earlier a tank shell exploded on the hospital grounds, killing one person and injuring eight others. The dead person was an architect whom he knew, and he remembered the moment when she was brought into his emergency room. "Almost all of her organs were gone," he said, speaking in a clinical way, as though to a group of interns. "Her stomach and chest were gone. But she was alive and she was even conscious of her wounds. She said, 'You cannot help me. Help somebody else.' She knew it was bad. We didn't even start an operation." He gave me her name and home address.

As I was leaving his office, I asked why he thought the hospital had become a target. "It happens every day, all the time," he replied. "They want to destroy our state. They want to destroy anything that has economic value, and they want to make us panic, to make us feel that there is no hope. That's why they shell civilian objects, especially the hospitals. They want us to surrender or lay down so that they can slit our throats."

The architect had lived on the top floor of a three-story building in Baščaršija, a heavily Muslim neighborhood, not far from the hospital. A death notice was posted at the entrance, a piece of white paper bordered in black, a Muslim crescent in the middle, her name printed at the top, the day of her death underneath. I climbed the stairway with Minka, my interpreter for the day, and knocked softly on the door.

A woman opened the door, and I noticed, behind her, people in dark clothes. Minka explained who I was, why I was there, and the woman invited us inside, telling us not to bother taking our shoes off, though we did, because it is the custom in Bosnian households. A dozen mourners were in the living room, which was quite large and quiet, filled with whispers and the soft, reassuring sound of socks treading on a thick carpet. Someone whispered to Minka that the burial had just taken place, and now the family and friends had gathered for a wake. Minka whispered that we would leave if that's what was best, but we were told to stay, and, within moments, a man who had the dignified appearance of a college dean came up to me and shook my hand, saying he was honored to have me as a guest in his house.

This was Tajib Saltagić, who had buried his wife an hour earlier.

Minka and I were shown to a couch, and Tajib sat opposite us, in an armchair next to his daughter, Amara. Their friends drifted to an adjoining room, leaving us alone, relieved, perhaps, not to have the burden of consoling Tajib during the worst moment in his life, or relieved, perhaps, that the outside world was taking notice of his wife's death. In Bosnia, most people wanted to talk about their tragedies, they wanted the outside world to know of the injustices they were suffering, they wanted to squeeze a bit of enlightenment out of the death of a wife or husband or infant son, and so they put their grief aside and gave a visiting journalist all the time he wanted, all the information he wanted, and then, when everything had been said and you were ready to leave, the grieving husband or wife or father might give you a gift, as though you had done them a favor, just listening.

I did not know, until Tajib began speaking, the terrible irony of his wife's death. Tajib, like his wife, was an architect, and they were working together at the hospital on a project to identify every location at which the hospital had been bombed and assess the structural damage caused by each bomb. No one knew more about the dangers at Koševo Hospital than Tajib and his wife. Tajib was at his office in the diagnostics building when his wife stepped outside just before the bomb landed.

"I felt the detonation of the shell," Tajib explained. "I thought the worst had happened. After my wife did not return to the office, I went outside and found the place where the shell fell on the pavement. There was a pool of blood three meters away from the entrance. I didn't know it was my wife's."

I was silent. There was no need to ask questions, and, in fact, any interruption would have been a travesty. Tajib explained everything step by step, with an architect's precision, as though he was tracing a blueprint, or because he hoped an absence of tears would mean an absence of pain. He walked to the emergency room, where Dr. Kulenović told him his wife had been sent to the surgery building. Tajib walked there. He found the chief surgeon, and before a word was exchanged, Tajib knew his wife was dead.

"It was in the surgeon's eyes," Tajib said, and, for the first time, his voice cracked, slightly, like a twig. His daughter took a tighter hold of his hand. He looked down, composed himself, and spoke with a child's innocence. "I am surprised at the reaction of the civilized countries. They don't have feelings of sympathy for the nice people living in Bosnia. Why haven't they helped us for almost a year?"

On the day his wife was killed, Tajib was applying the finishing touches to a layout of the hospital compound on which he and his wife had drawn black circles denoting direct hits and black triangles denoting near misses. He gave me a copy of the layout, which had 96 circles and 81 triangles, a total of 177 bombs. The one that killed his wife, and which he had not yet drawn on the layout, was number 178. It landed in front of the diagnostics building, so it would count as a near miss, a triangle.

Tajib wore a black tie, a dark jacket, dark pants. He had the kind of handsome face, topped by thick black hair, that men aspire to have when they reach their late forties or early fifties; his age showed, but it dignified his face, rather than ravishing it. He had wrinkles, but they were clean wrinkles, moving across his cheeks in smooth and symmetrical lines, as though he, an architect, had drawn them. He retained an unusual form of honor as he talked of his dead wife; he had the grit to avoid sobbing, but not so much as to appear callous. He spoke in a soft voice.

"For us, this is the most tragic moment. But we have the strength to finish the project. My daughter is an architect and she will continue the work of my wife. I hope that my son will be a doctor in Koševo Hospital."

The son, Faruk, was studying medicine at the University of Texas and had not yet been informed that his mother was dead. Tajib did not know how he would do that; the problem wasn't in finding the right words, but in transmitting the words. Sarajevo was cut off from the outside world. No phones, no mail, no telex.

"We have satellite phones at the Holiday Inn," I said. "I can arrange for you to use one."

"You can? But those phones are very expensive, aren't they?"

"Don't worry about it," I replied.

The journey from his home to the Holiday Inn would take nearly an hour on foot and take him past the city's worst sniper zones, so I picked him up in my car the next day, in the afternoon. His daughter, Amara, came along, and, when the moment of truth arrived, she took the handset after I dialed the number in Texas. Her brother was living in an apartment with several other students, but no one was home at the time. She left a message on the answering machine, saying she would call again the next day. She said nothing about her mother's death, but I am sure that when her brother got home and heard the message, he knew something terrible had happened, and I suspect he listened to her message over and over again, trying to read into her inflections the bad news that was sure to come; I imagine he did not sleep that night.

I picked up Tajib and Amara twenty-four hours later and drove to the Holiday Inn once more. The cramped Reuters bureau—a double bedroom converted to an office—was a mess because a mortar explosion in the morning had shattered its window, and a workman was using a hammer to bash out the cracked glass. A reporter and interpreter were working in the room as well. Tajib and Amara would not have the luxury of quiet or solitude. I dialed the number and gave the handset to Amara.

Faruk answered the phone. Before he could say anything—*What's happened, Amara? Tell me, now, what's happened?*—she broke down in tears and gave the handset to her father. She collapsed into a chair and began wailing. Tajib said a few words and then read from a text he fished out of his pocket. I don't know what he said, and I thought it odd that he would recite a speech to his son. I have thought about it since then, and I think I understand his actions. He had so much to say, so little time to say it, so he did not want to waste a second, or a word. He read quickly, very quickly, pouring words over the phone, a deluge of information after a drought.

I had to leave the office, which was a madhouse. There was the workman and his shattering glass, Amara and her howling, the reporter and his interpreter, Tajib and his tragic soliloquy. The corridor outside was freezing, but it was a sanctuary, and I leaned against a wall, closed my eyes and wished that I could be anywhere but in Bosnia. After a few minutes, I returned to the office. When the call was finished, Tajib embraced his daughter, and then turned to me.

"My son is strong," he said.

We returned to his apartment and had a cup of coffee. As always, it was Turkish coffee, powerful as a locomotive, served in tiny saucers. Tajib seemed satisfied, for he had dispensed with a horrendous burden, that of telling his son that his mother was dead, and I sensed that Tajib felt sorrier for the son than for himself. We talked for an hour, and when it was time to leave, Amara pressed a gift into my hand, and Tajib offered to show me his wife's grave. We walked downstairs and across the street, to a small cemetery with tombstones dating back several centuries, joined in the past year by modest wood markers for new graves. Munira's was the newest of the new, a mound of fresh earth rising several feet above ground, covered by a light layer of snow, like powdered sugar. Tajib spoke up.

"I was born in Sarajevo. My greatest loves are my wife, my children and this town."

▶ *Five*

IN SARAJEVO, you could experience every human emotion except one, boredom. If I was at a loss for something to do, or too tired to go outside, I could draw back the curtains in my room and look down at a small park in which men, women and children dodged sniper bullets, occasionally without success. Before Bosnia went mad, the park was a pleasant place with wood benches and trees and neighborhood children playing tag on the grass. The war changed all that. The benches and trees vanished, scavenged for fire-wood. The stumps and roots were torn out, too—that's how cold and desperate people were in winter. What remained was a denuded bit of earth that became an apocalyptic shooting gallery in which the ammunition was live, and so were the targets, until they got hit. Serb soldiers were just a few hundred yards away, on the other side of Sniper Alley, a distance that counts as short-range in the sniping trade. The park, like Bosnia, fascinated and repulsed me.

It was a pleasant winter day, and the gods were providing perfect shooting weather, no rain or fog to obscure a sniper's view, just a fat sun conspiring with mild temperatures to entice people outdoors. On days like that, it was best to resist the temptation to go outside, better to stay indoors behind the grimy walls that kept out sunshine and bullets. Clear days were the deadliest of all. A sniper, hiding behind one of the tombstones in the Jewish cemetery on the other side of the front line, was having a great time with his high-powered rifle. Usually he squeezed off single shots, sometimes several at a time, and occasionally he harmonized his shooting finger with the cadence of a familiar song. Name That Tune, Bosnia-style. After a while, things like that didn't seem strange.

I hated the snipers more than anything else. First you heard the crack of their shots, then the whistle of the bullet, then the echo of the crack and then silence. Everything happened in a millisecond. Crack, whistle, echo, silence. The sound was uniquely chilling, in a way that made it feel more menacing than a mortar blast or the rat-tat-tat of a machine gun. A sniper shoots one bullet at a time, a bullet that stands out as distinctly as a single, piercing note from an opera diva overpowering her chorus. You hear that lone shot and you know, instinctively, that the bullet is aimed at somebody, per-haps you, and this is quite different from mortars fired, as many were around Sarajevo, without any particular target in mind. It is the sound of a professional assassin.

The sound makes you feel naked, as defenseless as a baby in a crib. You might, in fact, be wearing a flak jacket, but regardless of the physical protection it offers, the mental security it provides is negligible, if not negative. Putting on a flak jacket can make you feel more vulnerable. You realize how many parts of your body you cherish and do not want to leave unprotected. Your feet. Your hands. Your throat. Your face. Your—it's hard to be polite about this—balls. You realize that a bullet to your head is a death sentence, and you realize how soft human tissue is, that a tiny piece of shrapnel, no larger than a paper clip, can take out your eye or slice off your thumb or sever your spine or, of course, kill you. A slightly larger piece, the size of a tube of Crest, can decapitate you. Even if you are sitting in a room at the Holiday Inn, out of the line of fire, the sound of a sniper's bullet gives you the chills. It is full of meaning.

The Holiday Inn became a grandstand from which you could watch the snipers at work. A journalist could convince himself on a slow afternoon that he was doing his job by peering through a window at people running for their lives. Some people didn't bother to run—they were too tired of being scared to give a damn any longer, and there were stories of people who could take no more and committed suicide by intentionally walking into a sniper zone. In the park, old people who weren't suicidal shuffled as quickly as they could, and mothers dragged their children by the arm. Watching them was work, not voyeurism. Just ask any of the photographers who found safe spots near a sniper zone and waited for someone to be shot.

I was in my room writing a story about a war crimes trial when I heard a shot and then a terrifying human scream. I moved to the window and looked down at the park. The sniper had got somebody.

A man was stumbling along the park in a disjointed way, like a drunk chasing after a taxi. He looked young, and he let out a scream, "Help me! Help me!" He had been hit in the torso but his legs were still working, more or less. He would have been face-down in the mud if it had been a head shot. His howl went up and down in intensity, like a siren running out of power. It was a sound you would expect to hear in a mental hospital, a mad howl of a person pushed over the edge. It came from the lungs, from the heart, from the mind. There's a moment in Sarajevo that's almost too horrible to express in words, so sometimes it came out in a howl that meant, *"I've been shot! I'm dying, my God, I'm dying!"* As the man stumbled through the park, I thought of a thoroughbred horse moving down a racetrack when, suddenly, one of its legs breaks. The horse starts hobbling and slows down but still steps on the snapped leg, lurching with each horrendously painful stride.

He fell to the ground a few yards from the safety of an apartment building. He had gone as far as he could, and if no one came to rescue him, he would die right there, perhaps in a few minutes or, if the sniper felt like finishing him off, in a few seconds. He got lucky. Several men dashed into the exposed area and carried him off. A hospital was less than a half mile away, and on the next day I found him there, in a basement bathroom that had been turned into a recovery ward. His name was Haris Batanović, and the bullet had passed through his abdomen and shattered his left arm. Bullets fired by snipers travel at an extremely high velocity and create enormous damage when they hit their target. Haris's arm, held together by shiny metal rods that stuck out of his skin like screwdrivers, would never be the same again. Haris was a skinny kid, a college student before the war, and he looked so sad in his bloodied bed, doped up on morphine, that I figured he wanted to cry into his mother's breast. He could not do that. His mother had been killed by a Serb shell two months earlier.

When a sniper got active in an area, it cleared out, especially if somebody got shot. The place turned silent. Nobody went into the open, and cars screeched by at full speed. A warning sign might be put up—*"Pazi! Snajper!"*—but usually there wouldn't be a sign. Who had a pen or paper handy in a city under siege? And so, perhaps a half hour later, somebody would walk by, a person who had no idea that a sniper had been at work, and if that person did not get shot, and if another newcomer did not get shot, then foot traffic returned to normal rates. It was a risky game. On one day, three people were shot at a water well near the Skenderija ice-skating rink, one of the main facilities for the 1984 Olympics. After the first person was shot, the area emptied. Then an unsuspecting woman walked to the well to get water for her family, and she was shot. The area remained deserted for a while, until another woman fetching water for her family went to the well, and she was shot.

About forty minutes after Haris Batanović screamed like he had never screamed before, two schoolgirls started walking through the park. They did not know of the drama that had preceded them. A bullet whizzed over their heads. Crack, whistle, echo. They dove into the mud, and stayed there, frozen, their faces in the muck. Curtains parted in the surrounding buildings, and hundreds of frightened eyes looked down on the girls. A couple of men who were in the secure shadow of the Holiday Inn shouted directions to them. Stay low! Crawl! The girls slithered like snakes along the ground for about thirty yards. It took a minute or two. They then did what they should not have done, they jumped onto their feet and darted through the final stretch, zigzagging like angry fireflies. Their scarves floated in the wind behind them. The men shouted, No! No!

The girls were lucky. The sniper did not shoot. Lord knows what he was thinking. He certainly knew that it's hard to hit running targets. Perhaps he wanted to save his ammunition for high-percentage shots. After so much activity in a day, he might have been afraid that the Bosnian Army had sent a sniper into the area, waiting to pick him off as he emerged from behind the tombstone for another kill. Better to keep his finger off the trigger and have a shot of brandy instead. There's always tomorrow.

In Sarajevo, I could stand at my window, out of the line of fire, and watch more drama unfold in five minutes than some people might see in a lifetime. It was all there, within a 200-yard radius of my room at the Holiday Inn, the best and worst of *Homo sapiens*. When I started covering Bosnia, I sensed that I might learn why people are willing to risk their lives to commit good or evil, why some people fall so easily into a murderous trance when a Big Lie is repeated over and over and why others resist the lure of hatred and become heroes. But I had no idea that all of these questions would be raised by gazing at a park, and that some of the questions, if I gazed long enough and pondered hard enough, might be answered.

▶ *Six*

THE REUTERS bureau at the Holiday Inn had a radio transmitter that enabled its correspondents, equipped with walkie-talkies, to keep in touch as they moved around town. Each correspondent had a code name, as though they were in the Special Forces. I asked why they needed code names, and was told it was for security reasons, because the correspondents didn't want eavesdroppers to know who was where. I was not told who represented the security threat. The Serbs? The Associated Press?

The bureau could listen to military communications, Serb and

Bosnian, and this turned into a form of entertainment at night, when commanders were asleep and their foot soldiers started drinking. The airwaves came alive as men on both sides of the front line talked to each other, swore at each other and sang songs. A Bosnian soldier would chat over the airwaves with a Serb friend, now a soldier on the other side, exchanging gossip about their families and mutual acquaintances. In other conversations, old friends might no longer be so friendly, and they would taunt each other, one of them perhaps firing a shot across the front line, and shouting, "That was for you, asshole. Here comes another one." And he would shoot again.

I was in the Reuters office late one night, having a drink with Samir, a reporter, and for amusement we skipped from one frequency to another, checking out the frontline chatter. We came across a Serb soldier who was cursing Bosnia's president, Alija Izetbegović, and, when he tired of that, belted out a comically slurred medley of Frank Sinatra tunes. You have not lived life to its fullest until you hear a sloshed war criminal crooning "I did it my way" in Serbian.

Samir, in a mischievous mood, picked up the handset and interrupted the Serb.

"Heh, Chetnik, did you hear the news? Clinton just dropped an atom bomb on Belgrade."

The singing stopped. There was silence. Samir winked at me.

"Chetnik, did you hear me? Clinton dropped an atom bomb on Belgrade. What are you going to do now?"

The Serb, who perhaps was drunken enough to believe Samir for a few startled seconds, recovered his equilibrium. He knew exactly what he would do.

"I'm coming to Sarajevo, and I'm going to fuck you, Alija."

And he started to sing, once more, "My Way."

This was an intimate war. It was not a war in which fighter pilots took off from one country, flew a thousand miles to another country, dropped their "payloads" and then returned to the country they took off from, never seeing the people they killed, never hearing a word of their language, never seeing a drop of blood. It was hardly a war of missiles, in which a soldier pushes a button and sends five hundred pounds of explosives on a rocket-propelled trajectory toward a city he has never seen, which is only a spot on his military map, too far away for him to hear the explosion, or feel its impact or listen to the screams. These are scenarios of high technology wars, wars of remote-control murder, in which not only the weapons are different, but the language, too. In Bosnia, you never heard the phrases "collateral damage" or "saturation bombing" or "heat-seeking missiles." Sniping and raping and pillaging—yes, you heard those words every day.

We have a tendency to equate high technology with progress, but I prefer the low-tech style of Bosnia's warfare, which had the cruel virtue of limiting the carnage each soldier could accomplish. Is a soldier who slits another person's throat more barbaric than a soldier who pushes a button that launches a missile that kills one thousand people? I suspect not. In the pecking order of barbarism, Bosnia's war could be topped. The war had its own perversity, of course, a perversity of boozy radio chats between grammar school friends who talked nostalgically in the evening and then tried to kill each other during the day. It was, at times, a miniature war in which you could leave the Holiday Inn at ten o'clock in the morning, nearly be killed by a sniper's bullet, and then, at eleven o'clock, be on the other side of the front line, talking to the sniper who tried to murder you just an hour before, and watch as he took aim at your friends as they left the Holiday Inn.

Sarajevo was not a whole city under siege; it was three quarters of a city under siege. Serb rebels controlled a crucial neighborhood, Grbavica, which was separated from the rest of the city by the Miljacka River. The Holiday Inn was located just a few hundred yards from Grbavica, on the opposite bank of the river. There was no secret about the origin of the sniper fire that gave journalists the jitters when entering or exiting the hotel garage at full throttle. It came from Grbavica, from men and women whom, if we were foolish enough, we could have waved to as we sped away in our armored or unarmored vehicles (known in military lexicon as "hard" or "soft").

On a slow day, Kevin and I persuaded a colleague from the BBC to make the roundabout journey to Grbavica in his armored Land Rover. The crossing point through the front line was at the U.N.-controlled airport, several miles away from the Holiday Inn and Grbavica. We raced down Sniper Alley to the airport, got permission from the United Nations to cross the tarmac to the Serb side and then went to Serb military headquarters for permission to visit

Grbavica. We were given an escort, an attractive female soldier who applied a fresh coat of lipstick before heading to the front line with us.

Grbavica was built on a gentle hill that descends to the Miljacka River, and the strip of flat land near the river was covered by large apartment buildings. These buildings were smack on the front line, and the apartments that faced the river, toward the Bosnian side, were deserted except for the snipers who crept from one apartment to another, firing a few shots from one, then moving on before soldiers on the other side figured out which window the bullets were coming from. One of the snipers was named Slobodan Žarković, a casino manager before the war, a gambler by nature, and he kindly offered to give us a tour of his favorite perches.

Slobodan, a small man, perhaps five foot seven, wore a maroon parka, a Chicago Bears ski hat, Hi-Tec tennis shoes, black leather gloves, and had a brown beard. We met him a few hundred yards behind the front line, at a canteen where soldiers were eating a midday meal of fresh bread and stewed vegetables, a feast by the malnourished standards on the Bosnian side of the river. Slobodan was excited and, it seemed, genuinely honored to serve as our host, to the point that his behavior became obsequious, like a waiter constantly coming to your table to ask if you are enjoying your food. "No problem, no problem," he laughed, almost childishly, when he noticed our caution as we left the canteen and headed to the front line. It had snowed the night before, so our boots crunched in the powder as we sprinted through exposed stretches of open space. We were men of military age, and this made us fair game for Bosnian snipers. No problem, no problem. I could think of no more ironic way of getting maimed or killed in this war than to be shot by, of all things, a Bosnian.

Slobodan led us into a building, then into its basement, then deeper still, into a nuclear fallout shelter. The building, like those around it, was built during Tito's time, when civil defense was at a premium because of fears that Yugoslavia could be attacked by the Soviet Union and its allies or America and its allies. The shelter was pitch-dark, so we turned on our flashlights as Slobodan led us through a maze of connected shelters that felt like tombs. Soldiers were living down here, or at least resting up, for I could smell stale cigarette smoke and noticed, in the beam of my flashlight, an occasional steel-framed bunk bed. Slobodan beckoned us forward, into narrow passages that we had to crawl through, into more chambers of concrete and blackness, an underground world, and he tried to reassure us with his giggly refrain of "No problem, no problem." We had no idea where he was taking us. I did not feel lost or afraid, just stupid.

We finally spotted a hint of daylight ahead of us, ascended a concrete stairway, passed through a set of bomb-proof doors, exited the underworld and found ourselves in another building's stairwell. Slobodan motioned for us to follow his path up the stairs, littered with fallen plaster, and he was like a parrot that would not shut up, No problem, no problem. Every door we passed had been forced open, and quick glimpses inside indicated the apartments were ransacked. Slobodan shoved open a door on the fifth floor, and we followed him inside, bending down as he did. Sunshine filtered through the windows, and if we stood up or made too much noise, bullets might filter through, too. We stood back a foot or two from a kitchen window and peered outside.

There, three hundred yards dead ahead, was the Holiday Inn, a familiar sight, except that I was seeing it from a new angle, from the Serb side of the Miljacka River, from one of the buildings where sniper fire came from, from one of the snipers' perches, from behind the shoulder of one of the snipers, a small, anxious-to-please guy who kept saying, "No problem, no problem." I noticed the satellite dish outside the Reuters bureau on the fifth floor, room 509, I knew it well. I looked at the fourth floor, below Reuters, and saw a cracked window that I also knew well. It was the window of my room. If Slobodan would lend me his rifle, I could shoot out my window, or shoot out the window of Kevin's room and perhaps hit Džemal, who might be dozing on his bed at that moment. I also had a direct line of fire at a room occupied by a journalist with whom I had gotten into a ferocious argument the night before. Oh yes, we could have a great time, Slobodan and I.

"You see yellow building?" Slobodan pointed with his pistol. "Is Holiday Inn. No problem! No problem!"

I didn't know whether he meant that it was no problem to kill the hotel's guests, or whether I should not be worried about staying at the hotel. He aimed his pistol at a few people sprinting along the exposed boulevard in front of the hotel.

"I can shoot! Look, look, people. Pistol, pop pop!" he laughed. "No problem, no problem. No shoot people. No, no shoot."

What he was saying, in his kinetically broken way, was that he did not shoot civilians. I played along and did not ask whether he had fired at our Land Rover as we left the Holiday Inn that morning. I asked, instead, when he last shot a "soldier." He responded enthusiastically.

"Today, no. Yesterday, yes. Pop pop!"

▶ *Seven*

HIGHER up in the hills circling Sarajevo, in a mountain town called Pale, the leader of Bosnia's Serbs, Radovan Karadžić, amateur poet and professional warlord, lived in a chalet at which little of importance happened until darkness fell, and then everything happened, everything became possible, as though a spell had been cast. Truth became lies, lies became truth, and if the spell worked properly, you could not tell one from the other. Shortly after my visit to Grbavica, I made the trip from Sarajevo to Pale, and during the journey I encountered Karadžić, one of the most loathsome characters in the war, and I encountered Hansi Krauss, one of the most endearing characters. What follows is an account of that strange journey, of the events that followed it and of the fates of those polar characters. I hope that I am not giving away too much of the story by saying that its moral is quite simple: Justice is a matter of happenstance in our world.

There were several Bosnian enclaves in Serb-held territory at the time, and one of them was Žepa, where as many as 25,000 people were living, though barely. For a few weeks, the media spotlight swung its powerful arc on Žepa, and this prodded the United Nations to try to deliver food and medicine there. An emergency convoy was put together, setting out from Sarajevo, and the media were permitted to tag along in their own vehicles, so I rode shotgun next to Hansi Krauss, an Associated Press photographer. We had met the night before, matched up by an AP reporter who heard that I was looking for a ride in a hard vehicle, and wanted Hansi, who was new to Bosnia, to travel with someone who had a bit more experience.

Journalists were instructed to rendezvous at six in the morning at the Marshal Tito Barracks, where the U.N.'s Ukrainian battalion was stationed. This we did, and of course the Ukrainians were not ready to leave. They had a fuel problem; they had sold it all on the black market. Ukrainian soldiers were legendary for making illicit fortunes by siphoning gas from the huge tanks of their armored personnel carriers and selling it on the black market. Eventually our convoy did leave, after the French or Egyptian battalions loaned a few hundred gallons of gas to their crooked colleagues.

By lunchtime we reached Rogatica, a Serb-held town notorious for the obstinacy of its checkpoint commanders. True to form, they demanded to inspect each vehicle, which meant unloading the trucks, opening the boxes of food and medicine, shaking sardine tins to make sure bullets weren't hidden inside, seizing any box that was not listed on a truck's manifest, impounding our spare jerricans of gasoline (on the excuse that we planned to deliver it to soldiers in Žepa; in fact, the Serbs wanted the gas for themselves and refused to hand it back on our return journey), and demanding that the Ukrainians provide a complete inventory of their weapons and ammunition, down to the number and caliber of bullets. The Serbs always promised to allow unhindered movement for U.N. aid convoys, and the U.N. Security Council had given its troops in Bosnia the right to use "all measures necessary" to deliver aid, but when crunch time arrived, the United Nations backed down, and the Serbs called the shots, especially at Rogatica.

Hansi and I had plenty of time to chat. He was thirty years old, German, nearly bald, and he spoke English with an accent, but in a lightly sarcastic tone, as though he was mocking the way in which Germans attack the English language, trying to master it with force rather than finesse. In his spare time, Hansi was a top-notch rock climber, and he had climbed difficult peaks in America and Europe, including El Capitan in California's Yosemite National Park, a place I had visited many times as a backpacker. He loved the outdoors as much as I did, so we talked without interruption about the mountains we both knew well. I had never climbed El Capitan—this was a two-day climb, one pitch after another, sleeping on the mountain face, risking your life on the security of a piton wedged into a fickle wall, something far beyond my beginner's abilities—but he had climbed it, and I quizzed him intensely about the experience.

It is not that far from El Capitan to Rogatica. The qualities that make a good climber are the same ones that make a good photographer. A willingness to take risks, and an ability to choose wisely which risks to take. A genuine interest in the craft, rather than a cowboy's desire for thrills. There were plenty of thrill seekers in the photography crowd, guys who loved the adrenaline and gore and boasting, and were covering the war for little else but that. Combat photographers have always had a reputation for recklessness, and I suspect the reputation is becoming more and more deserved because almost anyone can shoot a picture these days. Twenty years ago, you actually had to set the f-stop and shutter speed, and in order to do it properly, you had to have experience and, if you wanted to be great, the intuitions of an artist. Now, you just point and shoot, like a pistol; anyone looking for a thrill can do it. I was surprised in Bosnia at the number of former soldiers who had swapped their guns for cameras. Hansi was not part of that crowd; he was too smart and too conscientious for that stuff.

The weather was mild for a winter day in the Balkans, so Hansi and I sat in the back of the Land Rover, which was uncovered. I had not felt so good for several weeks. Instead of being trapped in Sarajevo, worrying about snipers and mortars and the cold, I was sitting outside, feeling the sun against my face, relaxed, warm, not concerned in the least about being shot at, because at Rogatica there was no fighting. I remember that spell of pleasure well, because it was so sweet, so simple.

The convoy was released from purgatory at four o'clock, and we drove slowly through Rogatica, past its burned mosque (the Muslims were cleansed months earlier) and up into the hills. Žepa was twenty-five miles away, but after ten miles we were stopped at the mother of all roadblocks. Its commander was a short, chubby guy with a double-pump shotgun and crooked mustache. On his left was a monster the size of a pillar who had an unkempt black beard and hair to his shoulders, reminiscent of Rasputin, though less handsome. Coils of bullets were slung around his chest, bandolier-style, and looped casually under his right arm was a heavy machine gun, the kind usually bolted atop an armored personnel carrier. On the commander's right was someone with a linebacker's physique, wearing a camouflage jumpsuit and black headband strapped across his forehead. Rambo carried enough weapons for a platoon, including half a dozen grenades dangling from his breast pockets and belt, and an Uzi machine gun in his left hand, casually pointed at us. Quite obviously, these were men accustomed to settling arguments with their trigger fingers.

Darkness was falling, and the temperature was dropping like a rock in a dry well, for there were no clouds to keep the day's warmth close to the ground, and in a Bosnian winter, no matter how warm the weather is during the day, the nights are bitterly cold. We were on the top of a hillside, lunar in its barrenness, and a sharp wind shot the coldness through our clothes and through our skin.

The commander, whose name was Rajko Kušić, said the convoy could not pass. After some debate, he said the U.N. vehicles could pass on the next day, and must stay where they were, on the hillside, overnight, but that the journalists must leave the area, because we did not have authorization to cross the front line. When one of the journalists produced an official Serb pass to cross the front line, Rajko waved it off with a rough flick of his hand. Žepa, he said, "does not need journalists." An hour later, Rajko gave us five minutes to get lost and said that anyone who failed to leave would be arrested. For once, I was not entirely unhappy to be turned back from a roadblock.

There were four press vehicles, about a dozen journalists in all, and we drove straight to Pale, ninety minutes away, keeping our cars close together yet going as fast as possible. It is like that in countries at war; darkness is danger, a time when you do not want to dawdle on isolated roads where an irate soldier can change the course of your life. We raced along, assuming the exhausting day was coming to an end. We were, of course, mistaken.

We arrived, around 10:30, at the Panorama Hotel, headquarters for the Serb leadership. The Serbs had assured the United Nations that foreign journalists would be permitted to enter Žepa, so we decided to lodge a protest with Radovan Karadžić. He was not at the hotel, but was expected to return soon from a dinner engagement, and his aides guessed that he would be glad to meet with us. Karadžić does not shy away from the spotlight; he loves it, as an actor loves the stage. We bought a few glasses of fruit juice from a basement snack bar, and waited in a conference room. A few people smoked cigarettes, while others lay their heads on the table and fell asleep.

The door opened and Karadžić's spokesman, Ljubica Raković, walked in.

"Is Peter Maass here?" he asked, loudly.

I nodded my head and raised my hand.

"Ah, Mr. Maass, I have wanted to speak to you for some time. Do you know that we now subscribe to the *Washington Post* news service?"

Washington Post stories are distributed over a computer system that anyone with a modem can subscribe to for a fee.

"And do you know what our password is?" he asked.

Every subscriber has a password for billing purposes.

"It is 'Muslim.' Do you understand? 'Muslim!' "

He was the only one laughing.

"Do you know, Mr. Maass, we read your stories very carefully. I personally was very interested in the stories you have written about so-called mass rapes by Serbs."

He placed copies of my stories on the conference table. One of them was a recent front-page feature on the girl from Višegrad, Mersiha, who had been raped by the town's warlord, Milan.

"We read *all* of your stories with great interest," Raković emphasized.

I nodded my head, said I was grateful for their interest in my work and waited for him to berate me for being biased, anti-Serb, a liar. It didn't happen. He left the room with a smile that said, *You have been warned.*

I am a big fan of satellite communications and laptop computers because they allowed me to transmit my stories halfway around the world. The mechanics of a global village meant not just that I could inform my newspaper's readers, almost instantly, of what was happening in Bosnia, but anyone in the world could find out, almost instantly, what I was writing in my newspaper; for example, Ljubica Raković. I didn't care whether, as a result, he berated me about my work; I was accustomed to criticism from lackeys like him and from readers who wrote letters to my editor declaring that I was anti-Serb, or anti-Croat or anti-Muslim. However, I did care what Milan, the warlord, might think, because he was, by all accounts, a psychopathic killer, and I had done him no favors with my rape story.

Just because you're paranoid, as Woody Allen may well have said first, doesn't mean somebody isn't trying to get you. I had this very much in my mind after Raković left the conference room.

At 12:45 a.m., the doors burst open and Radovan Karadžić made his entrance. When Karadžić arrives in a room, you notice his presence instantly, as though six trumpeters in red coats blared their horns to proclaim his presence. He is a bear of a man, six foot four, wide as an oak tree, who loves being the center of attention, loves to talk and boast, eat and drink, tell jokes and recite poetry. If it were possible to put the matter of the war to the side, I would say he is quite enjoyable to be around. He makes fun of other people and doesn't mind if others make fun of him. He is, in that way, a classic Serb—engaging, opinionated, macho, charming. An evening with him is never dull. Neither, unfortunately, is a war with him.

He has an incredible amount of hair. It is gray and settles over his head in massive waves that bounce when he walks and flutter over his forehead in the slightest of breezes. Karadžić has another facial feature of note—a dimple on his chin. His is not the face of a warlord, even though that's how he is regarded in the West. I recently came across a useful passage in a novel by Christopher Isherwood, who wrote of the Nazis: "That is how they wish you to imagine them, as unconquerable monsters. But they are human, very human, in their weakness. We must not fear them. We must understand them. It is absolutely necessary to understand them, or we are all lost." The passage, from *Prater Violet*, published in 1945, applies very well to the men and women in Pale, too.

Karadžić sat at the head of the table and waited politely as microphones were placed in front of him. He nodded hello to the journalists whom he knew, and then made a general apology for keeping us waiting. His contrite tone, very much in his character, was a considerable contrast to the behavior exhibited by his soldiers. It was the Balkan version of good cop, bad cop. Karadžić acted polite and feigned displeasure over the behavior of his soldiers, the bad cops. Of course, as we knew, the bad cops were following his orders to the letter. The most remarkable thing about Karadžić was his knack for telling lies with disarming sincerity. Not little lies, white lies, or deceptions, but whopping lies, lies that were so big, and so incredible, that you wanted to laugh, to say, in response, Hold on, Radovan, you expect me to believe this?

One of the ironies about Karadžić is that he was the leader of

Bosnia's Serbs, yet he did not come from Bosnia, and he was not Serb. Karadžić was born in 1936 in a mountain village in Montenegro, a Yugoslav republic adjacent to Bosnia. His father was a shoemaker, his mother tended a herd of cattle. He lived in Montenegro until moving to Sarajevo to attend university. Montenegrins are cultural brothers to Serbs, and it was not unusual for a Montenegrin to move from his native republic and transfer his blood allegiance to Serbia, a far more powerful and prestigious nation. To prove their Serbness, some Montenegrins act more Serb than the Serbs, like defenders of the faith.

After university, Karadžić became a psychiatrist whose clients included the Sarajevo soccer team, which he tried to pull out of a slump by using group hypnosis. In his spare time, he was a poet whose talents were modest, at best, and he existed on the margins of Sarajevo's rich cultural life. He was, according to some accounts, snubbed by the literary elite, and this, the theory goes, contributed to his desire to punish the city that turned its back to him. (To a surprising extent, this was a war of poor rural Serbs against wealthier urban Muslims, a *Deliverance* scenario.) In 1985, Karadžić spent eleven months in jail on fraud charges related to a home loan. After that, he dabbled in politics but was not known as a nationalist; he joined a Green party before taking charge, in 1990, of the Serbian Democratic Party (SDS in Serbian). In an interview with a Belgrade magazine a few days after being appointed SDS president, Karadžić said, "In Serbia, the media are wrongly speaking of the dangers of fundamentalism in Bosnia. . . . The situation is quite different. . . . Our Bosnian Muslims are Slavs, of our same blood and language, who have chosen the European life along with their Muslim faith. In my estimation, it is not necessary that the Serbs once again defend Christian Europe in the fight against Islam. We Serbs are closer to our Muslims than we are to that Europe."

Two years later, Karadžić slipped out of Sarajevo and took up residence in Pale, back in the mountains again, overseeing the destruction of Bosnia's Muslim community.

The press conference began with our protests about being turned back outside Žepa, and Karadžić replied that it was beyond his control, because local commanders had the authority to decide who crosses the front lines. The questions became more general, about the causes of the war, the tactics, the destruction, the war crimes and so on. Karadžić responded enthusiastically, explaining that, No, Serbs were not bombing Sarajevo, the "Muslims" were doing all that and blaming it on the Serbs. Somebody asked him whether this meant that Serbs had not fired incendiary shells that gutted the National Library and its precious contents at the beginning of the war. Karadžić rose to the challenge.

"Listen, they always play games to blame Serbs and gain international sympathy. Whenever a very important person comes to Sarajevo, the Muslims shell the city. They even killed the people in the breadline. And they burned down their library. You know why? Because they don't like Christian civilization in their city. They never liked that library building. It is from the Austro-Hungarian times. It is a Christian building. They took out all of the Muslim books, left the Christian books inside and burned it down."

What about the Serb prison camps? Surely he couldn't deny the pictures of emaciated prisoners who looked as horrible as survivors of Auschwitz.

"We opened our entire prisons to the media, and the media focused on one very thin boy," Karadžić said, speaking in English. "All the other prisoners were good-looking, but the media only focused on this one skinny boy. He was skinny, that's all. Maybe he had cancer. I was skinny like that when I was a young boy." He smiled and rubbed his considerable belly.

"The Muslims want to force Serbs to live under *sharia*," I heard him say, referring to Islamic holy law. "Our women would be forced to wear chadors. . . .

"We do not want to conquer Sarajevo. We should divide the city with the Muslims. It can be like Beirut. . . .

"There was no ethnic cleansing as a part of our policy. Never. We never contributed to the shifting of people. The Muslims wanted compulsively to leave. We couldn't stop them from leaving. . . .

"I don't see what's wrong with a Greater Serbia. There's nothing wrong with Great Britain, so what's wrong with Greater Serbia?"

The press conference ended a few minutes after two in the morning. We gathered up our gear and drove in convoy to the Olympik Pension, ten minutes away, the usual place where journalists stayed in Pale. It was unheated when we arrived, so we could see our breath indoors, and there were not enough beds to go around. I slept on the floor.

The after-hours encounter with Karadžić had a hallucinogenic quality. His ideas were so grotesque, his version of reality so twisted, that I was tempted to conclude he was on drugs, or that I was. I knew Bosnia well, and I knew that the things Karadžić said were lies, and that these lies were being broadcast worldwide, every day, several times a day, and they were being taken seriously. I am not saying that his lies were accepted as the truth, but I sensed they were obscuring the truth, causing outsiders to stay on the sidelines, and this of course was a great triumph for Karadžić. He didn't need to make outsiders believe his version of events; he just needed to make them doubt the truth and sit on their hands.

He needed, for example, to make everyone question whether the Bosnians were bombing themselves, and in fact everyone did wonder about that, because each time a lot of Bosnians were killed by a mortar in Sarajevo, Western governments asked U.N. soldiers for a "crater analysis" to figure out where the offending mortar came from. "Crater analysis" is not always an exact science, and the U.N. soldiers had a hard time pinning the blame; the incoming direction of the shell could be determined, but not the precise position from which it was fired. If Karadžić denied responsibility, and if the United Nations could not prove scientifically that the Serbs were responsible, then we should hold off on punishing them, right? Right. Thankfully, we have not always been so circumspect, and did not demand, during World War II, that Winston Churchill provide proof that the bombs exploding in London were German rather than British.

We returned to Sarajevo the next day, a slippery drive down icy mountain roads, past small log cabins that kept the snipers warm while they kept the city under siege, across the airport tarmac, along Sniper Alley and back to the Holiday Inn. We arrived in Sarajevo just in time for the funerals of eight men, women and children killed by a shell as they stood in line to fill up their plastic jugs with water. Up in Pale, the Serb leadership was claiming that the Muslims had, once again, bombed themselves.

Hansi and I stayed in touch over the next few weeks. Journalists depend on each other for camaraderie and information about what's going on. In a place like Sarajevo, you can't stay on top of everything, so the more friends you have, the more you will know about what's happening. A few days after returning from Pale, I ran into Hansi at the morning U.N. briefing.

"Have you heard about the fashion show?" he asked.

"Fashion show? Are you serious?"

"*Ja*, there's a fashion show at the new pizzeria opposite the presidency at one o'clock tomorrow."

"I'll see you there."

There's a saying about the three ingredients for success in retailing: location, location, location. The pizzeria had neither of the three. It was in one of the worst sniper zones, an intersection adjacent to government headquarters. Snipers had a clear view along the street, so patrons occasionally burst into the pizzeria at a run, except on foggy days when the snipers could not see through the mist, and you could make a proper entrance. Once inside, you were safe, no matter the weather, because the snipers could not angle their shots inside the joint.

Esad Češko owned the pizzeria. He imported women's clothes from Italy before the war, and during the war he seemed to have turned his business skills to the black market, where he appeared to be doing quite well, judging by the fifty-pound sacks of flour and pasta piled up in his kitchen with labels on their sides, "Humanitarian Aid: Not for Sale." Esad made no apologies about providing pizzas to the wartime elite. "My purpose is to help make this town lively," he smiled. "Making a profit is not my purpose. I will not lose money, that's for sure, but it doesn't matter. We need to let the world know that this city has not died." He wore a toupee that undercut the sincerity of his words.

The pizzeria was crowded with soldiers and photographers, all male, with the exception of a reporter for *The Sunday Times* of London, who was the center of attention until the models showed up. There was the usual haze of cigarette smoke, and the aisles between tables were clogged with an obstacle course of flak jackets, AK-47s and Nikons. Hansi had already arrived, so I joined his table.

The models arrived, and they were quite beautiful, with long legs, short skirts and blood-red lipstick. Perhaps they had lost weight during the siege, but models are supposed to look underfed, so they seemed ready for Parisian catwalks. Somebody at the table, noticing bare legs longer than a summer's day, remarked that the only other place where you could see that much flesh in Sarajevo was at the morgue. At a table of photographers, it got a few laughs. The show itself was a disappointment, because the number of models totaled three, and two of them were sisters, and they merely wore their nicest clothes, which they had brought to the pizzeria in plastic bags. So they walked along the aisles, bearing that bored, disinterested look models are supposed to have, whether in Paris or Sarajevo, and after five minutes of pathetic titillation, it was all over. They disappeared into the back, changed into their grubby war clothes and dashed out the front door, models no more, just targets. I felt empty, because the fashion show was not a fashion show, just a reminder that normality could not be attained in Sarajevo.

Hansi did not bother to take pictures. The fashion show was a stunt arranged by Esad, the man with the toupee, and it was hardly newsworthy. That didn't affect other photographers who figured, rightly, that the outside world would enjoy a few pictures of a leggy girl in Sarajevo's first wartime "fashion show." Hansi, nobody's propagandist, was more honest than that. As we put on our flak jackets and headed outside, he laughed a bit and said, "*Ja*, nice girls, bad show."

A few days later, I visited Hansi at his office, which was in a building of the apocalypse. For journalistic purposes, it was perfectly located, across the street from army headquarters and one hundred yards from government headquarters. For survival purposes, its location was less than desirable, because it was sandwiched between the city's main targets. The building's exterior was made of glass, or had been, because most of it was shot out. The Associated Press was the building's only occupant; every other office was ransacked and deserted. You had to walk through a maze of cold, looted corridors before reaching the AP office, where a blazing wood stove gave the room a snug feel, like the log cabin in *Little House on the Prairie.*

On the previous day, I wrote a story about a two-year-old girl who had been sleeping on her family's couch as they gathered for an evening meal when a tank shell smashed through the roof, sending shrapnel into the girl's heart, killing her. It was an ordinary tragedy by Sarajevo standards, and as such, a good story, because the outside world had not yet been desensitized to Bosnia's misery. Her funeral was the next afternoon, and I decided to find out as much as I could beforehand about the macabre syndrome of funerals being shelled and strafed by the Serbs. One of the experts on the subject was Hansi Krauss.

I showed up with a colleague from United Press International, a competitor to the Associated Press, and I knew Hansi would not mind, because competition is a stupid thing in a war zone. It's like climbing a mountain; as much as you want to get to the top alone, would you cut the ropes of other teams trying to make it there? Some people would, and one of them was Hansi's boss, who hardly said hello to the UPI reporter and ordered Hansi not to divulge any information about funerals. Hansi smiled, said of course he wouldn't do that and proceeded to tell us everything he knew.

Hansi attended more than a dozen funerals at Lion Cemetery, the fastest growing cemetery in the world, expanding every day, as though it were alive, drawing nourishment from the dead. The cemetery took its name from a statue of a lion at its gates, and the lion, fittingly, was disfigured by shrapnel. If you stood next to the brooding lion and looked westward, you saw the ruined stadium at which, in 1984, the world's finest athletes gathered for the Winter Olympics. You would be well advised not to spend much time next to the lion, pondering the irony of Sarajevo then, Sarajevo now, for the graveyard was located on an unshielded hillside beneath Koševo Hospital, an easy mark for snipers higher up in the hills, hiding behind an abandoned zoo. When snipers opened fire, mourners dove for cover behind one of the remaining trees, behind the mounds of dirt, behind the tombstones, made of slats of wood, or into an open grave, the best shelter of all.

"One time, I was at a military funeral, and the honor guard just ran away when the first shots were fired, so only three people stayed for the burial," Hansi said. "But you know what? The imams and priests are used to it. When there's sniping they don't jump into the graves. They only do that when there is shelling."

After nine weeks in Sarajevo, Hansi was rotated out for a rest in Germany, and on his last night he had a farewell party at the Belvedere Hotel, where he lived with the rest of the AP staff. When I arrived, Hansi and two photographers were slumped in a booth at the back of the bar, obscured by a forest of empty champagne bottles, and I think they were asleep. The bar was small, just a few tables and tacky Christmas lights hung along a wall, lazily blinking on and off, as though they were falling asleep. Hansi roused himself to life, gave us exaggerated hugs and insisted on opening a fresh bottle, although I could tell he had had enough, and he knew he had had enough, but celebration was in order, even if it was a bit forced. Farewells often turned out to be bittersweet, because it didn't matter how happy you were to leave, you wondered what you could possibly do, or experience, as an encore to Sarajevo. We toasted each other and I knew that I would miss him.

I accumulate friends carefully, after a long period of time, so I was surprised at how quickly we had become friends. How was this possible? There are lots of clichés about wars, myths of valor and nobility and manhood, and most of them are rubbish, because there is little nobility in war, what passes for valor is driven by fear, and manhood, I believe, is not achieved by killing other men. One of the clichés, however, is true, and it concerns friendships. They are made quickly, and they last for a long time, not just between soldiers, who experience the worst of things, but among journalists, who rarely experience the worst of things, and most often watch soldiers endure it all.

In a war, the masks and makeup you wear to disguise your personality, or enhance it, are torn away. War magnifies your weaknesses and strengths. It is hard to fool other people, and hard for them to fool you. Hansi and I didn't need to waste time with the formalities involved in slowly getting to know each other. Our social genetic codes had been zapped with the same sort of mutating X rays. We looked at each other and knew what we saw, and so we became friends.

After returning to Germany, Hansi was sent to Mogadishu, where the U.S.-led effort to pacify Somalia was falling apart. One morning, U.S. helicopter gunships killed more than seventy Somalis in a failed attempt to catch the warlord Mohammed Farah Aideed. Later in the day, Aideed's men went to the hotel where journalists were living and invited them to inspect the massacre site; protection was assured. Nearly a dozen journalists decided to go along. The journalists convoyed in several cars until gunfire forced all but one of the cars to return to the hotel. A mob of Somalis soon attacked the lone car, quite literally tearing its passengers to pieces, for the simple reason that they had white skin, and men with white skin had just killed men with black skin, so revenge was in order. Four journalists were murdered, including Hansi Krauss, who was just thirty years old, an accomplished mountain climber, a dedicated photographer and a friend of mine.

I was in Budapest, in my apartment, sifting through news service stories on my computer, when I read a bulletin about Hansi's death. I was, for a few moments, stunned. Then I became angry. I paced around my apartment, checked for more information, because I had a hard time believing Hansi had been killed, perhaps it was a mistake. I paced around some more. A few months after starting to cover the war, I began keeping an informal diary, a place where I could channel my anger. It was therapy, I suppose, and it helped. Words are my tears. After learning of Hansi's death, I eventually cooled down and started writing. I wrote of the futility of Hansi losing his life in a war that nobody really cared about, that would be forgotten in the next news cycle. I wrote of the agony he must have suffered in his last minutes, as strangers hacked away at his body, which, when it was recovered, was riddled with bullets, gutted by machetes, smashed by rocks. I wrote of the unfairness of it all, that Hansi Krauss was dead while Radovan Karadžić was alive.

▶ *Eight*

DURING the Vietnam war, the U.S. military held daily briefings in Saigon, and because the briefings were so deceptive and absurd, the sessions were known among the press corps as the Five O'Clock Follies. Enemy casualties were exaggerated, American casualties were downplayed and there was forever a bright light at the end of the tunnel. Michael Herr described the briefings as "psychotic vaudeville." A generation of journalists who had believed in the basic integrity of the American government learned, soon after arriving in Saigon, that they had been terribly naïve. The same process of disillusionment took place decades later in Bosnia as, day by day, the United Nations betrayed almost every principle that my generation hoped it stood for.

The United Nations hosted its own version of the Five O'Clock Follies, a morning briefing at the sandbagged headquarters of the U.N. Protection Force. The briefing began with the "weather report," which was UNPROFOR's tally of the previous day's bombardments around Sarajevo. The U.N. was laughably incompetent at stopping bombings but amazingly adept at keeping count of them, so every morning we got a scorecard of the number of mortars, tank shells and artillery shells fired by each side. This was followed by a breakdown of the number of food convoys, and the numbers were impressive, perhaps fifteen convoys a day, ten tons of food on each, and so on. The impression you would get was that UNPROFOR was doing a good job of feeding Bosnia. It was the same sort of bullish impression you might have gotten at the Five O'Clock Follies in Saigon about the advances made by our boys against the Vietcong. The impression, of course, would be the reverse of reality.

Food was being delivered, but to whom? The food situation was pitiful in Sarajevo, where many people were down to one meal a day, of rice or pasta, yet their plight was far preferable to what we were hearing from the isolated enclaves of Goražde, Žepa and Srebrenica, where nearly 200,000 Bosnians were, we heard, on the verge of starving to death. U.N. officials refused to give a precise breakdown of where the food was going. At a briefing, a spokesman for the U.N. High Commissioner for Refugees cut off questioning on the subject by saying his agency did not care whose stomach the food went into so long as it went into someone's stomach. But they were trying their best to get food to the people who need it, he added.

A year later, the truth emerged when Bosnia's government got hold of U.N. statistics that showed Serbs in Bosnia were receiving one third more relief food than Muslims. Serbs didn't really need the food—they had plenty of farmland at their disposal and open borders with Serbia, and they were, after all, the ones who started the war—but they demanded it in exchange for letting U.N. convoys cross into Sarajevo and other enclaves. It was blackmail, and the United Nations went along with it, which meant that a relief effort designed to feed the victims of war had the side effect of fattening up the aggressors. The blackmail included, ironically, mail itself: Under Serb pressure to keep Sarajevo isolated from the rest of the world, UNPROFOR restricted the number of letters foreign journalists could take out of the city on U.N. planes; the limit was six. The official excuse was that without the limit we might be tempted to take huge amounts of mail out of the city for personal financial gain.

The countries that controlled Bosnian policy at the U.N. Security Council—America, Britain, France and Russia—had made a decision not to use force to impose their will on the Serbs, and as a direct result of that, the officials and soldiers who carried out U.N.

resolutions in Bosnia had little leverage. If they wanted to get a convoy across front lines, they had to bargain with the outlaws rather than threaten, and when you start bargaining with the devil, you are inviting disaster. For a glimpse of this, you needed to look no farther than Sarajevo's airport, where Faust was working overtime.

The airport was a few miles from U.N. headquarters, at the end of a road that passed through a no-man's-land—there were many of these around Sarajevo—in which snipers were the only survivors, like roaches after a nuclear holocaust. This was a road famous for its dangers and the number and types of people who were shot while traveling on it: journalists, soldiers, babies. UNPROFOR had several checkpoints that were deadly nuisances because you had to wait for clearance at each of them, and you could be machine-gunned while waiting in your car. Plenty of people had been shot along the road, including a French journalist who made the mistake of painting a slogan on the back of his car, "Don't waste your bullets, I am immortal."

The airport's sole runway was a supremely valuable piece of real estate because of the checkerboard pattern of areas around it. The areas at either *end* of the tarmac were controlled by Serbs, and the areas on either *side* were controlled by Bosnians. On one side, in the Dobrinja neighborhood, which was the press village during the 1984 Winter Olympics, you were within besieged Sarajevo; on the other side, in Butmir, you were outside of the siege. If you could travel the few hundred yards from Dobrinja to Butmir, across the tarmac, you became free. When the war broke out, Serbs agreed to let the United Nations use the runway for relief flights. The United Nations, in turn, quietly agreed to make sure that Bosnians did not cross it.

The statistics spooned out at the briefings included the number of "intercepts" made each night on the tarmac. An intercept consisted of stopping somebody from trying to run between Dobrinja and Butmir. Before I arrived in Sarajevo, the number was quite low and U.N. officials said the traffic consisted of a few black-market dealers smuggling supplies into Sarajevo or soldiers sneaking from one side to the other, depending on the need for reinforcements inside Sarajevo or outside it. Being intercepted by U.N. troops and sent back to their starting point was the least of these people's worries. Serbs, remember, controlled either *end* of the tarmac, and they shot at anybody slipping across the U.N. dragnet during hours of darkness.

The intercepts grew in November, more so in early December and then, when the first cold snap arrived, the numbers soared to 500 a night. U.N. officials recited the statistics without comment and avoided questions about what was going on at the airport. After getting stonewalled at a briefing, I hopped aboard a U.N. armored personnel carrier that was going to the airport and, once there, headed to the security battalion's barracks. The airport was being guarded by French troops who lived in a hangar converted into sleeping quarters, with each room lined with a dozen bunk beds. The soldiers were conscripts in their early twenties, good kids. Color posters hung on the walls, one of Michael Jordan dunking a basketball, suspended in the air like Baryshnikov, the other of George Foreman, posing in the center of a boxing ring, a statue of fat and muscle. The room had the feel of a college dorm.

The soldiers' lives had consisted of little but sentry duty and sleep. They were like most UNPROFOR soldiers in Bosnia, kids who didn't even pretend to understand the war and felt uneasy about the job they were doing, because they didn't know whether they were helping the good guys or the bad guys.

I asked what they thought of their sentry duties.

Silence.

"The number of intercepts is quite high these days," I said. "Are the people you intercept women and children trying to escape the siege?"

Silence again. They were not supposed to talk to journalists. I spoke up again.

"How do you feel about it?"

"We're obliged to stop them," one of the soldiers finally said. "It's hard, it hurts us, but we have no choice. We are here to obey orders."

The silence was broken, and their hesitancy turned to confession. One spoke, then another, and another, and the voice was always the same, the voice of confused youth.

"It breaks our hearts. They cry, they plead with us for help to cross. They even offer money, but we're under orders to stop them," one of them said.

"They are taking the risk of dying to cross the tarmac," another said. "Even old people. There are people who are caught, taken back, and then we catch them again, two, three, four times. The only soothing thing is that they understand. They know we are just soldiers and that we have higher orders."

This was a wave of women, children and pensioners trying to escape a siege that was killing them. Their escape was stopped not by barbed wire or mines or Serb bullets, but by the United Nations.

As honest as the soldiers were being, there were some details that they could not bring themselves to divulge, as I later found out. They didn't just stop people. They confiscated food. A man who was risking his life to bring a sack of potatoes into the besieged city for his family would not only be stopped and taken back to Butmir, outside the siege line, but also deprived of the food he was carrying. These were the orders. The confiscations were carried out because the Serbs demanded it, and the United Nations went along.

U.N. soldiers had special night vision equipment allowing them to spot escapees as soon as they began their dash from the perimeter, and when this happened, an armored personnel carrier would hunt down the escapees, shining a spotlight on them to ease the chase. The problem was that Serb snipers opened fire as soon as someone was caught in a spotlight. It reminds me of movies about prisoner-of-war camps in World War II, of scenes in which escaping prisoners were caught in the dreaded sweep of a spotlight and, instantly, cut down by machine-gun fire from the guards.

I later talked to a girl caught in the spotlights. Her name was Almira Zalihić, eighteen years old, and I found her in a bed at Koševo Hospital, where her leg was in a cast after being broken by a sniper's bullet. She had tried to escape the siege with a group of nine people running across the tarmac. They almost made it to the other side, to Butmir and freedom and food and a gateway to the rest of the world, but thirty yards short of the finish they were "lit up," as she put it, by a U.N. patrol. They had been coached to hit the ground immediately if this happened, because the lights were always followed by bullets, as though the United Nations and Serbs worked in tandem, one shining the lights, the other pulling the trigger. Almira put down the romance novel she was reading, *My Happiness Is in Rome*, and explained what happened.

"We tried to lay down on the ground and there was heavy fire from a machine gun. I was not very fast to hit the ground, and a bullet hit my leg. I crawled behind the APC for cover. Five of us had been hit. Two died. The UNPROFOR soldiers gave us first aid and told us it happened all the time."

At the time, the ringleader of the U.N.'s psychotic vaudeville was a spokesman named Mik Magnusson. Among the unending rotation of spokesmen, he had a reputation for being more hostile than most. The best thing that could be said about Mik was that he spoke fluent English. The U.N. command had a habit, when it didn't want to comment on an issue, of rolling out a Spanish officer named Pepe as the spokesman of the day. Pepe spoke beginner's English. He didn't understand our questions, we didn't understand his answers, and this was as his bosses wanted it. (Spanish journalists had no greater luck; Pepe, kept out of the informational loop, was clueless in his own language.) Mik initially said the decision to prevent Sarajevans from escaping the siege had been made by the U.N. Security Council in New York. "They establish the rules under which we are operating," he said.

This seemed far-fetched because the Security Council was not known to micromanage U.N. operations in Bosnia. The decision was made at UNPROFOR headquarters. We sarcastically asked at which Security Council session the policy was decided, and Mik flashed us the grim look of a high school teacher trying to keep things under control in a remedial English class. A few days later, Mik announced that the policy, which had come under heavy criticism, was being reconsidered and stood a high likelihood of being reversed. He would not say who was reconsidering it, and again looked grim when somebody sarcastically said, "Oh, and when did you say the Security Council would meet to take a vote on this?"

The policy, in fact, was not changed. UNPROFOR soldiers continued to police the siege. For them, it was a necessary evil. If it was not done, the Serbs would close the airport and stop the airlift, undercutting the Security Council's policy of providing food and medicine to the war's victims. If the policy failed, and food and medicine could not be delivered, the Security Council would be faced with only one option, to abandon its passive policy and take sides against the Serbs. This, of course, was an option that the four key Security Council powers were determined to avoid. Whatever devil's bargains had to be made to ensure the "success" of the food-but-no-weapons policy would be made, even if it meant that in order to feed Sarajevo, the United Nations had to help keep it under siege.

In Bosnia, the goal of the "international community"—a vague and overused phrase that should be replaced with the names of the four men who determined policy, President Bill Clinton, Prime Minister John Major of Britain, President François Mitterrand of France and President Boris Yeltsin of Russia—was appeasement, and the United Nations was chosen as the instrument to carry it out. This was one of the tragedies of the war in Bosnia. Our world would be a better place if there was an unbiased organization that functioned as an arbiter of national interests, that acted according to principles rather than interests. In my younger days—an era that I now realize ended when I first stepped foot in Bosnia—I had thought, like many others, that the United Nations might fulfill this role after the Cold War. We learned in Bosnia that the U.N. flag deserves no more trust than any of the national flags in front of its New York headquarters. Integrity is like virginity; you can't get it back once it is gone, and the U.N. lost it in Bosnia.

I was in Sarajevo at a moment when the Bosnians seemed to be preparing a major offensive to break the siege. The focal point of the supposed offensive was Mount Igman, one of the highest peaks south of the city, and a strategic point from which the Bosnian Army could carve out a corridor to freedom. At the end of December, a U.N. official in Geneva announced out of the blue that the Bosnian Army had sent 10,000 troops to Igman and warned that they should be withdrawn. "The *concern* is that there may be a major offensive in preparation by the Bosnian government to try to regain lost territory or possibly even to try to liberate Sarajevo," said Fred Eckhard, spokesman for U.N. peace talks. The italics are mine. *Concern.* The implication of his remarks was made clear two days later by Mik, who announced, "We would discourage any military activity from any side at any time."

The United Nations wanted Bosnia's army to halt any efforts to liberate Sarajevo, and signaled its desire by divulging sensitive information on troop movements, a boon for the Serbs. Don't fight, the United Nations was saying, our negotiators will arrange a peace. But Bosnia's leaders suspected that the United Nations's vision of peace entailed partition in a way that would give Serb rebels control of most of the country. The Bosnians had an instructive precedent to look at: Croatia.

In July 1991, as Croatia declared its independence from Yugoslavia, Serbs who lived in Croatia teamed up with the Yugoslav National Army, dominated by Serbs, and seized control of almost one third of Croatia. The war lasted for six months and left at least 10,000 people dead. It cooled down in January 1992 when the U.N. mediator, Cyrus Vance, a secretary of state under President Jimmy Carter, brokered a truce under which thousands of U.N. troops were dispatched to the Serb-held areas. The U.N. troops were supposed to protect the Serb rebels, who in turn were supposed to relinquish their weapons and permit Croat refugees to return home. The Serbs refused to hold up their part of the bargain; soldiers tore army patches off their uniforms, put police patches in the same place and said they were policemen. They refused to let Croats return home. U.N. peacekeepers ended up serving as a buffer force that turned the front line into a de facto border. Croatia pleaded with the United Nations to enforce the mandate and disarm the Serbs, but the United Nations did not. Eventually, Croatia got what it wanted, though not through the good offices of the United Nations. In August 1995, the Croatian Army launched a military blitz, pushing aside the U.N. peacekeepers, and recaptured most of the occupied territory.

Bosnia's leaders feared that the same type of do-nothing cease-fire was being prepared for them. I visited the Presidency building, where Vice President Ejup Ganić had his small office and a prized satellite phone linking him with the rest of the world. The building, which housed Bosnia's skeleton government, was a few hundred yards from the Miljacka River, and the hills above it were controlled by Serbs, so hardly a day went by without the place being raked by machine-gun fire or mortars. The regal building would have crumbled early in the war had it not been built decades before of thick brownstone walls that could absorb direct hits without caving in. It was unwise to dawdle outside the building, but once inside, you were relatively safe, even though secretaries had been targeted by snipers while sitting at their desks.

Ganić spoke excellent English because he had earned a doctorate in thermal and fluid sciences at the Massachusetts Institute of Technology, after which he taught for six years at the University of Illinois. He was a tall man with dark hair and slightly abstracted looks that made him seem far more suited to academia than warfare. Give him a tweed jacket with elbow patches, stick a pipe in his mouth, and you have the image of an American college professor. Entering his office, a cupboard placed in front of its only window, I had the impression of being a guard entering a cell to speak with a prisoner who has been rapping a metal cup on the bars, proclaiming against his unjust imprisonment. You nod your head, you write down his message and you assure him that you will show it to the warden, but you really believe that nothing will come of it, and he will remain in his cell forever.

Ganić deeply believed Bosnia would not be saved by the United Nations or by the European countries that voiced sympathy for its plight. He knew that, historically, France and Britain had sided with Serbs against Germany, and that France and Britain might rap the Serbs on their knuckles for misbehaving but would never go to war against them or lend real military support to the "Muslim" nation they were dismembering. The end of the Cold War meant a return to old habits, and Ganić felt that Europe's big powers were returning to the habit of appeasement, a replay of 1938, when Britain and France gave their blessing to Hitler's annexation of part of Czechoslovakia.

Ganić stared at me intensely, leaned forward in his chair and whispered, like a half-mad prisoner, "Those leaders in Europe are creeps." He then got to the heart of the matter. "There is something missing here. Americans haven't been present. Americans wouldn't accept this Middle Age approach of keeping a city under siege."

Bill Clinton had been elected president but had not yet taken the oath of office. Ganić understood the reasons for political paralysis in Washington and figured, as I did, that it was just a matter of time before America, under a new president who promised in his election campaign to get tough with the Serbs, became involved and straightened things out. Until then, Ganić and Bosnia would have to deal with the likes of Boutros Boutros-Ghali, the U.N. secretary general, who would arrive in Sarajevo in less than twenty-four hours. "The U.N. has supervised the Bosnian tragedy," Ganić said. "The word 'supervise' is precise. I mean it. This is a very large biological experiment supervised by the United Nations." I left the office feeling more pity than ever for Ganić, and feeling, after his mention of a giant biological experiment, that he was going mad, and that if I were in his shoes, I would be going mad, too.

I returned to the Holiday Inn and visited Kevin and Džemal. We had swiftly fallen into a pattern of spending our spare time together, because we made one another laugh, and this was as necessary for our minds as food was for our stomachs. The hotel manager had found some gasoline on the black market, so we had a bit of heat and electricity; the television even worked, a mind-bending experience, because the satellite dish on the roof enabled us to watch MTV, and Bosnian television broadcast an array of films, from *The Blues Brothers* to *The Great Gatsby* and *Blazing Saddles*. If the Bosnian government was, as its enemy shouted, trying to establish an Islamic republic, it was moving very slowly in the audiovisual department.

▶ *Nine*

HISTORY tells us that when a foreign leader chooses to visit Sarajevo, he must choose the moment carefully. The assassination of Archduke Franz Ferdinand made that abundantly clear. Historians still cannot quite understand how the heir to the empire's throne could have made such a colossal error, for Sarajevo was filled with armed Serbs who despised the Austrians, and the Archduke had chosen to make his visit on Saint Vitus's Day, one of the holiest Serb holidays. The only surprising event of that day was that the Archduke managed to escape a first assassination attempt in the morning, when a bomb thrown at him by a young Serb radical went high and wide of its mark. A few hours later, the Archduke's motorcade took a wrong turn, prompting his car to come to a halt, and, in the kind of happenstance that would be dismissed as woefully contrived in a work of fiction, his car idled a few feet away from Gavrilo Princip, a conspirator from the earlier assassination attempt who was still at large and had just finished drinking a cup of coffee in a nearby café. Princip couldn't believe his good fortune in having another chance to get the job done, so he quickly pulled out his pistol and lunged toward the Archduke, firing an accurate shot at the Archduke's heart. The Archduke's wife, Sophie, was killed by a second shot. Princip, who would die in jail, became an eternal hero among Serbs.

With history in mind, if you were in Sarajevo on December 31, 1992, and if you were asked whether the time was right for U.N. Secretary General Boutros Boutros-Ghali to make a goodwill visit to the city, you would have laughed out loud and said, "Are you mad?" Boutros-Ghali's trip to Sarajevo must be viewed as proof that history repeats itself as farce.

The spectacle began in the morning at the Presidency building, whose north side faced Marshal Tito Street, the city's main thoroughfare. There, on any day, at any time, you could watch the traffic of human misery, men, women, children, grandmothers and invalids, pushing or pulling jugs of water in baby carriages or sleds, sawing branches off trees in the park alongside the street, or, if they were not strong enough to do that, just picking up twigs from the frozen ground. I talked to some of these people, and they said much the same thing, that the world powers must get serious, because their efforts so far had been useless. "I would tell Ghali to release us from this siege or kill us," one old man said. "This has been going on for too long."

Arriving in an impressive armored motorcade, the elderly secretary general wore a business suit and, over it, a blue flak jacket several sizes too big, lending him the look of a child in hand-me-downs. He was ushered upstairs to an ornate reception room, where he sank into an imitation Louis Quatorze chair alongside Vice President Ganić and several generals, all of them surrounded by a small army of journalists allowed to observe the diplomatic exchanges. Ganić, forever the inmate appealing to the warden for freedom, did not let the opportunity slip away. "Sarajevo is the world's biggest concentration camp," he said, softly tapping Boutros-Ghali on the forearm for emphasis. "People are dying slowly. Old people and children are suffering enormously. All the visits by foreign dignitaries produced hope, but after they left the situation continued to get worse. We hope that after your visit things will become better."

Boutros-Ghali replied by wishing Bosnia-Herzegovina a happy new year. He said the United Nations would help defend Bosnia's territorial integrity, and that, for example, it had set up a standing committee for peace talks, six working committees, and hired two cochairmen on a full-time basis. The secretary general noted that the Security Council had passed a series of resolutions condemning the crimes committed in Bosnia, and he told Ganić not to worry. "I want to assure you that we will solve your problems, but we need your assistance and cooperation. You must negotiate with your enemy in spite of all that has happened."

A crowd had gathered outside, and although they could not hear the dialogue in the reception room, they must have sensed things were not going well, that Boutros-Ghali had nothing new to say, for they began chanting so loudly that Boutros-Ghali glanced in their direction. In the distance, an artillery shell exploded. The make-believe world of diplomacy was being shoved aside by the sharp elbow of reality. I moved to the windows and looked down at the crowd, several hundred strong, jeering and shaking their fists, carrying a variety of placards that were essays in simplicity, proclaiming ideas like "Ghali Fascist."

I returned to the semicircle of chairs and heard Ganić plead with Boutros-Ghali to make a brief tour of Sarajevo. "This is a custom here. Please spend forty-five minutes where we have spent nine months." It was an offer the secretary general could not refuse, and he made the best of it by smiling and saying he would be honored. They headed downstairs, to the sedans and jeeps and armored personnel carriers that were crowded around the entrance, and to the protesters, who surged forward when they saw Boutros-Ghali. There followed the type of scene that you would expect, a crescendo of passion from the crowd, panicked security guards forming a tight circle around the secretary general, photographers swarming around them in a second circle, and, amid it all, I heard Ganić shout into Boutros-Ghali's ear, "Don't worry, these are not dangerous people."

Boutros-Ghali is Egyptian, and, at that time, an Egyptian battalion was stationed in Sarajevo, so they provided security for their compatriot. The Egyptians were the most likable soldiers in Sarajevo; they were not as rude as the French, not as corrupt as the Ukrainians, and they were pitifully unprepared for a Balkan winter, having brought desert clothing and armored vehicles without any heating. Few spoke English, so they were, in some cases, humorously inept at getting their job done. Egyptians were stationed at a perimeter bunker one hundred yards from the U.N. commander's residence, but they were incapable of pronouncing the tongue-twisting (to them) names of Western visitors over their walkie-talkies to the French soldiers inside the residence. When I would visit, they shouted one word, and one word only, over their walkie-talkies: "Peter! Peter!" They couldn't understand the response, whether clearance had been given or withheld, but they would wave me through, no matter what they heard. They were the gang that couldn't shoot straight.

Things were different when Boutros-Ghali came to town. Their

shirts were tucked in, their helmets were not tilting to one side or
the other, and their weapons had been cleaned. Boutros-Ghali drove
off with the top U.N. generals in the Balkans, Philippe Morillon and
Satish Nambiar, in a special staff car that had little blue U.N. flags
fluttering from its hood. The muscle was in front, in back and to
the side, a dozen armored jeeps and personnel carriers in all, with
Egyptian soldiers standing alertly in gun turrets on top of the vehicles or hanging from the sides on running boards, scanning the
crowd and rooftops. The stern expression on their faces meant business, and I thought it had been a mistake to view the Egyptians as
hapless soldiers.

Džemal and I ran to our car and fell in line behind the last vehicle
of the U.N. motorcade, an amphibious French jeep with a propeller
mounted at the rear of its chassis. Why it was deployed to a besieged
city in a mountainous country, I have no idea. The motorcade
headed away from the center of town, edging along the Miljacka
River, just past the spot where the Archduke was assassinated, and
slowed down in front of the National Library, which had been gutted in an attack of incendiary shells at the outset of the war, destroying the largest repository of Bosnian history—the intent of the
attack. The motorcade curved around the side of the library and
went back into the center of town, heading straight into an ambush
of venom.

The earlier protest outside the Presidency building had been arranged in advance, but what occurred on Marshal Tito Street was
spontaneous. Everyone knew that Boutros-Ghali was coming for a
visit, so when people walking along the street noticed a special motorcade inching along, they knew precisely what it was for, and they
knew who was inside the U.N. staff car. The reaction was immediate. I saw one old man stare at Boutros-Ghali's car and draw his
finger across his throat, execution style. Another man gave the finger. Someone else shouted, "The bastard should be killed," and another jeered, "Go away, we don't need you idiots!"

The first stop was a hospital on a narrow street. The visit was
quick, no more than ten minutes, and then it was time to head off
again. Boutros-Ghali, Morillon and Nambiar returned to their car,
locked the doors and waited to be driven away. And waited. The
secretary general's motorcade was stuck. The vehicles needed to
make a U-turn, because the next stop was in the opposite direction,

but the armored personnel carriers could not manage the maneuver, so Boutros-Ghali sat in his car, motionless and vulnerable, while his Egyptian escorts tried to sort out the mess.

A man stepped forward carrying a small briefcase, wearing a dark overcoat and sporting a neatly trimmed beard. Ismet Spahić happened to be walking along the sidewalk when Boutros-Ghali's car got stuck in the traffic mess. Ismet did a double take when he noticed Boutros-Ghali, looked at me and a few other people standing a few feet away, looked back at the car and became filled with rage.

"It's Ghali! It's Ghali!" he shouted in English. "Killer! *Killer! Killer!*"

He looked back at us again, perhaps in search of a more animated response from us, wondering how anyone could be so listless in the presence of these famous and, in Sarajevo, reviled men. He started gesturing madly, flailing his arms about and jabbing his finger at Boutros-Ghali, who stared straight ahead, acting as though he had not noticed that a man, perhaps a lunatic, was a few inches away from him, separated only by a car window, and was carrying on as though he wanted to murder the secretary general of the United Nations.

"Killer! Ghali, *killer!*"

The Egyptian soldiers had their hands full trying to untangle the traffic jam, and seemed to succeed only in making it worse, so they did not notice that a "situation" had developed. Ismet carried on without any interference. He put his face against the window, cupped his hands along his forehead to cut out the glare and took a deep look inside, trying to make out the other occupants. It didn't take him long to notice his amazing good fortune.

"Look, look!" he shouted, "It's Morillon. He's a killer too. Killer! *Killer!*"

Ismet's face was so close to the window that his spittle started to collect on it. He paused for a second, stared at the man in the front seat, stepped back again and took a deep breath, because he needed the oxygen and because he was absolutely stunned. He had used up a day's worth of energy, and there was just enough left for a final explosion.

"And that's Nambiar! He's the worst. Killer! *Killer!*"

Ismet stopped yelling, stepped back onto the sidewalk and wiped his brow with a handkerchief. He was sweating now, his chest heaving, worked up by the yelling and the passions he had vented, finally, after nine months of war and frustration. His overcoat had come undone, revealing a jacket and tie underneath, the clothing not of an assassin but of an office worker who probably had a college education and had thought, mistakenly, that he lived in a decent world that would not permit medieval sieges in twentieth-century Europe.

The most striking thing about Ismet was not the violence of his outburst, but the lack of it. He screamed and jabbed his finger at the car but never touched it, never pounded on its hood or kicked one of its doors or broke a window, never threatened Boutros-Ghali or his generals. He called these men killers, holding them responsible for deaths that occurred while they held negotiations which handed the Serbs more time to finish cleansing Bosnia, but he did not say he would kill them. The difference is notable. Ismet was Bosnia's Everyman, angry beyond articulation yet refraining from the mindless violence unleashed upon him and his people by the men in the hills. He was civilized, even if the world around him was not.

The trouble continued an hour later, inside U.N. headquarters, where Boutros-Ghali made his last stop for a wrap-up press conference. It was not going to be an ordinary press conference, that much was clear, but nobody was prepared for Vedrana Božinović, a young reporter for a Sarajevo radio station who asked the first question. Just as Ismet could not let pass his moment of opportunity, Vedrana had to speak up when she got hers, even though the things she wanted to say were not the sort that are supposed to be uttered by a journalist to the secretary general of the United Nations. A journalist is permitted to ask sharp questions, but not to invest any emotion into it, and not to turn a press conference into a morality play. But this was Sarajevo, and the ordinary rules of conduct did not apply, which was understandable, because the rules were being ignored by all sides, including the United Nations, which made promises and issued resolutions that it never honored. During a war, rules are for suckers, and Vedrana, young as she was, had learned that lesson over the past few months.

"You too are guilty for every single raped woman, for every single murdered man, woman and child," she said. "You are guilty—"

"Excuse me," interrupted Mik Magnusson, the U.N. spokesman. "What is your question?"

Vedrana ignored him.

"We think that you are guilty for our suffering. What do you want before you will do something? How many more victims are needed before you act? Aren't 12,000 enough? Do you want 15,000 or 20,000? Will that be enough?"

Her voice was cracking with emotion, and she was about to break into tears, so she stopped, bringing a deep silence to the room, and everyone's eyes, which had been focused in amazement on Vedrana, shifted toward Boutros-Ghali, who, to his credit, replied with dignity rather than arrogance, even if his message was not the one Vedrana wanted to hear.

"If I am guilty, then mea culpa," he said, spreading his hands across the table, palms facing up. "The way that we want to find a solution is through negotiation and more negotiation. I understand your suffering, but there is not a solution but to talk to your enemy. We are doing all we can."

At this point, Boutros-Ghali veered into the realm of the in-explicable.

"You have a situation which is better than ten other places all over the world. I can give you a list of ten places where you have more problems than in Sarajevo."

I remember thinking that the secretary general was mad. Kabul was worse than Sarajevo, that's true, and perhaps Huambo, a hellish city caught in the middle of Angola's civil war. Mogadishu had been scratched off the list because the U.S. Marines had just landed there. His number stuck in my mind. *Ten?* It seemed so absurd that neither I nor any other reporter in the room bothered to ask him to name the ten.

Vedrana was crying.

"We are dying, Mr. Ghali, we are dying."

"Let us have time to find a peaceful solution before thinking of something else," he replied.

"How much time?" Vedrana asked.

"I cannot give you a target date."

Within twenty minutes, the press conference was finished, and Boutros-Ghali returned to the airport, leaving Sarajevo as he had found it, frozen and bitter.

Much time has passed since that day. Of the many tragedies spawned in Bosnia since then, one of the saddest is the fact that

Vedrana and Ismet can no longer be counted on to express their anger with words. Now, I would not be surprised if Ismet, walking again past a car carrying the U.N. secretary general, would behave quite differently, following an example set at the beginning of this century, and draw a pistol from his overcoat, aim at his target's heart and pull the trigger without hesitation.

▶ *Ten*

PHILIPPE MORILLON is a genuine charmer, a Maurice Chevalier with four stars. The French general has twinkling blue eyes, a sweet accent when he speaks English, thinning white hair and a trim physique of which he is proud, for his combat jacket in Bosnia was tapered at the waist, drawing attention to his flat stomach. He loves to smoke cigars, calls favored journalists *"mon ami"* and employed a Swiss chef at his Sarajevo residence, which was stocked with fine wines and creamy cheeses. Invitations to dine with the general were eagerly sought.

Morillon was not just a colorful character in Bosnia, he was a pivotal one. As commander of U.N. forces, he had to carry out the strategies drawn up by distant politicians. Unlike them, Morillon had to watch, every day, as Serbs gutted Sarajevo, and Morillon had to justify doing nothing about it. He had to perform the dirty work of appeasement. It takes a special man to accomplish this task, a man of steel who can sleep soundly at night no matter what he has seen or done during the day. Until he snapped and turned on his masters, General Morillon was such a man. His metamorphosis showed that even a toughened general could not find the nerve to carry out the United Nations' strategy.

This tale of intrigue begins—where else?—in Casablanca, *the* Casablanca, where Morillon was born during the era of French colonialism. He returned to France for an education and graduated from Saint-Cyr military academy, France's West Point, after which he was dispatched to Algeria as a lieutenant in the Foreign Legion. In 1961, Morillon sided with extremist generals who were plotting a coup against President Charles de Gaulle, hoping to prevent him from granting independence to Algeria. When the plot fizzled, Morillon escaped punishment because he was a low-ranking officer, but he learned a lasting lesson about the folly of disobeying political authorities. It was part of the mental baggage he carried to Sarajevo, where he was, for the first few months, a loyal supporter of a real-politik that leaked credibility by the barrel.

A week after Boutros-Ghali's visit, I was at the Holiday Inn when a statement on the radio came at me like an artillery shell: "Turajlić has been assassinated." Hakija Turajlić was Bosnia's deputy prime minister. The radio report said only that he had been killed by Serbs while traveling near the airport in a United Nations vehicle. My deadline was hours away, so I walked to General Morillon's residence for an evening briefing that could be expected to yield fresh information about the killing. I knew that it would be a long night, because assassinations in Sarajevo are, as history had shown, volatile events.

If a first-time visitor arrived in Sarajevo in the darkness of night, he would have no problem finding General Morillon's residence, because it was the only place in the city that had electricity and lights around the clock, thanks to the military generator parked in the backyard. Morillon often complained that his residence was a target of nighttime shellings and strafings, which it was, and he viewed them as intentional provocations, but I have a different explanation, that the brightly lit residence was the only building that the Serbs in the hills could see, so they fired at it.

The residence, known as the Delegates' Club, was one of the finest villas in Sarajevo. Once Morillon moved in, the residence was ringed by barbed wire and protected by a sandbagged bunker at the front gate. I always got the jitters when visiting the residence for the evening briefings, because the Egyptian soldiers made journalists stand outside the gate while they went through their hopeless dialogue with their walkie-talkies, and it did not matter that mortars were landing a few hundred yards away, or that machine-gun fire seemed to be getting rather close, or that the bunker had been strafed an hour earlier—they would not let you inside the grounds or inside their bunker until they heard back on their walkie-talkies from the French soldiers inside the residence.

The briefings were informal, unlike the morning press conferences, and tea or coffee was served in porcelain saucers with gold trim as we sat in a reception room chatting with a member of Morillon's staff. His staff lived at the residence, so there was a constant

march of officers in fatigues who cast suspicious looks at us as they
went upstairs, wondering how the riffraff got inside.

The dining room was Sarajevo's Shangri-la. I peeked at it one
evening to confirm the tales I had heard. It was not large, perhaps
the size of an average American living room. The floor was made
of polished parquet, with a Persian rug in the middle, under a ma-
hogany dining table that had a smooth finish. The table was set for
eight diners, and each setting had a folded linen napkin, crystal water and wine glasses, and silver cutlery. Even though December had
just passed, a Christmas tree was still in the corner, and it had flashing lights, a sign of true decadence in Sarajevo. I had been told of
the menu on New Year's Eve, when the general and his staff began
their celebration with an appetizer of smoked salmon, then moved
on to a main course of roasted duck and washed it down with
French champagne. Outside, Sarajevo was dying.

I do not begrudge the general his luxuries. Anyone who volunteers
to serve in Sarajevo, whether a relief worker or French general or
foreign journalist, deserves some reward. Morillon's standard of living might seem callous, given the conditions that existed outside the
perimeter, but Morillon was no Mother Teresa, nor was I, nor any
other journalist on winter safari in Bosnia.

About a dozen journalists were in the reception room. Morillon's
spokesman came downstairs and handed out a press release that said
Hakija Turajlić was shot dead in a U.N. armored personnel carrier
that had been halted at a Serb roadblock near the airport. Turajlić
had gone to the airport to meet a Turkish delegation, and on his
return trip the APC was surrounded by several dozen Serb soldiers
and two Serb APCs outfitted with heavy-caliber machine guns. A
French colonel, Patrice Sartre, respected by both Bosnians and Serbs,
was dispatched to the standoff but made a crucial error—and vio-
lated U.N. operating procedures—by agreeing to open the back
doors of the APC to show the Serbs that there was only one person
inside rather than, as the Serbs suspected in a fit of paranoia, a unit
of Turkish mujahadeen. Colonel Sartre's mediation effort came to
an end when a Serb soldier unloaded the contents of his pistol into
Turajlić. This was the Achilles' heel of the U.N.'s conduct in Bosnia:
Negotiation doesn't work with bullies.

"I've always wanted to cover a story about a political assassination in Sarajevo," a friend from the BBC whispered.

At the next morning's briefing, General Morillon read out a statement that sounded like a college term paper on existentialism. His hands trembled and his voice wavered. I still cannot figure out whether his statement was a sign of madness or enlightenment. One thing is for sure, it was not the declaration of an iron-willed military commander. "Bosnia-Herzegovina is afflicted by a human illness— fear of others, fear of the other," he said. "It is this fear which gave strength to the arm of the assassin. It is this fear which is feeding all the soldiers in the battles we have not yet managed to bring an end to. It must be overcome."

Journalists love nothing more than official ineptness, and if the ineptness leads to death, we get more excited, because it gives the story greater value, particularly in a place like Sarajevo. American journalists tend to be analytical in reporting on such things, twisting the knife of blame slowly, with calculation, never showing their enjoyment or anger, but making sure that the victim feels every twitch of the blade. European journalists tend to be more vocal about such things, more emotional, because their style of journalism is partisan, stabbing at the victim with vigorous thrusts of the knife. I am thinking of Alfonso, a prominent Spanish journalist who was in the front row and hardly waited for Morillon and Sartre to finish their statements before shouting at them and waving his arms like a lunatic, which, at the moment, he was.

"How could you let a man who was under your protection be killed? How? You did not even fire one bullet! *Not one!* You are soldiers! Have you no honor? Are you not men?"

Morillon looked shell-shocked and did not reply. I had the impression that he submitted himself voluntarily to this humiliation, because he knew, somewhere in his soul, that he deserved it, and he wanted to show that at least he had enough character to accept a punishment that was entirely warranted. He did not leave the room in a huff, nor did he shout back. He just looked sadder and sadder, and spread out his hands in a gesture that seemed to say, "I am sorry. I am responsible."

Alfonso was not satisfied. "Turajlić was under your protection! You are soldiers, no? You have guns, yes? Is this your job, to watch Serbs assassinate Bosnians?"

Sartre was handling it much better than his boss, and I must begin by explaining his physique. Sartre was the shortest soldier I have

ever seen. Perhaps he was five foot six, though I might be overesti-
mating by an inch or more. Short people can have a hard time commanding respect, especially in the military, where brawn is what
matters, the more the better. Sartre was a colonel, the rank just
below general, so he had done quite well in the army, and he was
still a young man, on his way up, in his late thirties, I believe. There
was no mystery about his success. Small as he was, he exuded tough-
ness and intelligence. You could see it in the sharpness of his eyes,
the athleticism of his walk, the confidence in his voice. There was
something in the man that sent out a message, *Don't try it*. Sartre
was fearless, fearless even of Alfonso's paroxysms, which crystallized
into a single question: Why didn't you fire your gun?

Sartre shrugged his shoulders, as though he was surprised at being
asked a question that had such an obvious answer. "Fifty men
against two or three," he replied lazily.

Sartre had been outnumbered at the checkpoint. If he had refused
to open the back doors and called for reinforcements, perhaps the
Serbs would have backed down, but perhaps not, in which case he
might have had a shoot-out on his hands. This was the last thing
that Sartre's superiors at U.N. headquarters in New York wanted
to see happen, and this was known to Sartre, who received the Legion of Honor upon his return to France. By not protecting the
deputy prime minister, he had fulfilled his mission.

At six o'clock, I went to Morillon's residence for the evening briefing. Morillon did not make an appearance downstairs but let it be
known through his spokesman that he would be willing to see journalists individually in his office. He had been so shaken by Alfonso
and the howling pack in the morning that he could not bear the
experience for a second time. Each journalist would be allotted ten
minutes with him.

Soon I was led upstairs, over the soft carpets, and escorted into
Morillon's office by his chief of civil affairs, Viktor Andreyev, a roly-
poly Russian who always looked nervous and burdened by worries.
Morillon welcomed me with a big handshake and called me *"mon
ami américain."* He was a new man, relaxed and confident again,
full of charm, lacking any trace of penance. The change was so
thorough that I was tempted to think that France's defense minister
had beamed into Sarajevo and confronted Morillon after the morning press conference, slapping him sharply on his cheeks, as George C.

Scott did to a shell-shocked soldier in *Patton,* and shouted, "Get a hold of yourself, man. You're the commander. Act like it, damnit."

I asked the general whether he regretted coming to Bosnia, and he laughed lightly, and smiled, "No, I will never regret anything. There is a song by Edith Piaf that is very good." He sang its most famous lines: *"Non, je ne regrette rien, / Non, rien de rien."*

A day before, the deputy prime minister of Bosnia had been assassinated while traveling under U.N. protection. Bosnian protesters had strung a banner across the barbed-wire perimeter at U.N. headquarters that said, "Morillon—Killer." The U.N. mission in Bosnia was falling to pieces. I therefore walked out of Morillon's office knowing that something was wrong, that one of us was out of touch, that, surely, this was no time for singing cabaret tunes. Viktor escorted me downstairs, and I confessed to him that I was surprised by Morillon's singing.

"Yes," Viktor replied, "he has a very nice voice, doesn't he?"

Morillon's moment of weakness at the morning press conference was caused by a hairline fracture of his loyalty to U.N. policy. His singing showed that he had bounced back by the evening, but he had not truly recovered. Hairline fractures do not heal quickly, and they get worse if you fail to take care of them. Athletes often overcompensate for injuries of that sort, playing harder than before in order to prove their well-being and preserve their place on the team, ignoring the occasional stabs of pain, the warning signs that something is wrong. Eventually, if it is ignored long enough, the hairline fracture turns into a clean, crippling break.

The next two months were filled with more humiliations for UNPROFOR as Serbs conquered more territory in eastern Bosnia. Morillon defended U.N. policy as best he could, downplaying broken promises by the Serbs and shrugging off one humiliation after another, but eventually UNPROFOR's failure became too obvious to ignore and too large to cover up. Serbs were seizing territory and killing civilians. The United Nations had failed to stop it. Peace talks were going nowhere. The Serbs were lying to Morillon every day. Tens of thousands of Bosnians might perish in the next month. On Morillon's watch.

On March 11, when the enclave of Srebrenica in eastern Bosnia was on the verge of falling to the Serbs, Morillon hit the road. He put together a convoy of armored personnel carriers and flatbed trucks carrying food and medicine, and headed to Srebrenica. The Serbs got in his way, telling him that roads were closed, or accusing him of trying to deliver supplies to Bosnian soldiers, but Morillon argued and bluffed his way through the front lines, sacrificing his cargo along the way, much of it extorted as "levies." He arrived in Srebrenica on March 12 with a small detachment of U.N. soldiers. The Serbs eased off their shellings when he arrived, but everyone knew the attack would pick up once he left, and that Srebrenica would fall. The presence of the commander of U.N. forces was all that stood between 75,000 Bosnians and death. And so, within hours of his arrival, Morillon became trapped. Civilians blocked his vehicles and refused to let him leave. Was he their guest, their hostage or their savior?

Srebrenica was one of the most desperate places on earth. Thousands of people lived outdoors, despite the winter weather, because many houses had been destroyed and intact buildings were packed wall-to-wall with refugees. Virtually every mortar shell scored a direct hit—with so many people in such a small area, the Serbs could not miss. Wild dogs fed off the torn corpses. At night, people dashed into the hills when they heard American cargo planes overhead, and then fought like wolves for the parachuted food, men against women, women against children. They even fought over the parachutes, for the cloth could be turned into blankets and clothes. Morillon saw it all and felt it all.

Less than forty-eight hours after arriving in Srebrenica, Morillon had undergone a conversion. He no longer asked to leave the town; he wanted to stay. After taking a nap on the afternoon of March 14, he went to the balcony of the local post office, where he had been staying, and addressed a crowd that had gathered outside, in fear and hope. They could not believe their ears. "I have now decided to stay in order to calm your anguish and try to save you," Morillon announced through a bullhorn. "I am here, and here I stay." He ordered one of his lieutenants to raise the U.N. flag over the post office, which became his temporary headquarters. If the Serbs wanted to conquer Srebrenica, they would be forced to do it over his dead body.

Morillon became an instant global hero. Journalists gave his conversion front-page play, and they were aided by live interviews he conducted with his satellite communications gear. In France, only

Jacques Cousteau had a higher popularity rating. Even among Bosnians, who had looked on him as an apostle of appeasement, a genuine sense of admiration emerged. Here, finally, was a man willing to stand up to the Serbs.

The Serbs had no choice. If they resumed their offensive, they would kill the commander of U.N. forces, and that would be too much. They backed off, allowing some food and medicine into the enclave, and some refugees out. Morillon claimed victory and returned to Sarajevo after the Serbs agreed to the deployment of U.N. troops in Srebrenica and the regular delivery of humanitarian supplies. Morillon was hailed as the savior of Srebrenica—but he had little time to enjoy his stardom. The Serbs soon renewed their attack on the enclave. On one occasion, a barrage of shells killed fifty-six people in less than an hour. Many of the victims were children caught in a schoolyard and blown apart. Chunks of flesh were snagged on fences surrounding the yard. Larry Hollingworth, a veteran UNHCR field officer in Bosnia, could not contain his anger when journalists asked him for reaction. "My first thought," he said, "was for the commander who gave the order to attack. I hope he burns in the hottest corner of hell. My second thought was for the soldiers who loaded the breaches and fired the guns. I hope their sleep is forever punctuated by the screams of the children and the cries of their mothers."

More important, insofar as Morillon's career was concerned, newspapers in Paris reported that his tenure in Bosnia would be cut short. Coming less than two weeks after his unauthorized defense of Srebrenica, the official reasons for his dismissal were vague and nonsensical. The real reason, everyone knew, was that Morillon had bucked U.N. policy by putting his life on the line to defend Bosnians. The United Nations had no need for heroes in Bosnia.

More than six months after Morillon's departure, a remarkable letter, written by a departing UNPROFOR soldier, was published on the front page of *Oslobodjenje*, Sarajevo's newspaper. Here is part of it:

> It is difficult for me to leave Sarajevo. This city is for me the reflection of a Europe I love: multicultural, multiethnic and multilingual. Your city, much like Brussels, where I live, is a city of crossroads. If Europe loses these crossroads, it will become substantially impoverished. I don't know

if what I say is clear to you, but you can't imagine how much I admire you all, Muslim, Serb or Croat, for your dignity during these trying times, for your fierce spirit of resistance and for the strong resolution with which you refuse to let die the spirit of Sarajevo. I don't know if you will succeed in your goals. The whole of Europe is stricken these days with a narrow nationalism that is more and more directed against the values of the "other" instead of being based on the peaceful expression of each culture. . . . The names of Sarajevo and Bosnia-Herzegovina will stay imprinted forever in my memory. I leave part of my heart in Sarajevo, and part of my European soul. I'm not sure if I have been able to do much for you—being a U.N. soldier can be quite frustrating—but you have given me the strength to go on defending your cause, wherever I will be in the future. Good-bye, Sarajevo, and I hope I will see you soon under a regained peace.

The author was Francis Briquemont, the Belgian general who replaced Morillon. Briquemont's tour of duty was supposed to be a year, but he resigned after just six months. He wrote that he suffered from "intellectual exhaustion."

▶ *Eleven*

IT WAS POSSIBLE for love to blossom in the rubble.

On occasion, a U.N. spokesman would be shamed into silence during the morning briefing, and one of these moments occurred when a journalist asked about an incident in which Serb soldiers seized several truckloads of firewood that UNPROFOR was transporting into Sarajevo. The spokesman went through the usual ritual of criticizing the Serbs and stating that negotiations were under way to get the wood back and assure that such things did not happen again. We had heard it many times before. An attractive reporter for *Oslobodjenje* raised her hand. "Sir, if you can't manage to protect a shipment of firewood, how are you ever going to protect Bosnia?"

This was Marija. She had dark hair and, as her question indicated, a sharp mind. Kevin became friendly with her soon after I arrived in Sarajevo, and I suspected he was spending more time with her than he let on, despite the obstacles. Love under siege can pose unusual problems. Where do you go for a date in such a place? Not to the movies, not to a romantic restaurant. You're not even supposed to go out at night, what with sniper fire and the curfew. One more thing: condoms. In a war, they are as precious among civilians as ammunition is among soldiers. The scarcity in Bosnia often forced the sexually active crowd to wash out and reuse their treasured loops of latex. The situation was particularly desperate in the eastern enclaves; I spoke on a shortwave radio with a man in Goražde, and when I asked what they needed, aside from weapons and food, he shouted back, "Condoms!"

Somehow the romance between Kevin and Marija took off; I knew things were serious when Kevin gave Marija a flak jacket. Džemal, who had been sharing Kevin's room, gravitated to my room in the evenings. I was occasionally called upon to drive Marija home at night because Kevin did not know how to drive a car, although he did know how to drive a motorcycle. (I could never figure that out.) I hated driving at night. The streetlights were shot out, and in any event there was no electricity to run them, and on top of that headlights attracted sniper fire, so you had to drive by the moonlight. On moonless nights, when you could not see more than three feet ahead, you drove blindly in the darkness, turning on the headlights for a second, then turning them off, trying to memorize the cratered road ahead, hoping you would not smack into another car without headlights. It was easy to get lost in the blackness, and driving Marija home one evening, I took a wrong turn and blundered into the front line, which became apparent when tracer fire swept by the left side of my car. I sped away, cursing myself, and eventually found Marija's home. It was the last occasion I served as her chauffeur.

It was time to take a break from Sarajevo. I had been in the city for nearly a month, filing a story almost every day. I was exhausted, so I packed my bags and got a lift out on a U.N. cargo plane. As I left, Kevin was talking about moving into an apartment with Marija. For Kevin, who came to Bosnia to escape the tedium of financial journalism in Singapore, things could not have turned out better. I was happy for him and for Marija, and this happiness made Bosnia seem a little bit less cruel, a place where good things could happen to good people.

A week later, I was in London, scrolling through news stories on my computer, when I noticed a headline that said three journalists were injured in Bosnia. I read the story. The journalists were traveling in an armored Land Rover and drove over a mine in Gornji Vakuf. One of them, a photographer whom I knew, was thrown out of the car by the force of the explosion and suffered minor cuts to her face. The second one, whom I also knew, sustained a badly broken ankle. The third one fared worse, absorbing the greatest force of the blast, which catapulted the vehicle's steel-lined floor up into his legs, shattering them like matchsticks. His heels, ankles and shins were broken in dozens of places.

This was Kevin. After the explosion, he pulled himself out of the car, came under sniper fire and crawled with a colleague's help to a nearby building. He was rescued by Bosnian troops and eventually transported to a U.N. field hospital, from where, a few days later, he was evacuated out of Bosnia and to a hospital in Glasgow, Scotland. Luckily, neither of his legs was amputated. I contacted him at the hospital, and he sounded remarkably cheery on the phone, talking about being back on his feet in a couple of weeks and back in Bosnia, with Marija, in a month or two. It sounded rather optimistic, but I didn't say so. I wished him a speedy recovery and promised to buy him lunch when he got out of the hospital. I hung up the phone and knew that I would not spend much more time covering the war in Bosnia.

MR. SUICIDE

IT WAS a Thursday afternoon and my business in Belgrade was finished. For a week I had been pestering the Information Ministry for an interview with Serbian President Slobodan Milošević, and duly written a respectful letter to him explaining that my paper's readers were eager to learn his thoughts, but I was not getting anywhere with it, so I decided to pack my bags for a journey to Croatia. It would be good to be on the move again.

The phone rang and my government contact said, "President Milošević has agreed to your request. Your interview is arranged for three o'clock on Monday." She sounded as surprised as I was. Warren Zimmermann, the last U.S. Ambassador in Belgrade, had to wait an entire year before getting an audience with Milošević.

The Bosnia crisis had just reached a new level of hysteria, and local newspapers had taken to printing maps of the city with red spots marking the likely targets that American F-16 bombers would hit. I expected my contact to inform me that a black, unmarked car would pick me up at two o'clock and that I would be blindfolded for the trip to a secret hideout, presumably an underground bunker outside the city. I asked politely where the interview would take place. "At the President's office," she replied, giving me an address. It was in the center of town, an old and regal building that was sturdy enough to have survived the Luftwaffe's saturation bombing of Belgrade in World War II. Earlier in the day, I had interviewed angry depositors at a failed bank across the street from it. A small crowd had formed around me, and a few people shouted that the bank's collapse was all America's fault for imposing sanctions. I felt nervous enough to back away from the crowd. Slobo, as he was known, might have been watching from a window above, and smiling.

"Be there early, a few minutes before three," she advised.

"What are the chances of the interview being canceled between now and then?"

"I don't know."

I knew her well enough to probe a bit more. I had learned the lesson that the United Nations Security Council was so reluctant to grasp—the shelf life of a Milošević promise was exceedingly short. I didn't want to waste a weekend in Belgrade and then get a phone call on Monday morning informing me that the interview was postponed indefinitely. My friend at the Information Ministry sympathized.

"I really don't know," she said. "It's quite unusual that he gives an interview. Wait until Monday."

I was staying at the Hyatt Hotel, which had the best restaurants in town, the best fitness club, the best phone lines. It had become the favored retreat of Belgrade's gangsters, a place where they could unwind in luxury with expensive girlfriends who competed to wear the shortest skirt and highest heels. The hotel management didn't mind or couldn't do anything about it. I didn't mind, either. It lent a Balkan quality to the place. A hotel worker had recently entered one of the suites and found Alexander "Knele" Knežević, one of the city's most flamboyant gangsters, wearing Air Jordan sneakers and carrying a huge wad of German marks in his front pocket. Knežević also had two bullets in his head and three in his chest, and he was very dead. His funeral a few days later was attended by a large number of dolled-up ladies, each of whom claimed to be his girlfriend.

I was left with a weekend to ponder the imponderable, a one-on-one with Milošević. He rarely came out of his shell or allowed others into it. I was not sure why he decided to talk to me. I recalled the thoughts of an American diplomat who compared Milošević to Hitler and hoped his job would never require him to meet the man. "I could not shake his hand. Never. What would I tell my children?" I don't have any children. The only people I answered to were my editors, and they were delighted that the *Post* was going to get an interview with the sphinx of the Balkans. The point, of course, was to forget while I talked to Milošević that he was, in some way, responsible for the murder of at least 200,000 people, some of them my friends.

My colleagues in Belgrade warned me to expect little from the man. I stopped by *Vreme* magazine, the nerve center of Serbia's anti-Milošević brain trust. A sojourn in Belgrade was incomplete without a pilgrimage to *Vreme*, which had the disorganized feel of a student newspaper. There were no neckties, no schedules, no money but lots of chaos and brandy, particularly on Friday afternoons. The magazine was run in the same way that many Serbs overtake cars on narrow roads. They pull into the opposing lane without looking, floor the gas pedal, swear as they pass the slow car and, after swerving back into the lane to avoid a head-on collision, swear at the oncoming driver for going too goddamn fast. Nobody wears a seat belt. *Vreme* was like that. It called the government fascist and ridiculed its bullying tactics. How long would the government tolerate *Vreme*? Who cares. Floor it.

I wandered into the office of Petar Luković, the editor. His office had all the neatness of a trash bin. Papers were almost as likely to be on the floor as on his desk, cigarette butts colonized the place and anything that was hanging on the wall seemed to be at an odd angle, like in *Batman*. Petar looked like hell. Everybody who covered the war looked like hell—it was a draining story, physically and emotionally—but Petar managed to look worse than most. His face was ghostly white, he hadn't shaved for days, and his graying hair went off in a hundred madcap directions. His mind was racing along at top speed, a frantic, brilliant machine. He was undergoing a Balkan version of Kafka's *Metamorphosis*. If you saw him on the sidewalk heading toward you, you might discreetly cross to the other side of the street. I had no idea how old he was. Thirty-five? Fifty-five?

Before the war started, Yugoslavs were no different from other East Europeans, who all looked ten years older than their health-conscious peers in America. Once the war started, the Serbs

and Croats and Muslims and Slovenes and Macedonians and
Montenegrins—they were no longer Yugoslavs—jumped ahead and
looked ten years older than their East European brethren, twenty
years older than Americans. The gap was widening all the time.

It was generally thought among the journalistic crowd that one
day in Bosnia equaled seven days elsewhere, a week equaled a
month, a month a year, a year a decade. We were referring to the
depth of experience and the wisdom gained from it, but the standard
held true for an aging process, too. After a separation as brief as a
month or two, I would notice that the hair of some colleagues had
gone grayer, that their faces had a few more lines, that they didn't
pay as much attention to the cleanliness of their clothes or bodies.
They were possessed by war, by the madness of war and by the
presumption that they were acquiring the ability to see into people's
souls. It was true. They were getting closer to the truths of human
nature, dark and horrible. But they would end up no better than a
man who leaps off the Empire State Building and, when somebody
sticks his head out a window halfway down and asks how it's going,
he shouts back, "So far, no problems." Until they hit the ground,
my colleagues would feel fine, but in the thrilled and doomed way
that a surge of adrenaline makes you feel fine. Eventually it would
catch up with them, as it was catching up with Petar, whose face
was a mirror that let me see my future.

"The man is much too smart for any of us," Petar said. "Milošević won't say anything stupid or anything that will hurt himself.
He'll just tell you the usual lies. It won't be interesting. Your editors
will be disappointed. Slobo is too goddamn smart. You want to
know how smart he is? Look at me. I'm here. That's how smart
Milošević is. He lets this little magazine operate because he knows
we cannot threaten him. Who reads us? A few professors, diplomats
and foreign journalists. Most dictators would not tolerate us, but
that's because most dictators are more brutal than intelligent. But
Milošević, he beats them all. He knows our existence is good for
him. We are proof that a bit of democracy continues in this fucked-
up country. And you know what? The moment our circulation
grows, Milošević will close us down."

"How would he respond to a question about the suicide of his
parents?"

Petar looked worried. "Don't ask him about that. I am telling you, as a journalist and a friend, not to ask him about that. You are American, and you have different traditions. You want to know everything about a politician's personal life. Fine. Write a thousand words about Clinton's sex life. But that's not the way it is done here. If you ask Milošević about his parents, he won't say anything to you. He will end the interview. And he will never let you back in the country, if you're lucky. It would be a big mistake."

He had a point. The rules are different in a country at war. When you are talking with a checkpoint commander in the Balkans, and he is heavily armed and only partly sober, you tend to stay away from provocative questions. It's the opposite in America, where a journalist wants his subject to get angry, to explode a bit, to lose control and say controversial things that he'll regret reading about the next day. In the Balkans, you often worked assiduously to keep powerful people calm, for they could, if they chose, do you harm. Nothing stood in their way, certainly not a baby blue press pass from the United Nations.

The conversation drifted onto another topic. I heard the voice of Miloš Vasić, the dean of the group, in the hallway. Petar's phone rang, and he started yelling into it. I slipped out of his office with a nod of my head.

"You must not ask him about his parents," Miloš said, sitting at his small desk in a cramped office with six or seven other journalists (nobody seemed to know the precise number of people who worked there). "It is not proper. Besides, he won't tell you anything. Milošević rarely tells the truth, and when he does, it's not because he feels a need to be truthful. It is because the truth, in that case, is useful to him. Whatever he might say about his parents would be lies, because their deaths reveal too much about him. He would hate you for mentioning the subject.

"Look, Milošević is suicidal. It's in his family."

I stayed away from the Hyatt on Monday. I did not want to be there to receive a phone call saying the interview was canceled. I showed up at Milošević's building a few minutes before three, and the two policemen outside the entrance cast a lazy, unconcerned look at me as I walked by them. It was a bright day, and I could barely make out the entrance corridor as I stepped inside. On the left was a small booth with a glass partition, like a bank teller's. A plainclothes security guard was inside it. Directly ahead was a walk-through metal detector and, on the other side of it, two more plain-clothes guards. I handed my passport and business card to the guard on my left, and pronounced the magic words, "I am here to see President Milošević."

I expected a rigorous security check, but the guard in the glass booth lazily returned my documents and told me to walk through the metal detector. It howled. I pulled a tape recorder out of my jacket pocket and showed it to the guards standing in front of me.

"Any guns?" one of them said and laughed.

"No, no. No guns," I replied, thinking, These guys joke about guns?

They didn't bother sending me through the metal detector again. I stood motionless, not quite understanding why they weren't doing something that would indicate this was not a part-time job for them. I could have had an arsenal of small weapons and knives hidden up my sleeves, nestled into the small of my back and tucked into my socks. A middle-aged woman appeared and asked me to follow her. I put the tape recorder into my pocket and did as instructed, wondering, Is this whole thing a joke? Is Milošević relaxing in his nuclear-proof bunker, chuckling over the runaround he's given the *Washington Post?*

The building was poorly lit on the inside, the interior precisely what you would expect of something influenced by the heavy hand of Austro-Hungarian architecture. It was cold and lifeless. The ceilings were high enough for a basketball court and the doorways at least twelve feet tall, making everyone who passed through them feel small, which was the point. The walls were dotted with gloomy oil paintings in browns and blacks. As we walked up a wide staircase and along a second-floor corridor, I realized something was missing.

People. I saw no one else. The building, a former palace, seemed uninhabited, like a museum after closing time. Where were the aides scurrying around with urgent faxes from New York, Washington or London? Where were the crew-cut security guards, positioned like statues along the corridors and whispering into their sleeves? Where was the sound of phones ringing, the rustling of military maps, the scraping of chairs against floors as meetings were adjourned, the curses of generals arguing over which city to cleanse next? Where were the lobbyists and petitioners and warlords?

The woman led me down the corridor and opened a door into a small room that had a green sofa along the wall.

"Please wait here," she said.

She was back in a minute and opened a set of doors at a side of the room.

"Please," she said, motioning me into an adjoining chamber.

I could see through the open doors that the next room was quite large and bright, with a row of paintings on one wall. I walked in and noticed, standing next to a window to my right, Slobodan Milošević.

▶ *Two*

BOSNIA is known as the powder keg of Yugoslavia, which itself is known as the powder keg of the Balkans, which in turn is reputed to be the powder keg of Europe. I would like to lengthen the list a bit by noting that Slobodan Milošević was the powder keg of Bosnia. He is also one of the most extraordinary men you could hope to meet in your lifetime, a Halley's comet of dictators, appearing once or twice a century. I had tried to become as knowledgeable about him as possible, an education that began months earlier in the dining room of Serbia's Parliament.

The dining room is nothing like its counterpart in Washington, D.C. In Belgrade, you do not need to be a member of Parliament to get a table. It is sufficient to know a member, to say you are meeting one there, to look important or menacing or to slip a small bribe into the headwaiter's open palm. You seat yourself. The ashtray on your table is full and will not be emptied unless you make a specific request to your waiter, whose presence at the table is occasional. You shout to get his attention. The waiters have a week's worth of sauces on their shirts. The menu is a rumpled piece of paper that looks as though it was fished out of a rubbish bin, and the prices, for such an establishment, seem steep: two million dinars for a salad, ten million dinars for a steak. You are not paying for exclusivity, but for war. The millions mean nothing, though, thanks to hyperinflation. In real terms, your steak and salad cost two bucks.

The word "eclectic" is an insufficient way to describe the gentlemen with whom you are dining. Some are criminals or warlords or both, as in the case of Vojislav Šešelj, who once boasted, "I am proud to have been proclaimed a war criminal by the United States." He is six foot six, has a hefty belly and, usually, a pistol stuffed into his pants. He does not need to shout to get a waiter's attention. The other members with whom you dine include former boxers who occasionally draw on their rusty athletic skills to settle parliamentary debates. Parliament also has its share of mystics and poets and flunkies, so the dining room, like the Balkans, is never a bore.

My education about Milošević started in earnest when I sat down one day for lunch in the dining room with Vlatka Mihelić, my interpreter. Within a minute a big guy with a mustache steamed toward our table. He was followed by what appeared to be several bodyguards, and he spoke two words that made me freeze: "Peter Maass!" I did not recognize him. He thrust his hand forward for a good shake, and I had to oblige him by offering mine in return. I didn't know what to make of it and thought of the scene in *The Godfather Part II* when Pacino plants the kiss of death on Cazale's lips. I had written enough stories to enrage dozens of Serbia's finest criminals-*cum*-warriors. Was this one of them?

"Peter Maass! You don't remember me?"

"Uhm, I'm afraid not."

"I am Laszlo J."

I couldn't place the name.

"Laszlo J., from Subotica."

Bingo. A year earlier I had gone to Subotica to do a story about the problems of the city's ethnic Hungarian population. Laszlo was a human rights lawyer whom I interviewed there and, after our chat, he agreed to interpret for me for the rest of the day. He was an ethnic Hungarian and despised Milošević. He also was a great interpreter, an excellent city guide and a good laugh.

"Laszlo, of course, how are you? What are you doing"—and I lowered my voice—"here?"

He laughed. "I am a minister now. Please, take my card."

His title was Deputy Minister for Human Rights in the federal Yugoslav government. Not bad. From interpreter to minister in a year's time. He had joined the federal government when Milan Panić, a Serbian émigré who made a fortune in Southern California, was appointed figurehead prime minister and made a surprise effort to get rid of Milošević. The puppet failed to oust the puppet master, and when Laszlo accosted me in the dining room, a humbled Panić was packing his bags for Los Angeles.

"Here," he said to Vlatka, "why don't you take one of my cards, too. I don't need them any longer. I am quitting today. There is no hope for this country now."

Laszlo sat down. He yelled at the waiter to bring some food. We talked, naturally, about politics. There was no need to worry about being overheard. One measure of Milošević's genius is that he tolerated a surprising amount of free speech. He was willing to harass or detain anyone who was a real threat, but few people were, and so Belgrade was crawling with dissidents and professors who quite openly called Milošević a fascist. Saddam would have cut off their heads, creating ten new enemies for every one he executed. Milošević let them ramble on, and the opposition, which chanted "Slobo, Saddam" at protests, remained pathetically weak.

We talked about the Vance-Owen peace plan, named after its authors, Cyrus Vance and David Owen, the former British foreign secretary. It called for the Serbs to withdraw from a quarter of the territory they held in Bosnia. The big question at the time was whether Milošević would force his puppets in Bosnia to accept the deal. I mentioned to Laszlo that the deal would be a setback to Milošević's goal of creating a Greater Serbia, and Laszlo just laughed as he told me the secret way to predict Milošević's every move.

"Don't ask what strategy is best for achieving a Greater Serbia, or what strategy is best for the welfare of the Serbs or the survival of this thing that everyone calls 'rump Yugoslavia,' which sounds like a kind of steak," Laszlo said. "Ask what strategy will keep Milošević in power, and that's the one he will follow. Every time. All of these things that he talks about, like nationalism and protecting Serbs, are just tools that he uses to stay in power. He doesn't care about them at all. He doesn't care about anyone at all. He cares only about staying in power."

Milošević was one of the most dangerous breeds of rulers that the world sees. He had no vanity, was infinitely mutable and possessed only the most primal of instincts—the desire to stay in power as long as possible, even at the cost of destroying his country and, eventually, himself. His ruthlessness was all-embracing. Of course Milošević disliked Muslims and Croats, but he also showed little affection for Serbs despite masterminding wars in Bosnia and Croatia to "protect" them. Neither I nor any of the colleagues I have consulted can recall Milošević making a single visit to a hospital to pin medals on wounded soldiers or to refugee shelters to console homeless Serbs. He never shed a tear in public. When running for reelection in 1992, he made just a few speeches. Milošević would do anything that was essential for staying in power, but nothing that was unessential.

He did not have the normal defects that bring down a dictator. He did not waste time on mistresses or material indulgences; he lived in a relatively modest villa with his wife and son and daughter. He could have decorated himself with medals, organized parades in his honor, created a cottage industry of books about his life. Saddam, Noriega, Somoza, Papa Doc, Mussolini, Hitler—they did that. Milošević, a light-year smarter than his peers, couldn't care less about that nonsense. You can travel to every town in Serbia, enter every office building, and you will not find a statue of Slobodan Milošević.

He lacked a master plan, and this was another strength. The "vision thing" is supposed to be important for any leader, whether he be an angel or a tyrant. But the drawback of having a master plan or final solution or whatever you want to call the goal of a madman is that the effort to achieve it might lead to disaster. Hitler wanted to build a German empire and exterminate all the Jews in Europe. He bit off more than he could chew. Saddam Hussein wanted Kuwait to become the nineteenth province of Iraq. He went too far. Pol Pot wanted to kill every educated Cambodian. He got only part of the job done. Slobo's master plan was to stay in power.

The story of Slobodan Milošević—his first name means "freedom" in Serbian—begins in the sleepy Serbian town of Požarevac, where he was born in 1941. Both his parents were from the neighboring and smaller Yugoslav republic of Montenegro, Serbia's little brother. Milošević lived his entire life in Serbia, and the worst thing you can do is question his nationalistic sincerity by accusing him of not being a full-blooded Serb.

His family background is a horror show. His father failed in the priesthood—there are many versions of why and when. He left his family, the rumor goes, and went mad, roaming the mountainsides in Montenegro and talking to rocks. One day he took a shotgun and blew his head off. Almost a decade later, when Milošević was in Belgrade, word reached him that his mother, a devoted Communist schoolteacher, was dead. She too had committed suicide by hanging herself in the family sitting room. A favorite uncle who was an army general also committed suicide by shooting himself in the head.

Predictably, Milošević had few friends, if any, while at university. People who knew him then say he rarely socialized and didn't play any team sports, an unusual trait in an athletics-mad country. He had a sweetheart, Mirjana Marković, who came from one of the country's most prominent Communist families. They got married, and it was a good match, because Marković had her own tragic family history. Her mother, a Communist partisan in World War II, was arrested by Nazi agents during Serbia's occupation by Germany and, the story goes, was tortured into divulging the names of partisan leaders. She was then murdered.

Milošević had an easy ride up Yugoslavia's power structure. He joined the Communist Party, called the League of Communists, at the age of eighteen in 1959, and organized party activities at Belgrade University's law school, from which he graduated in 1964. He worked in the information department of the Belgrade municipal government, specializing in economic affairs, and eventually became the director of the Tehnogas company in 1970. Later, he became president of Belgrade Bank and worked in the bank's New York City branch. His exposure to America, and his working fluency in English, would later prove invaluable as he outfoxed the American and West European governments. Milošević knew his rivals far better than they knew him. In 1982 he became a full-time official in the League of Communists, taking over as head of the party's Belgrade branch in 1984, then of the Serbian branch in 1986, and, a year later, assuming the presidency of Serbia. With it, he grabbed the role of undisputed strongman in Yugoslavia.

Until that moment, he was a Communist apparatchik and loyal follower of his mentor, Serbian President Ivan Stambolić. Milošević's first stroke of genius was to realize, far sooner than his counterparts in Eastern Europe or political experts in the West, that communism was doomed. Perhaps, because Yugoslavia was Eastern Europe's richest and freest country, the regime could hold on longer than others, but it would tumble, sooner or later. Milošević knew this. His second stroke of genius, this one laden with evil, was to realize that there would be only one way to survive the collapse and stay in power—by playing the nationalist card and telling Serbs to forget about Yugoslavia and concentrate on fighting their supposed enemies. He didn't even need to write his own *Mein Kampf*; the Serbian Academy of Arts and Sciences did the job for him in 1986, drawing up an infamous memorandum that Milošević eventually adopted as an ideological blueprint for his nationalist agitation. Instead of opposing the madness, Serbia's intellectuals concocted a justification for it, showing once again that education is hardly an antidote to barbarism.

This was the suicide card, too. Yugoslavia had no shortage of nationalist rivalries. Tito knew this and, until his death in 1980, suppressed nationalism and balanced the power of one nationality against another. He knew that if you open the lid and invite the rivalries to come out, and then—this is the crucial point—set one national group on another, the outcome could be war, especially at a time of economic distress when everyone is looking for a scapegoat. Milošević knew this, too. The difference between the two men is that Tito sought to stay in power by avoiding war. Milošević, after failing to keep Yugoslavia together on Serbia-first terms, sought to stay in power by going to war. There is an abundance of evidence that shows Milošević orchestrated the arming of local Serbs before fighting broke out, oversaw the incursions of paramilitary forces from Serbia into Croatia and Bosnia and, finally, ensured the collusion of the Yugoslav National Army. His efforts might amount to a suicidal strategy, but if there is one thing we should know about Slobodan Milošević, one thing that sets him apart from every Communist or post-Communist leader in Eastern Europe, it is that he is not afraid of suicide. He does not think of the long term; he evaluates each challenge that confronts him, and, because he is clever enough to outwit Machiavelli, he has overcome each challenge so far.

Milošević was poorly understood outside Yugoslavia. Many Balkan experts believed a violent explosion of nationalism was inevitable in Yugoslavia, and that Milošević was an actor in the drama rather than its director. Their theory is simple: The different nationalities that made up Yugoslavia have always wanted to kill one another, thanks to their tribal rivalries and centuries-old hatreds. Tito's death led to a thawing out of the enmities that had been put into the deep freeze, so the people could finally achieve their longtime wish to murder one another into extinction. Milošević was little more than an agent provocateur, and if he had not done the job, someone else would have. War was inevitable, and, facing the inevitable, Western countries had no choice but to watch, for the one-sided fighting had to be allowed to run its course, history was at work after all, and history ordained a victory by the stronger Serbs.

I have a hard time accepting this theory and deferring to the experts who promoted it so successfully. There was nothing spontaneous or inevitable about the explosion in Yugoslavia. "The breakup of Yugoslavia is a classic example of nationalism from the top down—a manipulated nationalism in a region where peace has historically prevailed more than war and in which a quarter of the population were in mixed marriages," wrote Ambassador Zimmermann. "The manipulators condoned and even provoked local ethnic violence in order to engender animosities that could then be magnified by the press, leading to further violence." I interviewed many experts who worked at Western universities and think tanks, and I often asked, at the end of the interviews, how many times they had visited Belgrade or Zagreb or Sarajevo in the past year or two. The answer, quite often, was "not at all." Unlike Zimmermann, who lived in Yugoslavia for many years and observed its collapse first-hand, they did not bother to spend much time in the places they spoke so authoritatively about. Jonathan Eyal, an expert who traveled extensively in the region and whose opinions were insightful and prescient, laughed when I asked why so many of his peers stayed at home. "It's an industry, an armchair industry," he chuckled.

The rise of Serb nationalism is similar to what happened in Germany in the 1930s and 1940s. Anti-Semitism was always a strong factor in Germany, as in most European countries, but Hitler pumped it up until it became a violent force. The Holocaust was the outcome. No one would suggest, though, that the Holocaust was an inevitable outcome of German anti-Semitism. Without Hitler's evil genius, it would not have happened. Likewise, without the evil genius of Slobodan Milošević, the wars in Yugoslavia could have been avoided. Yes, Serbia contained plenty of nationalist troublemakers, just as Germany contained plenty of anti-Semites, but none were as clever as Milošević, none could have accomplished what he accomplished. Whipping a nation into a nationalist frenzy, controlling what had been a feisty media, organizing a war successfully, keeping outside powers and internal rivals at bay—these are not easy tasks. It takes an enormous amount of skill, and some luck. Milošević had both.

His luck consisted of facing Western leaders who didn't want to get involved, and who were glad to be able to say that the wars stemmed from "centuries-old rivalries," even though, for example, the Serb-Croat rivalry is relatively recent and mild in the annals of European bloodletting (the rivalries between the French and the Germans, between the French and the British—these are genuinely centuries-old and led to many more wars, and far bloodier ones, than Serbs and Croats have fought). Once war broke out in Yugoslavia, a Serb victory was ordained not by immutable forces of history, nor by Slobodan Milošević, but by Western leaders who falsely said they could do nothing. It was as though President Franklin Roosevelt kept America out of World War II and shrugged off the problem between Germans and Jews as a "centuries-old rivalry" that outsiders should not meddle in.

Perhaps I should not throw around comparisons with Germany so lightly. I am not an expert on Germany, but I have looked at events there with more than an ordinary interest, and I think they are of more than ordinary relevance to Yugoslavia. Here are my credentials, and my biases: My mother's family, the Warburgs, came from the German port city of Hamburg, where they had established a banking dynasty. The bank, M.M. Warburg & Co., was prominent even though it was a Jewish establishment and faced anti-Semitism from its inception in the eighteenth century. When Hitler came to power, the bank was one of the main financial targets of his Nazi crusaders. They strangled the bank and forced the family to transfer it, for a pittance, to non-Jewish owners. The chairman of the bank, Max Warburg, my great-great-uncle, was of course expelled from German corporate boards before escaping Hamburg. He took it all with great dignity and, in the case of his 1933 removal from the board of HAPAG, a huge German shipping firm, he delivered a memorable speech.

The industrialists who ran HAPAG wanted to pretend that the aryanization of the board was anything but that. They arranged to retire two Christian board members at the same time that Max Warburg, the only Jewish member, was expelled. Being German and, as such, being sticklers for protocol, they held a traditional farewell meeting for the "retirees." One of the departing Christians began to make a speech that defended the contributions of my uncle but he broke down in tears halfway through it. Uncle Max sprang to his feet and finished the broken man's speech. When my uncle sat down, protocol called for somebody to carry on with the salutations—on retirement, a board member was toasted by everyone else. But none of the men at the table were in a mood to speak up for the "retiring" Jew. So Uncle Max tapped his glass, stood up again and made an ingenious speech that he addressed to himself.

"My dear gentlemen, dear Mr. Warburg," he began. "To our great regret, we have learned that you have decided to leave the board of the company and consider this decision irrevocable." My uncle listed the services that he and his bank had offered to HAPAG over the years, including financial rescue in times of crisis when no other bank was willing to extend loans. "We have never forgotten you for this," Uncle Max concluded. "And now I would like to wish you, dear Mr. Warburg, a calm old age, good luck and many blessings to your family." He sat down. There was a shamed silence around the table. His speech contained the only thanks he got on that sad day.

My family was lucky. They lost their assets, which were considerable at the time, but they were astute enough to get out of Germany before it was too late. My great-grandfather, Max Warburg's brother, had immigrated to America before the Nazis came to power and married well, so the family avoided the stateless and penniless fate of most Jewish refugees from Hitler's Germany, Pétain's France, Horthy's Hungary, Pavelić's Croatia and so on. The departure of Max Warburg from Hamburg on the eve of the Holocaust marked the first time in centuries that there were no Warburg men in Germany. The family history is an example of how Germany's ancient relationship with Jews came to an end in the 1930s, thanks to Hitler.

I would like to sit down for a chat about Bosnia with Uncle Max. He died in New York in 1946, a saddened and confused old man who, on his deathbed, imagined that his German coachman was preparing his splendid horses to take him back to his Hamburg mansion. He had lived through two world wars, an assassination plot, Hitler's Third Reich. He had dealings with American presidents, German chancellors and British royalty. I am sure that he could tell me a few things about the nature of people and politics, about "ancient hatreds" and "tribal rivalries," and I suspect that one of the things he would say is that the capacity for self-destruction exists in every society, and that its eruption into war depends not on the will of God but on the acts of men, especially their leaders. He might then stroke his mustache—most Warburgs of that era had mustaches, thick, fabulous ones that they groomed with excruciating loyalty—and remind me that you cannot have an Adolf Hitler without a Neville Chamberlain.

As late as 1986, few people outside of Yugoslavia, or inside it, had heard of Slobodan Milošević. He was, at the time, a loyal party member. "Nationalism is the card on which all enemies of socialist Yugoslavia play," he said in a 1986 speech. Within a year, when he realized socialism and Yugoslavia were faltering and that nationalism was the horse to bet on, he switched mounts. Milošević's transition from socialist to nationalist, from apparatchik to dictator, happened at a precise moment, on April 24, 1987, in an epiphany of mythical proportions.

At the time, he was head of the Serbian branch of the League of Communists. Milošević traveled to the province of Kosovo, a dirt-poor region dominated by ethnic Albanians. Serbs, outnumbered nine to one in Kosovo, had complained for years of being harassed by Albanians. The complaints touched a nerve that runs up the spiritual spine of most Serbs, who view Kosovo as their West Bank and Alamo and Statue of Liberty rolled into one, even though few of them live there or want to live there. It was in 1389, at Kosovo Polje, the Field of Blackbirds, that Tsar Lazar and his Serb army were crushed by the Turks. Kosovo is a place where Serbs feel their destiny is made, where the first Serbian kingdom was established, where the holiest Serbian monasteries are located. It is no coincidence that Milošević had his first encounter with fatal greatness there. He was attending a meeting in a municipal office as Serbs gathered outside to press their case. Police used truncheons to keep the crowd at bay. Milošević emerged and, with a boxer's scowl, shouted the words that set him on a new course, and Europe, too.

"No one will be allowed to beat the Serbs again! No one!"

As with most myths, the versions of what he said differ slightly according to who is telling the tale, and even the precise location of where he uttered those famous words differs. What's beyond doubt is that for the first time in his life Milošević vowed that the protection of Serbs would be his goal. His colleagues say he was "like a heated stove" when he returned to Belgrade, where his first order of business was to oust his mentor, President Ivan Stambolić.

The best way to understand Milošević's epiphany is to read a passage from *Catch-22* in which the chaplain of Captain Yossarian's bomber unit tells a lie for the first time in his life. The chaplain had checked himself into the field hospital and told the doctors that he suffered from a disease called Wisconsin shingles. The doctors were flummoxed. In fact, there was no such disease—the chaplain invented it because he no longer wanted to perform his duties. Delirious with pleasure, the chaplain confides to Yossarian, "I never told a lie before. Isn't it wonderful?" The book's narrator explains the rest, and although the subject is a fictitious chaplain in a fictitious American Air Force unit in World War II, it applies equally well to the thoughts running through Slobodan Milošević's mind on April 24, 1987.

"Everyone knew that sin was evil and that no good could come from evil. But he did feel good; he felt positively marvelous. . . . It was almost no trick at all, he saw, to turn vice into virtue, and slander into truth, impotence into abstinence, arrogance into humility, plunder into philanthropy, thievery into honor, blasphemy into wisdom, brutality into patriotism, and sadism into justice. Anybody could do it; it required no brains at all. It merely required no character."

▶ *Three*

THE MAN with no character glared across the room at me, as though I had kept him waiting.

"Hello, Mr. Milošević," I said.

"Why do you write lies about my country?" he snapped, walking toward me. "You are aiming to define Serbian people as terrorists, killers, murderers. It is just to make some impression with an audience in many countries, to have an excuse for moves against my people. It is very distorted picture. I believe that after a while the truth will get through and that lots of your colleagues will be really ashamed of artificial production of those informations, which were completely unbalanced."

This was his greeting, a bit awkward grammatically but crystal clear in its meaning. He moved ahead like a train sliding into a station, and stopped just before impact with me. He extended his hand. We shook. It was easy. I hardly remember it, neither a death grip nor a weak touch. Like his actions, the handshake left hardly a fingerprint.

"Please sit down."

It sounded a bit like an order. I chose one of the leather armchairs spaced around a circular coffee table. Milošević took the armchair to my left. Three feet separated us. He offered me a Dutch cigarillo from a box that lay on the table. The foreign cigarillos were one of his few extravagances. I declined. I don't smoke, which always put me at a rasping loss in a nation where smoking is as natural as breathing.

"Sanctions don't seem to be hurting you that much," I smiled.

"You know very well that in history there are no sanctions that can hold," he smiled back, lighting up.

I glanced around his office. It had, I must say, a pleasant and elegant feel. The floor was parquet, the walls flecked with oil paintings that, with the light pouring in from a row of bullet-proof windows, looked far cheerier than the ones I had seen in the dark corridors. The rear of the expansive office was presided over by a polished wooden table that served as his desk. I could not see any papers on it, nor any family photos. The socialist seal of Serbia loomed behind it on the wall, the only visible intrusion of politics. The room was inhabited by several potted palms, and its atmosphere was half aviary, half boardroom. It was, above all, peaceful.

The man with no character was wearing a blue double-breasted suit, a silk tie and white shirt. Tidy but not flashy, like a good lawyer. He was shorter than I expected, certainly no taller than five foot nine. His white hair was trimmed, as always, a few centimeters longer than a crew cut. His hairline, standing its ground in front but receding around his temples, formed a soft V at the top of his forehead. His hair was the bristly and abrasive sort, growing straight into the air like bamboo shoots.

His most remarkable feature was his chin. Everybody notices it. The chin sloped out like a ledge from a mountain, giving him the look of a boxer. His small, hazel eyes were set deeply under his forehead. His face was saved from angularity by a pair of puffy and cheery cheeks, like a grandfather's. He looked good. The Belgrade rumor mill said he suffered from diabetes. It might be true, but it didn't show. There were few wrinkles on his face, few signs of stress, no veins pushing to the surface. Either life had been good to him, or he was made of steel, physically and emotionally.

You would never describe this man as warm, but he did not come across as cold, either. His voice was unremarkable, moderate in scale, and when he spoke of wrongs committed against the Serbs, his favorite subject, there was a trace of whining in it, the sound of injury. He looked me in the eye for ninety minutes and told one lie after another, and he did it with utter sincerity. He sat three feet away from me and, without smiling or sounding sarcastic, he protested in a sweet voice, "I am one of the normal, simple citizens of Serbia. I don't believe I am something extraordinary."

I thought of Ambassador Zimmermann, who once said of my host, "He is the slickest con man in the Balkans." If you have ever been to the Balkans, you will understand that this accolade is quite extraordinary.

A waiter stepped in with two silver trays, each one holding a glass of weak orange juice and a cup of strong Turkish coffee, which reminded me of Bosnia. He slid the trays next to us on the table. His black jacket needed a pressing, as did his shirt. He backed out of the room soundlessly. Then it hit me: I was alone with Slobodan Milošević.

When an American journalist interviews a head of government, several people are usually in the room. There is likely to be a spokesman who takes notes; a foreign minister or top adviser; an interpreter, even if the leader speaks English; and a security guard or two. When I interviewed the South Korean president a few years back, his retinue included a linebacker-sized goon in a blazer who stood in a corner of the room and never took his eyes off me. I didn't make any quick movements. I didn't want him to get the wrong idea.

Paranoia is an occupational hazard of the job taken on by dictators. The one sure thing about their job is that someone else wants it and is willing to kill for it. A dictator has reason to be cautious and a bit fearful, to a limit. If you go beyond this limit, and start cutting off the head of everyone who disagrees with you, or jailing people who don't disagree with you but might some day, then you are on a slippery slope. It is the beginning of the end, because after a while your people will take it no more, or your political allies will strike at you before you strike at them, or the rest of the world will take it no more. You will be lucky to die of old age.

Milošević knew which people to jail, which ones to watch out for and which ones to treat with cigarillos. The lax security at his office, rather than a sign of sloppiness, was an illustration of confidence. Only paranoid leaders, like Saddam Hussein, who required visitors to take off rings, lest they be used for poisoned handshakes, would regard a *Washington Post* correspondent as a security threat. The record, Milošević knew, shows that of all the major political assassinations in the twentieth century, not a one was committed by an American journalist. In fact, the record shows that some assassinations have been committed by bodyguards who were supposed to protect dictators from journalists.

Milošević knew all that. His ministers and advisers worked in separate buildings and came to his office when summoned. He had nothing to fear from me, and so we were alone in his office and undisturbed. His phone never rang, the waiter never returned, nobody knocked on the door. One of the reasons he did not fear a palace coup was because no one of importance was in the palace.

His initial outburst tailed off into pleasantries. He had established himself and all Serbs as misunderstood victims. The discussion could commence.

"We are blamed for a nationalistic policy but I don't believe that our policy is nationalistic," the builder of Greater Serbia said. "I don't even think that nationalism has anything in common with the end of the twentieth century. The main rule existing is the process of integration, not the process of disintegration. If we don't have national equality and equality of people, we cannot be, how to say, a civilized and prosperous country in the future."

I asked him, Is the cleansing of Bosnia an act of integration?

"I was discussing that problem with my friends [in Bosnia] and they said to me that there was not absolutely any policy to press any Muslims to leave their cities. Of course in the circumstances of war, a lot of citizens want to go somewhere where they feel more safe. But I think those accusations of Serbs and ethnic cleansing are not fair. For example, in Banja Luka there are a lot of Muslims living equally and equally treated by the Serbs."

I pointed out that the situation appeared different to me, and to hundreds of other journalists and relief workers who spent time in Bosnia. I had been to Banja Luka and most of the other areas from which, Milošević said, Muslims and Croats left on their own accord. It didn't seem that way. Milošević shrugged and gave me a look of pity, as though he was saddened I was so misguided. I began to sense that my friends at *Vreme* were right; I would get nothing out of the man. It seemed appropriate to ask why Ambassador Zimmermann was telling the world that Slobodan Milošević was a con man. His expression of pity vanished, and now he looked a bit cross.

"Zimmermann was not properly informed," he said. "I don't pay any attention to him. I don't believe that the future of relations among the United States and Serbia relies upon the opinion of a few useless bureaucrats in the State Department."

I was curious to know what Milošević thought about war crimes. He seemed glad I had asked the question.

"It is the duty of any civilized country in our international community to punish war criminals," he stressed, looking deeply concerned about the issue. "Universal rights have to be protected all over the world. I am in favor of prosecution of war criminals. And I believe that in this bloody war, there are war crimes on all sides, no doubt about that. But any specific accusation has to be clarified."

What about the specific accusation that Slobodan Milošević is a war criminal?

"Those are only really dirty accusations, dirty accusations without any evidence," he replied, his deep concern turning to the indignation of a gentleman whose honor has been challenged. "They are accusations in the interests of those who are practically in favor of destroying Serbia. Everything will be clear after a while. Nobody can hide facts for a long time in this world."

Amen.

I would have had better luck trying to land a punch on a hologram. Milošević existed in a different dimension, a twilight zone of lies, and I was mucking about in the dimension of facts. He had spent his entire life in the world of communism, and he had become a master, an absolute master, at fabrication. Of course my verbal punches went right through him. It was as though I pointed to a black wall and asked Milošević what color it was. White, he says. No, I reply, look at it, that wall there, it is black, it is five feet away from us. He looks at it, then at me, and says, The wall is white, my friend, maybe you should have your eyes checked. He does not shout in anger. He sounds concerned for my eyesight.

I knew the wall was black. I could see the wall. I had touched the wall. I had watched the workmen paint it black. But many of the foreign visitors who lined up to speak with Milošević could not see the wall, which was called Bosnia. They had rarely been there, if ever, and they had rarely talked with cleansed Bosnians, if ever. They had read plenty about Bosnia, but when Milošević said with total sincerity that Serbs were not involved in ethnic cleansing, and that it was Muslims who tried to cleanse Serbs, and in any event he had no power over the Serbs in Bosnia, some of the visitors were confused. They might doubt his words, but they could not be sure what was true. The Balkans, the bloody Balkans, there is no truth here, right? And so they left Milošević's office wondering whether he might be a peacemaker. As Ambassador Zimmermann wrote, "Milošević makes a stunning first impression on those who do not have the information to refute his often erroneous assertions. Many is the U.S. senator or congressman who has reeled out of his office exclaiming, 'Why, he's not nearly as bad as I expected!' One congressman even invited him to a White House prayer breakfast. . . . Unfortunately, the man is almost totally dominated by his dark side."

These visitors were the naïve ones. There was another category of visitors who were not naïve, who knew what Milošević was up to but continued to meet with him and treat his version of events as credible, if not entirely truthful. These were the appeasers, the ministers and diplomats from Washington, London and Paris who were not duped by Milošević but played along with his lies, relieved that he possessed a civilized visage and sincere manner which allowed them to package him as a peacemaker, and in this way they did not appear unforgivably craven in their effort to draw up a peace plan that met his demands rather than Bosnia's.

I took another sip from my coffee. I was getting nowhere. I wondered, should I confront Milošević, call him a liar and a murderer, a Balkan Hitler, throw pictures of Bosnian corpses onto that nicely polished coffee table next to us? Yes, I could act differently. A British colleague of mine had a memorable standoff with Vojislav Šešelj, the notorious warlord whose paramilitary troops, the Chetniks, were responsible for the worst atrocities in Bosnia. Šešelj despised foreign journalists almost as much as he hated Muslims and Croats, so he charged $500 for an interview. My friend paid the fee. She secretly filmed the payoff and broadcast it in her televised report. Her interview was brief. Šešelj told the usual lies. No, his troops did not engage in ethnic cleansing, No, they did not torture prisoners, and so on. My friend got upset. She put down her pen and spoke her mind.

"The thing about your fighters is that they did not fight a brave fight. You were not fighting soldiers but attacking villages with women and children. I feel quite sick in my stomach talking to you."

Šešelj grinned.

"I can't do anything about your stomach. You'll need a doctor for that."

They then walked out on each other.

It would be unwise to walk out on Milošević. Perhaps I would have better luck asking personal questions. Nobody knew who Milošević was, whether there was a real person behind the smiles and war crimes, so I tried to find out. I asked if he had any hobbies.

He looked at me oddly, probably amused that I had asked such a silly question.

"I want to spend more time with my children," he replied. "I want to walk with them. I want to travel with them."

I asked what books he read.

Another odd look. He mentioned a novel about World War II called *Peaceful Crime*, but he had a hard time explaining the plot.

I asked him about the oil paintings on the wall. Why had he chosen them?

Another quizzical look crossed his face, this one more suspicious than the last, as though he was thinking, Art? He's asking me about art? What's he after? Does he really work for the *Washington Post*?

"There is only one painting that is my private painting," he said, courteous as ever. "The others were here when I came into the office. That one over there"—he pointed to a landscape near the windows—"is by Sava Šumanović. He was killed at the beginning of the Second World War, a victim of fascist aggression. He was killed by the Ustashe, Croatian troops. You know that Croatia was allied with Germany in the Second World War?"

I knew. Anyone who had watched five minutes of television in Serbia had probably seen the grainy pictures of Croatia's Nazi-era leader, Ante Pavelić, parading around Berlin with Hitler. Those pictures were usually followed by shots of Croatia's current leader, Franjo Tudjman, parading around Bonn with Helmut Kohl. Fascism on the border then, fascism on the border now. Only the dates had changed. The threat was the same, and so were the films, virtually every night.

Milošević had occupied the presidential office since ousting Stambolić in 1987, but he hadn't changed any of the paintings. It had a touch of the perversity of killing the emperor and taking up with his wife. Milošević knew only that one of the artists had been murdered by Croats, an odd form of artistic appreciation. I shouldn't have been surprised. The paintings did not matter to him, nor did the size of his office or the color of the telephone or the softness of his armchairs or the book he claimed to be reading or the walks that he said he wanted to take with his children. What mattered to him was power and holding on to it.

I still had the suicide card to toss out on the table. It was the wild card in my hand, and I toyed with it until it was dog-eared, wondering when to play it. Each of my personal questions had been preceded by a pause and a long introduction on my part. When I asked about his hobbies, I started off by explaining that Americans are interested in the backgrounds of political leaders. I prefaced my question about books with a remark about wanting to know the kinds of things that influenced him in his younger years. I was trying to decide whether, and how, to play the suicide card. Should I do it now? I looked at Milošević each time, and he at me, and I sensed that he was waiting for me to lay it on the table.

I folded. The idealistic journalist inside of me says I was a coward. Journalists are not supposed to let presidents stare us down. I have regrets about it. At the time I was thinking of what my Belgrade friends told me. *You won't get anything out of him. He's too smart. You'll just get into trouble.* They had a point. A country at war is no place for an amateur or an idealist. There are plenty of corpses scattered around the former Yugoslavia that, if they could speak, would say this: Don't fuck with Milošević. The Serbian leader had offered me cigarillos and smiled politely and even chatted idly about Los Angeles, my hometown—"I was there once. A very large city. You have to fly for half an hour from the airport before you land in the suburbs." He doesn't look the part of a dictator who brought death to 200,000 people and homelessness to a million or two more. But his smiles and words don't mean anything. Only his actions carry a meaning, and it is this: Don't fuck with Milošević.

He seemed bored while we talked. His lies were familiar to him, like a campaign speech recited over and over again. He was on automatic pilot. He certainly had reason to be bored, not only with me, but with all the journalists and diplomats who were shown through those dark corridors and ushered into his tranquil office. He might have thought we were pathetic, talking so politely, just like priests, careful not to raise our voices or swear. For the diplomats, who didn't need to fear retribution, it was probably a mistake to be so tactful in their choice of words, because the kind of language appropriate to Geneva will get you nowhere in the Balkans. If a Serb thinks his rival is an asshole, he will say so, and the rival is more likely to be impressed than offended. After all, what kind of man does not swear? *A weak man.* At the start of the war, Sarajevo Radio carried live transmissions of negotiations between Serb and Bosnian officials, who called each other lying motherfuckers. It was crude, and I suppose it confirms the stereotype of these people as primitives, but it was probably no worse than any of the "expletive deleteds" uttered by Richard Nixon in the Oval Office.

"Well," Milošević said. "It has been an hour and a half, and I thought the interview was only going to be a half hour."

"Yes," I replied. "Thank you very much. It has been very interesting."

We shook hands again, this handshake as unremarkable as the first one. He walked me to the door, and I stepped out, feeling a bit like a freed prisoner. I was glad it was over. You feel uneasy talking to Milošević because you know that you will not get what you want, that he is too smart to make a mistake, that he will get the better of you. Since he rose to power, Milošević had outwitted everyone who walked through that door. Diplomats got promises that were empty, journalists got words that meant nothing.

My story was on the front page the next day. "Serbian President Slobodan Milošević today expressed satisfaction with the Clinton administration's policy on the war in neighboring Bosnia, saying he believes the White House will steer clear of forceful measures against the Bosnian Serb faction," it stated. " 'I appreciate very much that the U.S. will not be the world policeman, to put everything in order in [its] own view,' Milošević said in an interview. Unlike the previous U.S. administration, he said, 'This administration is oriented to the essential problems of the United States . . . [and] will not try to hide internal problems by opening international problems.' "

I suppose that the reason Milošević agreed to talk with me was because he wanted to send a conciliatory message to President Clinton, to tell him that Serbia had no desire to get in a fight with America and was glad that America, obviously, didn't want a fight either. Clinton was embarrassed because the last thing he needed was a front-page compliment from a Balkan tyrant. Asked about Milošević's comments, Clinton vowed at a press conference to keep putting diplomatic pressure on Serbia. The olive branch was tossed into the garbage. Milošević responded by pouring more weapons and fuel into Bosnia to keep the war going. Also, his government refused to let me back into the country. I have been unable to visit Belgrade since then.

▶ Four

A DICTATOR does not qualify as the genuine article until his image seeps into the American consciousness and stays there, like a pop icon. Words and even deeds don't amount to much at the end of the twentieth century unless a visual image puts it all together, preferably in color. To achieve notoriety, a President or Maximum Leader or Marshal for Eternity or whatever he calls himself must provide America with at least one image, one in-your-face-take-this-America image, to seal his fate.

Manuel Noriega was doomed. Even when he smiled he looked like a grotesque cartoon character. He had a puffy, rutted face that you could not forget, no matter how hard you tried. He was called Pineapple Face. By his friends. But what really did it for Noriega, the moment when he ensured that Americans would not stop loathing him until he was behind bars in Miami, was when he picked up a shiny machete at a televised banquet in Panama City and, mid-tirade, began banging its flat side against the speaker's podium, ranting on about the Yankees, the Yankees, the goddamn Yankees. *Whack!* went the machete. *Whack! Whack! Whack!* Within months, America invaded Panama.

Saddam Hussein had an image problem, too. His impenetrably thick mustache was as foreboding as a nighttime jungle, which it resembled. He spoke Arabic, which, to many American ears, has a sound not unlike listening to an old man clear his throat. What we saw on American television was, most often, a picture of Saddam getting kissed on his cheeks by one of his adoring and unsmiling generals, who looked very much like Saddam—same mustache, same dark hair, same coldness in the eyes: Saddam clones. He never banged a machete on a podium, but he warned his people to prepare for a mother of all battles against America, and that, of course, ensured such a battle would take place. He made it easy for us to hate him. He dared us to attack.

In politics, it is very important to personalize the enemy. If a nation must go to war, it must be filled with the requisite amount of spite, it must not only be ready to kill, which is the task of any vigilant nation, but it must *want* to kill. And so it was with America and Noriega and Saddam. The wars against their countries could, in each case, be boiled down to two words. Get Noriega. Get Saddam. President Bush did not spend much time talking about the need to keep oil reserves in friendly hands, which was the real aim of the war on Iraq, or hold up pictures of the ousted Emir of Kuwait and say that our boys should spill their blood in order to permit this unlucky man to regain his feudal throne. (The emir, incidentally, is a rather unsavory-looking character. He wisely stayed away from the cameras.) We were hypnotized by one word, repeated over and over again. *Saddam, Saddam, Saddam.*

If the leaders of Iraq and Panama had been ordinary-looking and ordinary-talking men, would we have been able to hate them enough to go to war against them? What if they had been a bit smarter and shied away from the limelight, rather than basking in it, and pleaded with America for understanding, rather than challenging us to a duel?

They might, in that case, have been as successful as Slobodan Milošević. We hardly know him. What image comes to mind when an American hears the words "Slobodan Milošević"? Chances are, no image comes to mind. It's a blank. That's largely because the White House did not make any effort to demonize him. It didn't want to fight him. And Milošević was obliging. He didn't want to fight us. He learned from the mistakes of his peers and abstained from histrionics and refrained from bragging over the prostrate body of American foreign policy. Milošević discovered that it was possible to humiliate America without provoking it to respond. Machetes were for amateurs, and Milošević was no amateur.

▶ *Five*

THE LETTER was slipped under my door while I slept.

Dear Mr. Maass,

Due to the uncertain economic atmosphere and the consequent conflicting status of foreign exchange in Yugoslavia we have been compelled
to increase our dinar room rates with effect from 1st April, 1993. We
remain committed to our originally quoted U.S. Dollar room rate when
payed [sic] in actual U.S. Dollars. However, should you wish to settle
your account in Yugoslav dinars, your room rate is 4,290,000 per night
exclusive of local government taxes.

Yours Sincerely,

Srdjan Mileković, Director of Rooms

It was not an April Fools' joke. It was the second letter of its kind
that I had received at the Hyatt in two weeks. The nightly rate was
little more than a million dinars when I checked in. It doubled after
a few days, then doubled again and, if I didn't leave soon, I would
break through the 10-million-dinar-a-night level. Hyperinflation was
hitting its stride in Belgrade.

"Have you already paid your bill?" Dragan asked when he picked
me up the morning after my Milošević interview. A wily jack-of-all-
trades, Dragan was driving me out of Serbia.

"Yes."

"How did you pay it?"

"The *Post* is transferring the money into the Hyatt's Swiss bank
account."

Dragan looked upset as we pulled away from the hotel.

"You shouldn't have done that."

"Why not?" I replied. "I can't pay with a credit card, thanks to
the sanctions. If I paid in dinars, I would have needed a van to carry
the bills to the hotel. Sacks of money, Dragan."

My tab had come to more than 100 million dinars, which equaled
about $2,000, depending on the exchange rate, which depended on
the day I exchanged my money, at which hour I exchanged it,
whether the exchange was done at a bank or on the black market,
and whether I got robbed before, during or after the transaction.
There were so many variables in Serbia.

"If you paid the bill yourself you could make a lot of money," Dragan sighed.

"What do you mean?"

"Is simple," Dragan said. "You can pay the bill in dollars or dinars, right?"

"Right."

"Let's say you decide to pay in dinars."

"Okay."

"I get dinars for you."

"Okay."

"I get it from a friend. He is a bank."

"Dragan, a man cannot be a bank."

"I know. He is not bank, but he does what bank does."

"Change money?"

"Yes. But he gives better rate than the bank. Much better. Your bill was what?"

"About 100 million dinars."

"If you go to a bank and ask for 100 million dinars, they will ask for $2,000. Am I right?"

"Yes. That's the official exchange rate."

"But, my friend, when I ask for 100 million dinars, he will ask for only $1,000."

"The black-market rate," I noted.

"Yes. The official rate is *cheat*."

"Cheat?"

"Oh, sorry, *sheet*."

"Shit," I corrected him.

"Right. Is *sheet*. Nobody uses official rate. Have you been to bank?"

"Yes."

"What did it look like?"

"Empty."

"Right. So, because of my friend, you pay $1,000 for 100 million dinars. You then pay hotel bill yourself, with these dinars. Forget about Switzerland. Horrible country. The people don't laugh. Is against law. When you send your expense report, you tell your newspaper that you paid $2,000 for the 100 million dinars, the official rate. Your paper will pay you $2,000. But you only really paid $1,000. We have $1,000 profit."

I laughed hard.

"We, Dragan?"

He looked hurt.

"Yes. I am your friend. We are partners."

Milo Minderbinder would have been proud. He was the cook in *Catch*-22 who became a master dealmaker and, by the end of the book, supplied the American and German armies with food and ammunition. He was the sort of genius who could buy an egg for seven cents in Malta and then, after wheeling and dealing, sell it for five cents—and make a profit. The trick, after buying at seven cents, was to trade the egg for another product, then another and another and finally trade the last product for two eggs, which he would then sell for five cents apiece, thereby turning his original investment of seven cents to ten cents.

Dragan could do virtually the same thing with my hotel bill.

"But Dragan," I teased. "Isn't there something wrong with that?"

"Wrong? Wrong? What's wrong? The hotel gets 100 million dinars. It doesn't lose money. Your newspaper doesn't lose money because the hotel bill is 100 million dinars and 100 million dinars equals $2,000 at official rate. Your newspaper is important newspaper. It wants to pay official rate. It would punish you if you said you buy dinars on black market. American companies don't do things like that. You even have law that says your companies cannot pay bribes, right?"

"Right," I admitted.

"No bribes! Hah. How stupid. Of course Japan is winning."

He had a point.

"You see," Dragan continued. "Nobody loses. Not hotel. Not newspaper. Maybe bank, which loses profit it would make by changing money at official rate. But bank is owned by government, and government is criminal organization." He paused. "This is not my opinion. The United Nations says so."

Dragan was a fixer. In trouble spots across the globe, foreign news organizations have local fixers like Dragan. They get gasoline when none is available, they find hotel rooms when hotels are booked solid, they arrange interviews when no one wants to talk. They are a cleaner version of Harry Lime, the Vienna war profiteer played by Orson Welles in *The Third Man*. You ask the fixers to get something for you, you give them the money, and they will get it. You don't ask how. They are not the mafia but they know the mafia, which is why they are on your payroll.

Dragan was infrequently at his office. The only thing required of him was to take care of the tasks he was given. Where and when he did it was of no concern to the news agency that employed him. So Dragan had lots of side businesses, such as getting black-market sacks of money from his friends to pay the hotel bills of visiting journalists. He also drove journalists from Serbia to Croatia, via Hungary, for $450 a pop, and that's how the two of us met.

The Highway of Brotherhood and Unity, which linked Belgrade and Zagreb, was closed to civilian traffic since 1991, due to a pro-liferation of land mines and checkpoints along its brotherly asphalt. The journey now required a detour through Hungary. I could take a crowded, robber-infested train to Budapest, and then hop on an-other train from Budapest to Zagreb and arrive at my destination after fourteen hours of misery. Or I could pay Dragan an exorbitant fee to drive me out of Serbia, into Hungary and then to Hungary's border with Croatia, where a Croat friend of his would take me down the homestretch to Zagreb. The handoff was necessary be-cause Dragan, a Serb, could not drive into Croatia, and the Croat could not drive into Serbia.

Before the war, the direct highway journey took four hours and cost a few dollars in bus fare. Now it took eight hours and enriched people like Dragan.

It was a warm spring day, and the highway to Hungary was nearly empty, gasoline being scarce and expensive. We whooshed past a gas line that stretched for a mile or so. It was nothing like the lines in America in the early 1970s, when the Arabs learned to say "cartel." The Serbian lines consisted of trucks setting out on sanctions-busting runs to Hungary, and, unlike American lines, these ones moved infrequently. The drivers waited a day, two days, some-times three. Prostitutes worked the gas lines, waltzing from one eighteen-wheeler to another, a good business, given the truckers' high boredom and low morals. When a hooker reached the end of a line, she turned around and worked her way back to the front. An undisciplined driver could lose his gas money before getting to the pumps.

"*Sheet,*" Dragan said.

"What's wrong?"

"Fucking police."

A police car was flashing its lights behind us. We pulled over. The cops casually walked up to the driver's side of the car and began a conversation with Dragan. They didn't seem angry. Neither did Dragan. They talked like old friends. I knew they had stopped us for speeding. With few cars on the highway, Dragan was doing about eighty-five miles an hour. After a few minutes of chatting, one of the policemen filled out a slip of paper and handed it to Dragan, who handed over some money. We pulled away and accelerated until we were doing eighty-five again.

"What was that about?" I asked.

"This is perfect example of how stupid this government is," Dragan said. He handed me the slip of paper.

"You see, it says I was speeding and must pay a fine of 2,000 dinars. That is maximum fine law allows for speeding. What is 2,000 dinars now? It is nothing because of inflation. One hundredth of penny, maybe? It is less than cost of making the paper of policeman. When the government fines me 2,000 dinars for speeding it must pay 20,000 dinars for this piece of paper. So the government fines itself when it fines me. This is stupidity. Balkan stupidity."

"Dragan, you gave the policemen more than 2,000 dinars."

"Of course. Look at watch. Is lunchtime. They didn't stop me to collect stupid fine. They need money for lunch. I gave it to them. If I did not, they would stop me for speeding again or something else. Listen, before the war, the dinars the policemen earned were worth a few hundred dollars a month. Now it is twenty dollars. The government has fucked them, so they fuck me, and we all fuck government together."

Like everybody else caught in the madhouse of Serbia, Dragan was surrounded by stupidity. His government's and the world's.

"You know, sanctions will not work. Serbs are tough. You push us, we push you. We don't like to work, that's true. Milošević said in speech that Serbs don't work well but know to fight well. Is true. We are lazy workers. You want to know why? We never had to work. For forty years, it was you Americans who paid for our nice lives. You want to help Tito, because Tito hates Soviet Union, so you give him billions of dollars. You call it, what, loans? Loans! Croats, they are like Germans, they work hard and have nice beaches and had to share money with us. So we become lazy. Now nobody gives us money. Our good life is finished.

"But I work hard. I want to have money. I want to buy medicine for my wife if she gets sick. I want to have gasoline for my car. I want my children to go to good school. They are at French school. Is very expensive. Even my wife doesn't understand. She tells me is bad to work hard. Send children to public school." He laughed. "I am not a good Serb!"

I enjoyed listening to him. He did not give me history lessons, which is what most Serbs do when they talk about their country. Dragan did not try to convince me of the historical glories of Serbia, that Serbs were eating with forks and knives before the British, or that a Serb invented the spoon, or that Serbs are defending Christian civilization from the infidel Turks. He talked about life.

"I have cousins in Chicago."

He pronounced it "Chee-kago." Practically every Serb claimed to have a cousin there, and probably did, but no one could pronounce it properly.

"I have been there. New York, too. I could never live in America."

"Why not?" I asked. "Things are just getting worse here in Serbia."

"Yes, but here I have many friends. I do business with them. They help me, I help them. I would die for them. Look, if I meet you, and after a few months we become friends, then we do business. It doesn't matter when you pay. We are friends. Maybe you will do me favor later. This is Balkan way. In America, it's cold. You have lawyers and meetings and contracts. Friends and business are separate. I could never live there. Is too inhuman. I am from Balkans. I love Balkans." He chuckled for a moment. "Fucking Balkans."

Despite his denial, Dragan was a good Serb, or at least a genuine Serb. The Serbs lived for 500 years under the Turks, and as much as they despise the Turks, they absorbed much of the eastern, Ottoman way of life, beyond their bitter cups of coffee. The warmth and informality, the importance of personal relations, the easy mixture of business and pleasure, the generous hospitality, the long lunches and dinners and absence of urgency, even their music, it is all vaguely eastern, and it is the opposite of the efficient yet cold way things work in Croatia or Germany or America, whose cultures were, of course, untouched by Ottoman influences.

We reached the border. We avoided the main transit station, which was always clogged, and took a back road to a little-known border crossing that would not take hours to get through. I had the impression that it was kept open for the benefit of wily people like Dragan, who probably supplemented the salaries of the border guards, whose vigilance seemed to evaporate when we arrived. Dragan looked in dismay at the Serbs who stood by the border station trying to sell cheap cigarettes. The idea was that you bought cigarettes cheaply on the Serbian side and sold them for a higher price once you crossed into Hungary, which was now more affluent than Serbia.

"This is new Europe," Dragan sighed. "Before the war, Serbs did not behave like this. It was other way around. Hungarians, the poor stupid Hungarians, stood on their side of the border and sold cheap cigarettes to everyone heading into rich, smart Yugoslavia. Now we are poor ones. Very soon, like Bangladesh."

Dragan didn't drive nearly as fast in Hungary as he did in Serbia. Hungarian cops needed lunch money but lunch cost much more in Hungary and the cops didn't like Serbs. It was in Hungary that Dragan realized how much of a pariah his country had become, and how much this was hurting him. In Hungary, as in most European nations, Serbs were viewed as gunrunners or murderers or both. *You're from Serbia? Why are you killing those Bosnians? Why?* In the old days before the war, a Yugoslav passport was the best one to have because you could travel freely in both Eastern Europe and Western Europe. Now it was a curse because Yugoslavia was another name for Greater Serbia, and if Dragan wanted to visit London, he had to stand for hours in a visa line outside the British embassy, and once inside, he would be treated like an outlaw. *Why are you killing those Bosnians? Why?*

Our discussion about the war was short. Dragan felt uncomfortable with it, because he knew what I thought. He had spoken with many foreign journalists who covered Bosnia, and the discussion usually slid into a polite argument that ended with Dragan being told he was being duped by his government. Dragan didn't like Milošević, but what he disliked even more was being told by a foreigner that Serbs were guilty of committing the worst atrocities in Europe since Nazi Germany.

"I haven't been to Bosnia," he apologized. "But I can't believe that Serbs have done the things that everyone says we have done. The Muslims must have attacked first."

Dragan was in denial. So was Serbia.

▶ *Six*

I MUST borrow a line from a British colleague, Ian Traynor, who wrote that in Serbia, television was more important than history. It would be fair to distill his analysis further and assert that Serbs were brainwashed by television. Please do not be put off by the simplicity of this assertion; it is a reasonable explanation of how an entire nation composed of generally sensible citizens, people like Dragan, would follow their leader into an abyss of war and ruin. The same sort of process occurred in Croatia under the aegis of Franjo Tudjman.

Milošević controlled television absolutely, refusing to let independent stations have any national frequencies. State television maintained a monopoly, and Milošević, a well-trained Communist who understood the power and importance of propaganda, met or talked on a daily basis with the director of Radio-Television Serbia, whom he appointed and replaced, as necessary. Newspapers and magazines were largely irrelevant because few people could afford to buy them anymore. The most amazing thing about the role of television was that it not only had the power to form people's opinions, it could change those opinions overnight, like playing with a yo-yo. Let me offer two examples.

At the start of 1993, Milošević opposed the Vance-Owen peace plan, which would have split Bosnia into ten autonomous provinces, giving the largest amount of territory to Serbs, but not in contiguous pieces. State television reported, ad nauseam, that the plan was unfair. In April 1993, opinion polls showed that only one third of Serbians favored it. However, Milošević changed his mind when he sensed that America might intervene if Serbs in Bosnia refused the plan. Suddenly, Milošević was in favor of it. Suddenly, state television was in favor of it. And suddenly, Serbians were in favor of it. Opinion polls showed that in May nearly two thirds of Serbians supported Vance-Owen, virtually the reverse of what polls showed a month earlier. Milošević, like a drill sergeant, could shout "About face!" over the airwaves, and his subjects would turn on a dime.

This was hardly a fluke. At the end of 1993, far-right nationalists in Parliament staged a political rebellion, accusing Milošević of being insufficiently patriotic (in part because of his support for the Vance-Owen plan), and he responded by calling a snap election. His Socialist Party risked losing its status as the country's dominant political force, so state television went into overdrive, alternately ignoring and defaming the far-right nationalists while extolling the Socialists. This time, the most obnoxious nationalist, Vojislav Šešelj, who in the previous election was portrayed approvingly as a patriotic fighter, was now branded, of all things, a war criminal! Objects that had been described as white a year earlier were now called black, and nobody seemed to notice the inconsistency.

A survey showed that state television devoted twenty times more airtime to the Socialists than to their largest rival. The coverage was more slavish than before. After showing a series of Milošević speeches from 1988—he made few speeches in the 1993 campaign —an anchorman made the following statement: "There is no leader or party in Europe which can match Milošević and his party's accomplishments in such a short period." Accomplishments indeed. The Yugoslav Statistics Bureau had just disclosed that inflation was growing at a rate of 0.7 percent an hour, which translated into a monthly rate of 20,190 percent, which in turn translated into an annual rate of 286 billion percent.

When the votes were counted, the Socialist Party had picked up twenty-two additional seats in Parliament. Milošević's remarkable success had nothing to do with slick propaganda—the stuff was crude and badly produced. Dead bodies, stiff anchormen, more dead bodies, more stiff anchormen. It would be tempting to conclude that he succeeded in brainwashing Serbs, and succeeded with such ease, because Serbs were stupid and backward (and very different from us). The theory would appear to be supported by the fact that the war in Bosnia was so despicable that, as any outsider knew, only a nation of mildly retarded people could be conned into waging it. But this notion would be wrong. The propaganda succeeded because it imparted a clear, Reaganesque message: Milošević was defending Serbs who lived outside Serbia, and defending Serbia itself from the Islamic-Ustashe dangers lurking at its borders. Simple, clean, effective. Serbs swallowed it. In a similar situation, so might we.

I sought guidance from Miloš Vasić at *Vreme* magazine. The wall above his desk was papered with cartoons, one of which showed a map on which America was identified as "the United States of Serbia," and the caption said, "What's Serbian pacifism? Greater Serbia to the Pacific!" Vasić was a master at exposing the lies of nationalists and the conceits of foreigners, and he had a standard response when asked for the secret behind Milošević's brainwashing success: "You must imagine a United States with every little TV station everywhere taking exactly the same editorial line—a line dictated by David Duke. You too would have war in five years."

CHAPTER 6

PULLING OUT

IT WAS 5:45 in the morning, and the alarm clock next to my bed sounded as loud as a mortar explosion. I heard the sound again, a rumbling noise like thunder, and I knew it was not my alarm clock, a palm-sized device that beeped quietly when it tried to wake me up. It was often like that: something would shake me out of my sleep, a sharp sound or a bad dream, and I would keep my eyes closed and give my mind a few seconds to clear up and figure out where I was, whether I was in a bed or on the ground or under a desk, in a hotel or military barracks or somebody's living room, clothed or unclothed, safe or vulnerable.

I remembered where I was. Vitez, central Bosnia. I had arrived the previous evening with three colleagues, parking my jeep next to a sign that said "Kasem's Gas Station." I knew Kasem's because I had slept there on previous trips. Now came the hard part: what was happening around me? A thunderstorm? I hoped so, I deeply hoped so, but I didn't hear any wind or rain. I had to accept the possibility that I had been woken up by artillery fire. A training session? No, the Bosnians didn't have enough ammunition to spare. Okay, it was the real thing, but the battle might be taking place on the other side of the Lašva Valley, and I was hearing the echo. I opened my eyes after another thunderlike rumble, closer this time.

No, it can't be. I was like a person who refuses to believe his checking account is in the red, and does the calculations over and over again until he can't avoid the bottom line. I was caught on top of a thousand gallons of gasoline in a mortar attack.

It was dark when we had pulled into Kasem's eight hours earlier, and none of us noticed the fresh combat trenches surrounding it. We didn't pay much attention to the fact that the pump jockeys had AK-47s slung over their shoulders. Everybody's got a gun in Bosnia. I asked one of the soldier-attendants whether there had been trouble recently, and he casually replied, "Yeah, we got robbed three nights ago." In a war, robberies are the least of your worries. I felt fortunate that Kasem's had a few vacant rooms on the second floor, and paid $25 to check into the front line.

I should not have been surprised about what happened next. Nothing lasts for very long in Bosnia; safety passes into danger, danger passes into safety. We all knew this, but it was easy to become forgetful when you were safe and feeling good. When I checked into Kasem's and was the first to take a shower, I thought things were going well. I shared a room with Sasha Radas, my interpreter, and the adjacent room was taken by Cathy Jenkins and Adam LeBor, British journalists. We pooled our food and enjoyed a good meal that night, by local standards. Slabs of salami, some fresh fruit, cookies and a bit of brandy to top it off. In a country where most people went to sleep hungry and cold, we were warm, clean and had plenty of spare gasoline for our jeep. Vitez was quiet, as was the long stretch of territory to Tuzla that we were planning to drive through on the next day. I slept well, until 5:45 a.m.

There are some journalists who enjoy being under attack, the war junkies, but I am not among them. My hero is not George Patton or Peter Arnett or Robert Duvall in *Apocalypse Now*, loving the smell of napalm in the morning. My hero is Captain Yossarian from *Catch-22*. Like Yossarian, who knew the odds of being shot out of the sky during World War II and didn't like them, I consider myself a realist, not a coward. When I accepted the assignment to cover Europe's worst war in several generations I knew only that wars are a fundamental human experience and that I should try to learn why. I also knew that covering a war can do good things for a young journalist's career. It took a while to learn of the drawbacks, such as waking up to a mortar attack.

When I could no longer pretend that the shells landing around
Kasem's were thunder, I slipped out of bed, threw on my clothes,
lowered my flak jacket over my head and pulled down the groin flap
as low as it would go. The sound of mortars was joined by its evil
twin, the sound of machine-gun fire. My colleagues performed the
same hurry-up dressing routine and crouched with me in the hallway, where we had little time to ponder our next move before the
first bullets zipped through the windows, shattering the glass and
sending us face-first to the ground. Our reaction was immediate,
beyond instinctual. We crawled like alligators to the next safest
place, the stairwell, abandoning our bags in the hallway. We had
the same thought on our minds, *One direct hit and we're vapor*. It
could happen any second. I wanted to click my heels twice and be
in Kansas.

Tragedy and absurdity were moons circling the Bosnian war. I
realized this as we crouched in the stairwell trying to sort out the
least bad option. We could stay where we were. We could try to
find the basement, if one existed, and wait out things there. Or we
could make a run for it, jumping out the second-floor window or
dashing out the door on the ground floor. Instinct tells you to run,
to tear the hell out of the corner you're in and run, quite literally,
for your life, run faster than you have ever run, faster than you
imagined you could run. But, in fact, the run-for-your-life option
was less preferable than staying put atop the gasoline. If we made
it outside, which direction should we head? Which direction were
the shots and mortars coming from? I hadn't a clue. There was also
a terrified bear in a cage out back, and what if he had gotten loose?
The bear was named MacKenzie, after the U.N. general.

Then the phone rang. You assume that everything around you
stands still when your life hangs in the balance. Just as your body
shuts down its nonessential functions—you don't feel hungry anymore, you don't need that cup of coffee to wake up, and you can
skip the visit to the toilet you were planning—you assume that
phones will not ring, that dogs will not bark and that flowers will
stop growing. Time is standing still for you; it should do the same
for everybody else. But there we were, listening to mortars and machine guns firing at us, and the phone rang downstairs. The guns
stopped firing for a moment. Perhaps our attackers heard the ring
and thought it was a signal. Or maybe it was our attackers on the

phone, calling to demand our surrender. Better yet, perhaps it was somebody from the British Army, which had a base just two miles away, who had heard that foreign correspondents were in trouble at Kasem's. If only.

The guys with the AK-47s were not answering the phone. They had disappeared, taking up positions in the trenches around the station, from where they returned fire. Sasha, the interpreter, agreed to crawl downstairs and answer the phone. It was a brave act, because the phone was in a glass-enclosed office visible from three sides. He slithered into the office, hid under the desk, slipped his hand onto the desktop to grab the phone, pulled the receiver under the desk and put it to his ear. It was a woman calling who said she was the girlfriend of one of the pump jockeys. She lived nearby and heard the battle. Was her lover still alive? Sasha couldn't say. He asked her whether she knew anything about our attackers and could do anything about it. She whiffed on both queries.

Sasha crawled back to the stairwell. Time limped along at the pace of an old woman crossing a busy street. *Hurry up*, you think, *Hurry fucking up*. All that I remember of those minutes in the stairwell, looking at the faces of my colleagues trying, as I was, to look as though they weren't terrified, is that I took the jeep keys out of my pocket, dangled them in the air and announced that I was putting them in my right front pocket. The reasoning was simple—if I got hit and we needed to make a run for it, the others should know where the keys were. It was gruesome logic but hardly unusual. Before going to Bosnia, many journalists took out special war insurance policies. If you lose a finger, the insurer pays you, say, $10,000; for a thumb, you get $15,000; a lost hand nets $30,000; a leg is worth $40,000 if the amputation is below the knee, and $60,000 above the knee. A British colleague's policy awarded him $150,000 if he suffered "irredeemable dementia" after covering Bosnia.

There were shouts outside, and the gunfire ceased again. A linebacker-sized soldier with a black ski mask over his face and an assault rifle in his hands burst into the station. This was reassuring, because, after all, he was not shooting. *"Novinari! Novinari!"* we shouted, telling him we were journalists. The war was still at a stage when announcing yourself as a reporter was a protective measure rather than an invitation to fire. We held up our United Nations press cards. We didn't know whether we had been captured or liberated, or by whom, or what this jittery soldier planned to do with us. He had no markings on his camouflage uniform. Was he a Croat? Muslim? Serb? British? We dared to ask.

"You don't want to know," he snapped. "Who else is here?"

We told him no one, but he ran past us to the first floor and began kicking in the doors, SWAT-style, bursting into each room with the speed and precision of a gentleman who had done this many times before. Sasha whispered, "Maybe he is trying to show off." It was not a joke; at times like that, your mood is manic. One moment you are sure you are going to die, the next moment you think everything is okay, the masked storm trooper is just showing off, and you can relax now. But our trooper was not showing off. After destroying as many doors as he could find, he ran back downstairs and barreled through a couple of glass doors he found there. He located the basement and, rather than risk an ambush by venturing into the darkness below, pointed his rifle down the stairway and fired away until there were no more bullets in his clip. That was the basement we had thought of sheltering in.

Another masked soldier carrying the obligatory AK-47 ran inside and crouched next to a wall a few feet away. He was smaller, about six foot two, and his eyes were wild and bloodshot. "Who are you?" asked Sasha. The guy smiled through his hood and whispered one word: "Ustashe." This was the name of Croatia's World War II pro-Nazi movement, and five decades later, Croat extremists in Bosnia proudly referred to themselves as Ustashe, a one-word boast that meant, "We're the meanest sons-of-bitches around." More of them piled into the gas station.

The entire valley had turned into a battle zone between Croat forces and the Bosnian Army, allies until dawn broke, when Croats assumed the role of Judas, hoping to lop off a chunk of Bosnia for themselves. The gas station had been controlled by the Bosnian Army when we checked in but the management was changing hands, Bosnia-style. We told the Croats we just wanted to get out of the place and shelter at the British base down the road. No problem, they said, but you can't leave now because it's unsafe. We suggested they contact the base so that a British armored personnel carrier could fetch us. They said they would see what they could do.

My sympathies had shifted. Until the Croats seized Kasem's, they were attacking it and, by extension, attacking us. Now that they were in control of it, the Bosnian Army was counterattacking and, by extension, attacking us. I had the simplest of wishes, to get out of the madness.

A few minutes later, a soldier told us to get outside. I moved downstairs as quickly as possible with my backpack, computer bag, helmet and flak jacket. The pump jockeys were in the office again, but now their hands were raised in the air, and they were staring at the wrong end of an assault rifle. Their faces bore the look of death. Ustashe do not take prisoners.

I stepped outside. There was no British APC in sight. Sasha dashed out and said the soldiers wanted us to *run* to the British base. They didn't know we had a jeep in the parking lot, but even so, I didn't like the idea of driving through a battle in a soft vehicle. We could return to the building and wait for better times. I noticed a few houses burning a couple hundred yards away, saw a company of nervous soldiers crouching for cover behind the station and realized that better times would not be coming to this spot. I ran to the jeep, past an unexploded grenade that lay on the ground like a gum wrapper, opened the trunk and threw out one of the jerricans of gasoline. The fewer explosive materials we carried the better. My colleagues jumped into the jeep, and they had the same thought on their minds: He better not flood the engine again. Thankfully I didn't, and, as we screeched out, one of the Ustashe soldiers gave us a straight-armed Nazi salute. It was his way of saying good-bye.

My Russian jeep had a top speed of sixty-five miles an hour, or about a quarter of the speed I would have liked. I weaved from one side of the empty road to the other, making it more difficult for snipers to get off an accurate shot. It's a trick I learned in Sarajevo. It might be useful when I return to my hometown of Los Angeles, where commuters occasionally face gunfire on the freeways. There was total silence in the jeep, everyone scrunching down into their helmets and flak jackets like turtles trying to sleep. At moments like that I would try to believe that my fear exceeded the danger, that I was merely being paranoid, but the sound of gunfire contradicted such hopes. Sasha interrupted my thoughts. "Oh no," he said, pulling something from his pocket. "We forgot to return our room keys."

We barreled into the British base. We had survived, we had gotten a second chance to live our lives as normal people. *Okay*, God was saying, *I'll let you out of this one, but I hope you learned your lesson.* This was only one of many second chances I got while covering the war. Each time I got one, I continued the same unsafe behavior that put me into the position of needing to pray for deliverance from a lethal corner I had boxed myself into. Sooner or later, the odds would catch up with me, as they had caught up with friends of mine. It was just a matter of time.

We dashed into the command post. The duty officer was an incarnation of David Niven, standing straighter than a telephone pole and speaking without moving his jaw. "Right, there's quite a bit of fighting going on out there this morning, so you were bloody lucky to get out of it so well," he said crisply. "I would suggest that you march down to the canteen and have some breakfast and tea. I should think you could use a good meal after a fright like that." When Brits get nervous they drink tea. So long as they are drinking tea, everything is okay. Never mind the mortars, would you like one lump of sugar or two?

The base was a neutral haven. Shells screeched overhead, a few every minute, each one making a horrible sound as it sliced through the air, a gut-splitting noise that made you want to retreat as far away from the front line as possible. The biggest shells were fired by the Croats from a 155-millimeter howitzer known as Nora, which used to be pointed at the Serbs, but now was firing from its hilltop perch at the Bosnians, making the British soldiers mutter things like, "Nora's up to no good today." It was hard to understand why a weapon of death was given a name that belonged to plump aunts. There were lots of things that were hard to understand. Why, as I mentioned before, when the only people outside were soldiers trying to kill other soldiers, did a fat pensioner pedal past the base on an orange bicycle? I still chuckle over the explanation given by the officer who observed the scene with me: "Bosnian mind fuck."

The breakfast was great, an affirmation of the parallel universe that I had just escaped to. As I dug into my corn flakes, the captured pump jockeys a few miles down the road were probably being marched out of the gas station and ordered to stand in front of a ditch. As I got up from the table to fetch more jam for my toast, their Croat captors might have been taking aim. And as I sat back

down and had another sip of English breakfast tea with two lumps
of sugar in it, the young Bosnians who had been my hosts the night
before were probably being shot dead. The war spun off lots of
parallel universes. There was, for example, the parallel universe of
diplomacy, in which diplomats would sit down in plush chairs in
Geneva or Brussels or New York and concoct peace plans that wors-
ened the fighting.

Bosnian mind fuck.

The executions that I assumed were taking place down the road
were less troubling than the suddenly bleak outlook for several million Bosnians who supported their government and its notion of a
pluralistic country in which everyone would live together peacefully.
After a year of warfare, the government had lost two thirds of its
territory to nationalist Serbs, and the attack that woke me at Kasem's gas station was a sign that the remaining third was in trouble.
Croats in Bosnia, backed by Croatia proper, wanted Kasem's gas
station, wanted Vitez and wanted most of the territory not yet seized
by Serbs. They figured that if the Western world was letting Serbs
carve off a slice of Bosnia, why shouldn't Croats have a slice, too?

As I sat in the British canteen, a soldier next to me swallowed the
last of his breakfast sausages and let out a huge battlefield burp. He
got up from his chair, grabbed his SA-80 rifle with one hand and
his food tray with another and shook his head in pity. "If the West
is going to give weapons to these poor bastards, it better be done
real soon," he said. "They're going to get killed, the whole lot of
them." An obedient soldier, he then headed outdoors to help keep
the West's death watch.

▶ *Two*

WHY didn't they just give up? It is one thing to fight on a
single front, but it is something quite different to fight on two fronts,
which is what the Bosnians had to do when Croatia chose the Judas
option. Croatian President Franjo Tudjman, whose appetite for a
chunk of Bosnia was well-known but unsated, gave his forces a
green light to conquer as much of Bosnia as they could manage. The
trickle of food and weapons that had sustained Bosnia in the war's
first year came through Croatia, and this lifeline was severed when

the first mortar was fired at Kasem's. A year after the Serbs began cleansing and killing Muslims, Croats began doing the same thing, like the vulture after the predator. Extinction beckoned.

In America, we have a hard time understanding why people in places like Bosnia are willing to suffer so much in a futile war. The goal of imperial wars, which we are most familiar with, is to conquer and rule. The goal of nationalist wars, as in Bosnia, is to conquer and cleanse. These contests are winner-take-all. When you are faced with enemies who wish to expunge you from your land, and when those enemies offer a treaty that ensures their boots will stay on your throat, suffocating you one day, you have little choice but to keep struggling, even though the odds are against you and people who call themselves your friends are saying you should give up. Resistance becomes not an option but an imperative.

Emir Tica taught me the meaning of resistance. Emir was one of those Bosnians whom I only met a few times but cannot forget, and somehow consider a friend. He was in his early thirties, well under six feet tall, and had brown hair and blue eyes. He liked heavy metal. Emir lived in Travnik, an ancient, minaret-filled town that was a regional capital during the Ottoman empire, and the birthplace of Ivo Andrić, the famed writer. Emir worked as an adjutant to Travnik's commander, and because Emir spoke English well, he also served as an unofficial liaison with foreign journalists, which is why our paths crossed.

"It is becoming clear to me that we are completely alone," Emir said at army headquarters, a restaurant where a guard at the door was equipped with a laughably outdated Tommy gun. "We as a people are in danger of simply disappearing. I have never called myself a Muslim, but now I must feel like a Muslim, because European Muslims are faced with obliteration. I know history, from books and movies, and I know that in the Nazi times they tried to destroy a people, the Jews. We are now starting to feel like the Jews must have felt in 1940, when they realized it was for real. But we must survive, at least two of us. It is not a question of who will survive but that someone must survive. In order to kill a people, you must kill memory, you must destroy everything that belongs to that people. But if two people can stay alive, they can remember. The Jews can remember, and I expect they can understand what is happening here better than anyone else."

It was hard to escape the Jewish analogy, and perhaps that's why I found my travels in Bosnia to be increasingly depressing. My ancestors would have liked to consider themselves Germans, or German Jews, but in the end they were Jews, just Jews, not Germans at all, and they had to leave or die. Emir had made the same mistake. He thought he was a Bosnian, or a Bosnian Muslim, but in the end he was a Muslim, just a Muslim, and other people, stronger ones, wanted his land and were willing to kill him for it. The same dark forces of history were at work, although this time the victims had a better opportunity to resist, and so, even on two fronts, they resisted.

What's surprising is the fact that presidents and prime ministers in the West were surprised at Bosnia's stubbornness. It is entirely natural for a people to continue fighting for their land or freedom until they are no longer capable of fighting. Let me suggest an approximate parallel. Imagine, for a moment, that Mexico and Canada mounted a surprise attack and gained control of two thirds of America, cleansing the conquered territory. The bulk of the population is crammed into the Midwest, the only land still held by our government. The West Coast and East Coast are occupied by the enemy. Would we agree to a peace treaty that gave most of the country to the Canadians and Mexicans, leaving us sandwiched between them, at their mercy for supplies? Remember, tens of thousands of our men have been tortured and killed by the Canadians and Mexicans, and tens of thousands of our women have been raped. The question is a no-brainer; we would continue fighting until we won back our land or were driven into the Grand Canyon.

In such situations, you fight in whatever way you can, with whatever weapons you have. When the Croats attacked, completely shutting off the Bosnian Army from outside supplies, the Bosnians survived by improvisation. If the terrain was appropriate, explosives were packed into barrels and rolled downhill at the enemy. These were known as barrel bombs. When the Bosnians ran out of artillery casings, they stuffed explosives into fire extinguishers. They even turned soda pop cans into mortar shells and grenades. They were one step away from reverting to impalings. And it worked. They held off the Croats, who, a year later, called off their failed offensive and patched up their alliance with the Bosnians.

Just as resistance is natural in situations like that, so, unfortunately, is radicalization. Feeling betrayed by America and Europe, the Muslim leadership in Bosnia began turning away from Western notions of pluralism, and focused on Muslim nationalism. It was the cruelest of self-fulfilling prophecies: The Western world viewed them as Muslims, not Europeans, so they became Muslims, tough Muslims. They had little choice—with the United Nations as global cop, the meek shall not inherit the earth. I sensed the beginnings of this process, a sad process, when I met Selma Hećimović at the Center for the Investigation of War Crimes and Crimes of Genocide, located in Zenica, a few miles up the road from Vitez.

Selma, a young schoolteacher in blue jeans, had the appearance of a surfer girl, with blond hair, blue eyes and three silver earrings in her left earlobe. Her wartime job consisted of helping refugees fill out questionnaires about war crimes. It was an unusual questionnaire, using the kind of dispassionate language that might be found in marketing surveys for deodorants, yet it asked respondents to explain the types of torture they suffered. It offered a checklist of aftereffects: "Nightmares? Fevers? Anxiety attacks? Loss of appetite? Crying? Suicidal thoughts? Depression? Desire for revenge? Desire to kill? Paranoia?"

A box on Selma's desk contained a foot-high stack of these questionnaires, but I was less interested in the box than the color picture on a wall next to her desk. The picture was of Ali Khamenei, and underneath the photo of Iran's spiritual leader was a 600-word statement, in Bosnian, that assailed Western countries for refusing to lift the arms embargo, and said that Iran stood ready to help its stricken brethren in the Balkans. I was also interested in the silent man who sat in a corner of the room, and who, when I politely asked him where he was from, smiled and replied, "Iran."

"We had illusions about American democracy," Selma said. "How can we believe in your democracy when there are atrocities happening here and you do nothing? When Clinton sends American weapons, then we'll put his picture on the walls. But these people" —she nodded toward the photo of Khamenei—"are really helping us. They're giving us weapons." The Iranian smiled.

I asked Selma what she thought of *sharia*, Islamic law. She replied that it was good, and that women were treated equally under it. I mentioned to her that *sharia* meant she must swap her blue jeans for an ankle-to-head black gown, the chador. I mentioned, too, that in Saudi Arabia, which has imposed *sharia*, women are not allowed to drive a car. Was that the kind of equal treatment she wanted for herself in Bosnia?

The Iranian interrupted. No, he said, that is wrong. Women can drive cars in Saudi Arabia. They don't have to wear the chador.

I replied that this was inaccurate, but he insisted just as strongly that I was inaccurate, and he asked whether I had been to Saudi Arabia, and when I said that I had not, and he claimed he had been, and that he was telling the truth while I was lying, the argument was over, no matter how hard I protested, because it was his word against mine. I knew, without asking, whose version Selma believed. Why, after all, should she trust the word of an American whose government, in her view, had betrayed her people?

Within a few months, women in Zenica started wearing Muslim scarves over their heads, and alcohol and pork became more difficult to purchase. For the first time, foreign journalists were harassed by the city's Muslim soldiers. Those soldiers, dishing out the kind of punishment their people suffered earlier in the war, became involved in atrocities of their own (though hardly on the scale of the Serbs or Croats). In Sarajevo, the minister of culture, a Muslim, announced that mixed marriages were a bad idea. A new elite emerged, composed of black marketeers, army chieftains and militants from Alija Izetbegović's Party of Democratic Action (SDA in Bosnian). After a year of warfare, the virus of nationalism, carried by Serbs and Croats, was infecting Muslims and eating away at the multinational society they once belonged to. How far would it spread?

When they started the war, Serbs claimed that Muslims wanted to set up an Islamic state. It was nonsense, of course, and it still is. But what's true is that Bosnia's multinational society has been eroded by the corrosive effects of the long war; virtue is degraded rather than rewarded in protracted military conflicts. A year after the war started, well-educated liberals with connections outside Bosnia began leaving in greater numbers, thereby letting less tolerant militants get a stronger grip on the hearts and minds of those who remained behind. This is perhaps the saddest part of Bosnia's tragedy, that its unique mosaic of nationalities, held together by civic tolerance, may disappear forever even in cities controlled by the government. With luck, Emir and those who share his views might triumph, not only against Serb and Croat nationalists, but against

Muslim nationalists, too. My hopes are with Emir, but I am not hopeful. It would be a true pity for Bosnia, which has lost so many lives already, to lose its soul.

"I don't want to live in an Islamic country," Emir said. "I drink alcohol. I don't pray or go to a mosque. When I listen to music, I listen to Guns N' Roses, Neil Young, AC/DC. When I read books, I read Mark Twain. When I speak a foreign language, it is English. I don't know how to speak Arabic. My country is Bosnia, and Bosnia exists only with all its nationalities. I don't want to live with only Muslims. Can you imagine living in California with only white people?"

▶ *Three*

"Only the hypocrite is really rotten to the core."
—Hannah Arendt

I CAN recall the precise day when, finally, I fell spiritually sick. It was April 22, 1993.

In Washington, D.C., the Holocaust Memorial Museum was being inaugurated in an outdoor ceremony that featured an emotional speech by President Bill Clinton, who looked bravely into an unseasonably cold wind and hit all the right notes, as he usually does. "The nations of the West must live forever with this knowledge: Even as our fragmentary awareness of these crimes grew into indisputable facts, we did far too little. Before the war started, doors to liberty were slammed shut. And even after we attacked Germany, rail lines to the camps, within miles of militarily significant targets, were left undisturbed. Mass deaths were left to occur, enshrouded in our denial. . . . The evil represented in this museum is incontestable. It is absolute. As we are its witness, so we must remain its adversary. We owe that much to the dead, as we owe it to our consciences and our children. So we must stop the fabricators of history and the bullies as well. Left unchallenged, they would still prey upon the powerless, and we cannot permit that to happen again."

Elie Wiesel was on the stage with Clinton. A few months earlier, Wiesel had visited a Serb prison camp in Bosnia, and the haunted faces of the Muslim inmates reminded him of the doomed souls

jailed with him at Auschwitz fifty years before. He saw many par-
allels, too many. And so, when he reached the speaker's podium,
Wiesel, a writer of extraordinary conscience, had no choice but to
turn his perpetually sad gaze away from the crowd and look into
the eyes of William Jefferson Clinton, perhaps the only person in
the world who could turn things around. It was not the polite thing
to do, but it was the right thing to do. "Mr. President, I cannot not
tell you something," Wiesel said. "I have been in the former Yugoslavia last fall. I cannot sleep since for what I have seen. As a Jew
I am saying that we must do something to stop the bloodshed in
that country. People fight each other and children die. Why? Something, anything must be done!"

On that day, April 22, 1993, I was in Tuzla, staying in an apartment that lay under the flight path of Serb artillery shells, which
whistled overhead like evil songbirds. I cannot forget that day because of an interview I had with Nedret Mujkanović, a doctor who
had just escaped from Srebrenica, where he performed hundreds of
amputations without anesthetic because Serbs were besieging the
town and depriving it of food and medicine. The interview lasted
for three hours, one bitter coffee after another, and these were three
of the most amazing hours I spent in Bosnia. I never came closer to
crying; at several points in the interview, I had to look away and
not listen, and tell myself to hold on. People came to our table and
shook the doctor's hand, kissed his cheek, gave him a flower. Some
were friends, others were strangers. They were all on the verge of
tears and didn't know what to say to a man who in the previous
nine months had sliced off arms and legs with a dull scalpel as patients screamed in pure agony. Their words of thanks were brief.
We're proud of you, they said, we're proud of you.

To understand my sickness, you need to understand Dr. Mujkanović. When I first saw him, he looked like a war profiteer. I was
at Tuzla's airport to cover the evacuation of Srebrenica's sick and
wounded. Almost everyone who emerged from the U.N. helicopters
was on a stretcher or crutches, but not Mujkanović, who leapt onto
the tarmac with a burgundy fedora on his head, a silk jacket around
his wide shoulders and shiny Italian shoes on his feet. He strode
across the tarmac with his nose stuck up in the air, his back ramrod
straight. I figured he was the black-market kingpin of Srebrenica.
Who else would have the squeeze to get onto a U.N. evacuation

helicopter, and who else would have such nice clothes and walk like a dandy? A few Bosnian journalists knew better and surrounded him. It was chaos on the tarmac—the helicopter rotors were whipping up a storm of dust, the last evacuees were moaning in pain as orderlies loaded them into ambulances, and U.N. soldiers were running around and shouting orders, truly a scene from a Balkan version of *M*A*S*H*. Sasha and I wandered over to Mujkanović and heard him mention the number of abdominal surgeries he performed without anesthesia. We arranged to meet him the next day, April 22, 1993.

At roughly the same moment that President Clinton began lecturing his cold audience in Washington, Mujkanović sat down at a grubby outdoor café in Tuzla and began telling his story, dressed now in army fatigues and a white T-shirt. It was a hot day, like summer. We were in the shadow of the Hotel Tuzla, where Bianca Jagger was staying during a fact-finding trip. I remember seeing her and realizing that Bosnia had become a choice stamp to have in your metaphysical passport. Her presence helped turn the Hotel Tuzla into a theater of the surreal. A day earlier Bosnian soldiers paraded captured Serb soldiers in front of the hotel and, after roughing them up and firing their guns into the air, treated their bruised captives to a spaghetti lunch at a restaurant in the lobby.

Mujkanović, who was in his late twenties but looked a decade older, sipped Turkish coffee and smoked American cigarettes, a potent mixture. He was a surgery intern in Tuzla when the war broke out, and because Srebrenica was desperate for medical help, the Bosnian Army infiltrated him there through the siege lines. It was a foolish five-day journey in which, for the final stretch, Mujkanović and his escorts crawled at night past Serb soldiers, close enough to see the burning tips of their cigarettes. When he arrived in Srebrenica, all medical supplies had run out, even bandages and aspirin. There were 75,000 people in the town and just three general practitioners who were clueless about surgery. Mujkanović taught them what he knew, which wasn't much, and it didn't take long for him to become an expert in medieval surgical practices, a Bosnian specialty.

When Mujkanović amputated a limb, he coaxed the patients along by telling them it would be short, just hold on for another minute, be brave and stay still, don't mind the bombs, there we go, just a little bit more, only a few more slices on the bone, now we're almost done. "Nobody held them down," Mujkanović said. "They believed in me. And they knew it was the only way." Even so, many surgery patients died from blood loss or postoperative infection, for there were no antibiotics in Srebrenica. Instead of disinfectants, he washed wounds with boiling water. Instead of blood transfusions, he stitched arteries together as quickly as possible with sewing thread. Instead of surgical lights, he used candles. Instead of bandages, he used strips of bed sheets. Instead of decent food, Mujkanović and his patients ate bean soup and bread made from straw. He performed 1,400 operations in nine months.

The town's agony unfolded less than a few miles from Serb territory where there was plenty of medicine and food. Srebrenica was only a few hundred miles from Western Europe, perhaps a thirty-minute plane ride away. As vacationers schussed down ski slopes in the Alps, and as diplomats sipped fine wines in Geneva, Mujkanović tried to blot out the medieval screams of his doomed patients.

It was easy to interview Mujkanović, like shooting ducks in a barrel, because no question could miss. What achievement was he proudest of?

"When captured Serb soldiers entered the hospital, they lay side by side with Bosnian soldiers. They stayed in the same rooms, and they shared the food that Bosnian families brought to the hospital. I guaranteed that nothing happened to them. My greatest satisfaction as a humanist and a doctor is that they were carried into the hospital on stretchers and left on their legs. . . . One of the Serbs was in critical condition because he already had a gangrenous foot. I fought for ten days to save the foot, to avoid amputation. When we succeeded, when he started to walk, he said, 'Doctor, if we ever see each other again, you will see how thankful I am. I can't do anything for you now, but I know you have a son. I wish you could see your son.' That was the best way he could thank me."

None of this explained why the good doctor was dressed for a disco when he jumped out of the helicopter in Tuzla. The only clothes he wore in Srebrenica were army fatigues, and when it was time to go, the people of Srebrenica didn't want him to look like a military slob, so they went into their closets and pulled out the best clothes they could find. Somebody found a fedora, somebody else came up with Italian shoes and so on. That's the way it was in

Srebrenica. The people wore rags but they wouldn't let their doctor wear rags. After saying his good-byes in town, Mujkanović made a final stop at the hospital before boarding the last helicopter. All his co-workers were there, people with whom he had lived a dozen lifetimes during his nine months in Srebrenica. Everyone was crying.

"I said to them, 'I am not leaving you. I will be back in Srebrenica.' They asked me how, and I said, 'I will find a way back.' "

I used a satellite phone at the Hotel Tuzla to transmit my profile of Mujkanović to Washington, and I returned to my apartment, where I watched the local news on a black-and-white television. Thanks to the wonders of satellite communications, and thanks to the ingenuity of Tuzla's television engineers, the local news featured a long segment on the opening ceremony at the Holocaust Museum. I listened to excerpts of President Clinton's speech and wanted to believe that he meant what he said about standing up to the bullies in the world. I wanted to believe, in particular, his final words: "With God's blessing upon our souls, and the memories of the fallen in our hearts and minds, it is to the ceaseless struggle to preserve human rights and dignity that we rededicate ourselves. . . . We will never relent, and we will prevail."

It was a beautiful speech, and I wanted to believe he meant it, if only because it was delivered on such hallowed ground, the Holocaust Museum. Who would dare to be insincere on a day like that, at a place like that? But I knew otherwise, and so, I am sure, did Dr. Mujkanović and anybody else in Bosnia who had listened to President Clinton's speeches over the previous months and suffered at the mercy of an untouched bully named Serbia. It was just words, eloquent words of course, but words intended as substitutes for action rather than precursors to it. My disappointment in President Clinton—no, let me be precise, my *disgust* with President Clinton—turned to shame. I felt no personal responsibility for the fact that he was a hypocrite. But something new struck me: President Clinton was making hypocrites of us all, and there was very little that could be done about it.

As a Jew, I have a special reason for wanting to believe that "never again" really means never again, and I would like to think it does not apply solely to Jews. It has taken me more than three decades to learn the truth. I was born in 1960, at the tail end of the baby boom, and came of age as part of the post-Vietnam, post-

Watergate generation that believes governments deceive inherently and that politicians are scoundrels. Instead of Camelot and the Peace Corps, my generation got Ollie North and the contras, and whether we were Republicans or Democrats, we all underwent a full-body baptism in the murky waters of political cynicism. I never considered myself an idealist about the motives of my government, yet I assumed it would not stand aside while defenseless cities and civilians were attacked without mercy in Europe, right under the wingtips of Air Force jets that flew observation missions over Bosnia. I was terribly naïve.

On April 22, 1993, I realized that the time had come to pull out of Bosnia. I was exhausted, I could not escape the war even in my sleep, I was no longer curious about the war and I no longer believed that my reporting could make a difference. The American government was unmoved and many Americans were unable to figure out who were the good guys and the bad guys or had given up caring about the difference. The fruits of my labors were drifting into a realm of journalism that was known in the Bosnian press corps as "horror porn": the woman who was raped nearly every day for two months; the guy who crawled through a battlefield after both his legs were blown off; the morgue stacked full of frozen bodies; the massacre in which a boy was shot dead along with the puppy in his arms; the grandmother burned to a crisp in her home, or the doctor who amputated without painkillers. You were on the lookout for these stories, not because anybody back home was going to do anything about it, but because it was good copy. The agony of Bosnia was being turned into a snuff film. I couldn't see any wisdom in risking my life to help produce the final reel.

THE APPEASERS

GENEVA is one of the gentlest places on the planet, especially
in the summer, when you cannot find a sweeter combination of sunshine, beauty, orderliness and wealth. The city is shaped like a horse-
shoe around the end of a long lake, fed by glacial waters that flow
down from the Alps, and this lake tempts you to steal an hour from
the working day to join the young crowd on the jetty for a swim
in the water, which feels pure. You can, in that hour, take a nap by
the lake, gaze at the snow-topped peaks above the city, admire the
women who are sunbathing topless or count the Rolls-Royces with
tinted windows cruising along the boardwalk. You must look hard
to find something disagreeable, but why bother?

Geneva is what Europe aspires to be, and Sarajevo is what Europe
recoils from. They would seem to have nothing in common, these
two cities, except that when you are in one of them, you cannot
imagine that the other exists.

The truth, more complex than appearances, is that they are similar, underneath their contrasting garments, like a millionaire and a
beggar. There is much virtue to be found in Sarajevo, even beauty,
and much vileness in Geneva, even evil. All of this dawned on me
when I turned down further assignments in Bosnia and was dispatched to Geneva, where, instead of soldiers tearing Bosnia apart,

diplomats were doing the same thing. These diplomats were not Serbian or Croatian but American and British and French, and instead of preventing a crime, they acted as accomplices. The men with pens were every bit as fascinating and repulsive as the men with guns.

If you wished to create a perfect diplomat, you could do no better than Charles Redman. According to his official résumé, Redman graduated from the Air Force Academy in 1966, and then went to Harvard University, where he earned a master's degree in 1968. After serving for six years in the Air Force, he joined the Foreign Service in 1974 and had a succession of fast-track assignments in Washington, Paris, Algiers and Brussels. He served as the State Department's spokesman during the Reagan years, and in 1989 was sent to Sweden as ambassador. In 1993, after a brief spell as a presidential troubleshooter for Haiti, he was tapped as the U.S. special envoy to the Bosnian peace talks.

Redman is nearly bald, and the top of his head does, on occasion, sparkle in the reflection of television lights. He is average height, average build, and his speech patterns are average; no fancy words, no complex sentences, no witticisms. This does not mean he is unintelligent. He is quite smart, able to respond to sharp questions with evasive answers that, at the end of a long interview, leave you leafing through your notebook searching for something, anything, of news value. You come up empty, and you realize, too late, that the guy outwitted you again, talking and talking and talking and saying absolutely nothing.

The peace talks took place at the Palais des Nations, a huge concrete-and-marble edifice built in the 1930s as the headquarters for the League of Nations. The Palais, like nothing else on the planet, is the largest expression of an architectural style best described as neo-fascist. An official brochure suggests, diplomatically, that it combines "classical grace with modern severity." It has no less than 1,700 doors. The negotiations were mediated by David Owen and Thorvald Stoltenberg, the former foreign minister of Norway, and they talked constantly with the major players, bringing them together for face-to-face negotiations that lasted well into the evening and, occasionally, into the early morning hours. "Balkan time," as a diplomat explained.

Redman was a step removed from the roundtable sessions at the

Palais, which he did not join but monitored closely. He worked on two tracks. On one, he tried to cajole the Serbs into handing over as much land as possible, which turned out to be very little. On the other track, he tried to cajole the Bosnians into accepting the scraps offered by the Serbs. In public, Redman said the Clinton administration did not favor partition but would support it, with great reluctance, if that was what Bosnia's government wished. Behind the scenes, Redman joined his European colleagues in pressuring the Bosnians to accept the carve-up. The executioners, trying to keep their hands as clean as possible, wanted their victim to flip the switch.

Was Redman a monster, a good soldier, a tortured soul? A moment of illumination came during a briefing I attended with two other journalists. One of them, Christopher Dickey, knew relatively little about Bosnia, and because of that, he asked the best question, dealing not with mind-numbing minutiae of maps and troops but with morality. My tape recorder was running, so I have a precise record of the exchange.

"Did you have any misgivings when you were taking this job?" Chris asked. "You're being asked to preside over a fairly sordid incident in diplomatic history, in European history. Do you have any misgivings about that?"

For an instant, Redman didn't say anything, and his face looked completely blank, as though he was stunned by the question, so indelicate, so crude. This was unusual for such a practiced and smooth diplomat. He seemed lost, like a buck frozen in a car's headlights, unable to move as a sudden and terrible force bore down on him. After a few seconds, Redman recovered with a blink of his eyes, as though the headlights had been switched off.

"First, I would have to take objection to the word 'preside.' I don't believe we're really presiding—"

"Bearing witness?"

"You know, I am a career diplomat, and this is a tough issue, a large issue, a complicated issue, and in that context I am happy to do the best I can. Like any issue, and like any diplomat, I have to do that in the context of the foreign policy of our administration, and again I am happy to do that. I think, as a serious professional, that's the role I have to play."

"But, I mean, you weren't drafted for this job." Chris wouldn't let the subject go.

"Drafted? To the extent I could have said no? True. But, as I say, I think in spite of all of its complications, it is a major foreign policy issue for the United States and for Europe and it's one that is going to have to be worked on and hopefully resolved in the best possible way, a way that may not suit everyone's definition. But still within that context, I think it's an endeavor that needs to be undertaken, and I am happy to be part of it."

I cannot forget the frozen look on Redman's face at the beginning of the exchange. After listening to his answer, and after thinking over the meaning of it, I suspect that his loss of poise was due not to the rudeness of the question but to its nature. Redman had never thought of the job in terms of morality or immorality. It was a job, an important job, and he was blessed to have it, because he was a professional and it represented a potential step up the ladder. Sordid? What's that got to do with it? What does sordid have to do with anything in diplomacy?

Redman was a hit man. The dons of the political world had, with winks and nods and euphemisms, put out a contract on Bosnia. The dons, who in political parlance are called presidents and prime ministers, do not carry out the dirty work themselves, and they deny being involved with it, or having ordered it, and in fact they argue that they would *never* consider doing anything of the sort because it would be wrong, they would never appease or reward aggression. And, at the same time, they dispatch diplomats like Redman, with attaché cases rather than violin cases, to discreet places like Geneva, to get the job done, draw up the papers and get them signed, quick and clean. Like any self-respecting hit man, Redman would just as easily have worked to save Bosnia rather than destroy it; heads or tails, it didn't matter to him, the important thing was to finish the job. There is an old ditty that applies quite well: "Diplomacy is to do and say / The nastiest thing in the nicest way."

In such affairs, the role of diplomats is just as crucial, and just as hideous, as the role of soldiers; the relationship is almost umbilical, like executioners and torturers, the one finishing a job started by the other. The Redmans would say they were carrying out the policy of their governments, just doing their professional duty, but it is a weak excuse, no better than Serbs in Bosnia saying they were only following orders when their commanders instructed them to torch a house or cleanse a village. If there is a difference, it does not favor the Redmans, for they knew *precisely* what was going on, they weren't intoxicated by nationalist propaganda, they had studied Munich and 1938, and yet they nonetheless participated in the destruction of a European nation and a European people, even though disobedience would have meant nothing more severe than the loss of their job, rather than their life.

Bosnia was a circle, always leading you back to where you started, to the weaknesses of humans. It also, thank God, let you see the strengths of humans.

George Kenney quit his State Department job in the summer of 1992, and was followed a year later, in the summer of 1993, by three more diplomats, including Marshall Harris, the desk officer for Bosnia, whose letter of resignation became front-page news. "I can no longer serve in a Department of State that accepts the forceful dismemberment of a European state and that will not act against genocide and the Serbian officials who perpetrate it," Harris wrote to Secretary of State Warren Christopher on August 4, 1993. "I can no longer in good conscience allow myself to be associated with an administration that . . . is driving the Bosnian government to surrender its territory and its sovereignty to the victors in a war of aggression. Accordingly, I hereby resign."

The others who resigned—Stephen Walker, the Croatia desk officer, and Jon Western, who compiled war crimes evidence in the Intelligence and Research Bureau—made similar statements about President Clinton's policy. A few months after them, another diplomat, Richard Johnson, who headed the Yugoslav desk, let his dissent be known through a private report entitled *The Pin Stripe Approach to Genocide*, in which he wrote, "My thesis here is a simple one: Senior U.S. government officials know that Serb leaders are waging genocide in Bosnia but will not say so in plain English because this would raise the pressure for U.S. action."

My dictionary defines the Yiddish word "chutzpah" as "supreme self-confidence." It is the word that comes to mind when I think about the actions of the Redmans of our world, actions that occasionally are so outrageous, so hypocritical yet persuasive, that I am left to wonder whether it is all a big joke at our expense, that when the cameras are turned off and the journalists head back to their newsrooms, the Redmans have a great laugh among themselves, slapping one another on the back and chuckling aloud, "How are we ever going to top that one!"

I am thinking of a remarkable gathering, the International Conference for the Protection of War Victims, held in a large convention center in Geneva. The keynote speaker was U.N. Secretary General Boutros Boutros-Ghali, whose appearance was the culmination of dozens of lofty speeches by ministers and ambassadors who arrived at the conference center in spotless Mercedes limousines. Warren Zimmermann, the former ambassador to Yugoslavia and, at the time, still a loyal bureaucrat, represented the United States and, like every other speaker, condemned atrocities and genocide and insisted that war criminals be brought to justice and punished severely. "Our governments meet this week here in Geneva to say enough! No more! This barbarism must stop!" And so on.

It was difficult to figure out whether such speeches should be met with applause or laughter, for just a few hundred yards away, at the Palais des Nations, Charles Redman was meeting with Radovan Karadžić, leader of Bosnia's Serbs, and Slobodan Milošević, leader of Serbia, both identified by international human rights groups as the worst war criminals in Europe since Nazi Germany. Curiously, Karadžić and Milošević were treated with great respect during their frequent visits to Geneva, where, instead of arresting them, the United Nations arranged complimentary limousines for them and picked up the tab at their five-star hotels. It seemed an odd way to fight barbarism.

Back at the International Conference for the Protection of War Victims, on the other side of the Avenue de la Paix, the ministers and ambassadors wrapped up their speeches. You could almost hear the champagne glasses clinking against each other.

▶ *Two*

IN 1977, at the age of thirty-nine, David Owen, brilliant and handsome, became Britain's foreign secretary, the youngest person to occupy that post since World War II. He was among the best and the brightest in the Labour Party, and many of his colleagues expected him to reach the top, 10 Downing Street, in the years ahead. They agreed that one of the few men who could stand in his way was none other than David Owen.

The holders of high intelligence have a problem; they must be modest about their gift, because it will arouse jealousy, and, when they make a mistake, as they will, others will laugh and point their fingers and say, Yes, you see, that man is quite arrogant and not half as smart as he pretends to be. Especially in politics, the difference between a genius and a fool is not so large; what separates one from the other is a bit of modesty, and David Owen was lacking this. The dean of the Labour Party, Denis Healey, put it this way: "At his birth, the good fairies gave [Owen] almost everything—dark locks, matinee idol features, a lightning intellect. Unfortunately, the bad fairy added one other quality. She made him a shit."

Labour was booted from power in 1979 by Margaret Thatcher's Conservative Party, and Owen, believing Labour had drifted too far to the left, helped create the middle-of-the-road Social Democratic Party, which performed well for a few years but faltered by the late 1980s, prompting him to jump ship again and set up yet another party. In a special election for a parliamentary seat, his party's candidate won just 155 votes, fewer than the candidate of something called the Monster Raving Loony Party. By this time, the Queen had awarded Owen the honorary title of Lord, and this seemed to be the end of the road for him, a quiet retirement, and would have been, were he not so eager for a comeback, any comeback, even one that meant he might be regarded as a personification of appeasement. Enthusiastically, Lord Owen became, in late 1992, the lead mediator at the Bosnian peace talks, which turned into his show.

Appeasement is much harder to accomplish than it seems. It is not just a matter of saying to the stronger side, There you go, have what you want, it's all yours, just sign on the dotted line. The appeaser must accomplish two crucial tasks.

First, the appeaser must, to the greatest extent possible, disguise the fact that he is appeasing. He must portray himself as a peacemaker, as a man who has prevented or ended a war on decent terms. That is why, for example, British Prime Minister Neville Chamberlain, returning from Munich after handing a chunk of Czechoslovakia to Hitler, said in an address from Downing Street on the evening of September 30, 1938, that he had achieved "peace with honor," and that, as a thankful result, everyone should "go home and get a nice quiet sleep." He had not appeased; he had kept the peace. Now go to sleep, go to sleep. . . .

Second, the appeaser must persuade the victim to cooperate.

Chamberlain was fortunate in this case, because Edvard Beneš, the president of Czechoslovakia, had no viable alternative to surrendering the Sudetenland; his small country could not resist a German blitzkrieg, especially if Britain was on Germany's side. As a result, Chamberlain was able to present the carve-up of Czechoslovakia as a sort of diplomatic euthanasia that the victim agreed to. He was lucky. If the victim resists, the appeaser is in a bind, because euthanasia turns into murder, and, instead of being a benevolent guide, soothing the victim as it is put to sleep, the appeaser must hold down the screaming victim as the terminal injection is administered. It is a very nasty business.

As though reading a fifty-five-year-old script, Lord Owen tirelessly explained in Geneva that the alternative to an imperfect peace was more war and more suffering for the people of Bosnia, and he accused his detractors—particularly journalists—of being "laptop bombardiers." Owen should be given the benefit of the doubt; perhaps he was deeply moved by the suffering of innocent women and children in Bosnia, and perhaps he lost sleep over it every night. But I find fault with his logic, which, if applied, for example, to World War II, would have meant that America should have stayed at home and counseled Britain to surrender, because more war would just mean more suffering. Think, for a moment, of all the death and devastation that would have been avoided if we had not entered the war in 1941, and if Britain had dutifully given up, as France had done.

Owen's case for a flawed peace was not, on humanitarian grounds, strong enough to silence all doubts; the aroma of appeasement lingered. He promoted an additional argument—introduced by the Serbs at the start of the war, and adopted by opponents of Western intervention—that the war was not a case of aggressor and victim, but of aggression on all sides. The Bosnians, in other words, did not deserve our unequivocal pity, and the Serbs should not be viewed so harshly. "I don't think this war has ever been quite as simple as aggressor or victim," Owen said at a July 6, 1993, press conference. "There are elements of aggression, there are elements of civil war, there are elements of provocation *on all sides*." The italics are mine, the words are his, and they were not a slip of the tongue; he repeated the message at every opportunity.

The second task—persuading the victim to cooperate—proved es-

pecially difficult for Owen. The Bosnians wanted to regain lost territory, and although their military position was dire, it was not
hopeless, and surrender was not obligatory. Owen began drawing
up a new peace plan in the summer of 1993, and he sensed, correctly, that the Bosnians would reject it because it would be more
generous to the Serbs than the previous one (the Vance-Owen plan),
which the Bosnians had accepted grudgingly and the Serbs had refused. How could he persuade the Bosnians to cooperate in their
own demise? It was time for the appeaser to weaken the victim and
subdue the victim as the death sentence was carried out. To do this,
Lord Owen enlisted the help of Fikret Abdić.

During the Yugoslav era, Fikret Abdić headed a large agricultural
trading firm called Agrokomerc, based in the northwestern Bosnian
town of Velika Kladuša. Abdić, a Muslim, was tossed in jail for
corruption in the 1980s, and later was sought by the Austrian police
on fraud charges. He swung back into action when war broke out,
becoming warlord of the Bihać enclave and a rival to Bosnian President Alija Izetbegović. Abdić kept the Serbs at bay by engaging
them in black-market ventures that proved profitable to all sides
concerned. Izetbegović appreciated the fact that Abdić prevented Bihać from being overrun, but their cooperation ended in the summer
of 1993 when Abdić, counting on better business opportunities if
the war ended, said Izetbegović should sign whatever peace deal was
on the table. Owen, looking to weaken the stubborn Izetbegović by
encouraging dissent against him, invited Abdić to participate in the
Geneva talks.

Owen's new peace plan called for splitting Bosnia into three republics, one for each nationality. The "Muslim-majority republic,"
as it was called, would cover 30 percent of the country and be divided into four parcels of land connected to one another by tunnels,
elevated roads and bridges running under, or over, huge stretches of
territory belonging to the Serbs and Croats. Please do not laugh. I
possess a series of official maps outlining the paths of these projects.
The maps, like the calculations of a mad scientist, purport to show
the feasibility of creating a viable home for Bosnia's Muslims out of
a patchwork of Indian-style reservations. It is a bit reminiscent of
Dr. Frankenstein's trying to create a human being by stitching together the flesh and organs of dead people; what he ended up with,
of course, was a doomed monster.

"We are being asked to sign our own death warrants," Bosnian Prime Minister Haris Silajdžić noted. "There are people here who think Bosnians are retarded."

Owen's ploy with Abdić did not work out as planned, insofar as it did not force Bosnia's government to accept the peace plan. On the night of September 1, President Izetbegović walked out of the Palais des Nations and denounced the plan; its formal death came a few weeks later. Yet Owen's maneuver with Abdić had a lingering, sinister effect, in that it started a military rebellion against the government. Abdić declared independence for Bihać, christening it the "Autonomous Province of Western Bosnia," and signed his own treaty with the Serbs. This created an obscene battle of Muslim on Muslim, in which the Bosnian Army fought Abdić's private militia, chasing him out of Bihać and into the arms of the Serbs, who welcomed him as a friend and supplied his men with weapons to continue their insurrection against Bosnia's government.

These absurd events might have been the occasion for laughter had they not been so tragic. I watched and shook my head in dismay and tried to write stories that sounded reasonable, and I think I succeeded, which is too bad, because the events in Geneva and Bosnia were not reasonable, and they should not have been presented as reasonable. The language of journalistic discourse is inoffensive, the language of balance and objectivity, on the one hand this, on the other hand that, the truth is in the middle (or perhaps unknowable). Was this the proper way to report on a situation that was not balanced, that was anything but balanced, that was, in fact, supremely absurd and tragic and venal? I don't know the answer to that one; but I do know that the Bosnian delegation in Geneva was going mad.

The Bosnians had the help of an American constitutional lawyer advising them about the fine print at the bottom of the peace plans poured out by Owen's staff. The lawyer acted like a fireman, rushing around and pouring water on fresh blazes, instructing others how to fight the fires and prevent new ones from breaking out. He was going over the edge, perhaps because of exhaustion, because the human brain can take only so much trickery before it shorts out. At the end of a press conference at the Palais, in a grand conference room with a ceiling at least forty feet high, the lawyer finally let go: "I want to conclude by cautioning the members of the news media!

You cannot believe anything that Owen and his press spokesman are telling you! Lies, propaganda and disinformation are being put out as to what is going on here!"

The atmosphere was worse at the President Hotel, unofficial headquarters for the Bosnian government. The President, a tacky establishment by Geneva standards, was located alongside the lake's boardwalk, and in August the boardwalk was used as a festival ground, with a noisy array of rides for kids. There was a mini–roller coaster to the left of the hotel, bumper cars and trampolines directly in front, flashing lights everywhere, and to the right of the hotel, less than fifty yards away, there was a shooting gallery. You felt that someone was playing a cruel joke on the Bosnians, who, even in Switzerland, went to sleep listening to the pop-pop of gunfire.

The lobby contained a gloomy collection of imitation van Gogh paintings, and was cluttered with exhausted Bosnian officials who sank into overstuffed sofas, ties loosened, socks falling down to their ankles, sipping bitter cups of coffee. If, by mistake, you laughed about something, the Bosnians would turn their weary heads toward you and stare with their red eyes. Laughter? Here? Why? I chatted in the lobby with Mustafa Bijedić, a diplomat accused by the British embassy of publicly suggesting that Lord Owen deserved to die as an accomplice to genocide. Mustafa told me it was not true, he never said that, but he added, too tired to bother with a wink or shrug, that he would not mourn the passing of such a man.

"I have learned that in Europe there is no morality, no justice, no conscience," he said. "There is just self-interest, comfort and deceit. I would rather live on the moon."

I was intrigued by Owen and wanted to write a profile of him. When I asked for an interview, his spokesman responded with an eruption of laughter. Owen was taking a beating in the American media, including the *Post*, and would not do me any favors. I moved to Plan B—the ambush interview. We were staying at the same hotel, the Intercontinental, and late one night we ended up in the dining room at the same time, virtually alone and just a few tables apart. I resolved to finish up my meal and stroll by his table, introduce myself, get invited to share a brandy with him and then listen as he unburdened himself of the guilt that was weighing on his shoulders.

Owen settled down with a stack of British newspapers and ordered an omelet. The omelet did not arrive as quickly as he wished, so he inquired of the waitress about its whereabouts. She promised it would arrive shortly. A few minutes later, the mysterious omelet had not arrived, and this made Lord Owen very cross. He got up, strode toward me and addressed the two waitresses who stood behind my table. "If I don't get my omelet in five minutes I'm leaving. Leaving, right? I have waited long enough. Five minutes more and I'm gone, yes?" The waitresses offered their apologies and one of them retreated to the kitchen; the omelet arrived within three minutes, and the waitress smiled as she served it. If only the Bosnians had been so obliging.

Owen consumed half the omelet and settled back into one of his papers. It was time to make my move. I paid my check and walked over to his table. "Excuse me, Lord Owen, I would like to introduce myself. I'm Peter Maass from the *Washington Post*." He looked up at me. He smiled. He nodded his head. He didn't say a word. "I think we share the same views about this hotel," I offered. "The service is awful." He smiled. He nodded his head. He didn't say a word. "Well," I finished, "it was nice meeting you. Good night." He smiled. He nodded his head. "Good night," he said. As I walked away, I recalled that Bosnian officials referred to Owen, a physician before turning to politics, as Dr. Death.

I resolved to get the Serb point of view. Radovan Karadžić and his entourage stayed at one of two hotels in Geneva, either the Richemond or La Reserve, the latter being a resort with a private beach, heliport, four tennis courts and six restaurants, offering fine cuisine from France, China, Italy and Japan. Unlike Izetbegović, who laughed only in bitterness, and who felt at home in a gloomy hotel, Karadžić seemed to enjoy himself in Geneva, for he was living in splendid luxury, calling all the shots, and the United Nations was picking up the tab.

During an afternoon break in the talks, I presented myself to his bodyguards, who occupied a double room adjacent to their boss's suite. Their television was tuned to MTV, on which Donna Summer was singing "I Gotta Die," and a bedside table was stacked with a variety of revolvers. The room, I must report, smelled like a gym. I asked whether Karadžić was available for an interview, and the response was negative, because Karadžić was asleep. "He had a big lunch," one of them yawned. As I walked out and passed Karadžić's door, I thought I heard the great man snoring the afternoon away.

I found Nikola Koljević, a Shakespearean scholar before the war, now Karadžić's owlish deputy. We retreated to a conference room and sat on opposite sides of a polished table covered by several maps of Bosnia, with new borders drawn across them in red ink, and Koljević rolled them up and put them aside. We chatted for a few minutes about his previous life as a professor of English at Sarajevo University—Koljević said he missed teaching very much—and then the conversation turned to David Owen. Koljević spoke about Owen as a father would speak about a son who has proven his worth. "He has learned a lot during this conference. He has become more familiar with the nature of the conflict, and he has become more and more pragmatic. His approach is very good. . . . You know what he says, 'I don't mind. If you agree it's okay with me.' " If Owen was browbeating anyone, it didn't seem to be the Serbs.

You could not imagine Izetbegović snoring loudly, or sleeping soundly, or praising David Owen. In the evening, after he finished dinner, which could be past midnight, because the talks followed Balkan time, Izetbegović would leave his hotel for a walk along the boardwalk, deserted by then, because this was Switzerland, and everyone was tucked into bed by eleven. He would be trailed by one of his bodyguards, and if you noticed Izetbegović and did not know who he was, you would pity him, that lonely, slight figure walking in the dark, so slowly, stooped over, shaking his head. Poor man, you would think, he is in mourning, his wife has just died.

In a way, this would be true, for Izetbegović was tied to Bosnia as a husband to his wife. A devout Muslim with blue eyes—only in Bosnia could such creatures exist—Izetbegović was born in 1925 in the Bosnian town of Bosanski Šamac, later moving to Sarajevo. "I was fourteen or fifteen years old when the Germans entered Sarajevo," he told an interviewer in 1993. "They seized the city and its important facilities, but schools and shops functioned and nobody touched the civilian population, even though Germany and its army did not have a good reputation regarding humanitarian issues. It was an occupation but the present events constitute . . . a war of an organized, well-equipped army against a civilian population." After the war Izetbegović studied law at Sarajevo University, becoming a corporate legal adviser, but he was jailed for five years in the early 1980s for religious activism. After his release, he entered politics and set up the SDA, which gathered the largest share of votes in Bosnia's first open elections in 1990. He became president of the republic, still part of Yugoslavia. When war started in 1992, his Serb and Croat rivals tried to use a 1970 tract he published, *Islamic Declaration*, as proof that he was a fundamentalist; it was a distortion of the tract and of Izetbegović's intentions.

Izetbegović's greatest defect was his naïveté. While Serbs and Croats were obtaining weapons and organizing themselves for war, Izetbegović was calling for peace and trying to keep Yugoslavia together. His effort to prevent the federation's breakup undercuts, yet again, the Serbo-Croat contention that he always wanted to set up an Islamic state in Bosnia. When the Yugoslav National Army (JNA in Serbian) ordered the disbanding, in January 1991, of all Territorial Defense units (similar to our National Guard), Izetbegović fully complied, despite the objections of some of his supporters. Izetbegović had been duped; while the JNA, whose officer corps was dominated by Serbs, disarmed Territorial Defense units in areas of Bosnia inhabited largely by Muslims, it secretly supplied more weapons to units in areas inhabited largely by Serbs. When Bosnia's secession became unavoidable, Izetbegović believed that Western countries would use their diplomatic and military muscle to prevent an attack by Serbia. Here, too, he was naïve.

In Geneva, Izetbegović's mood often shifted from agitation to introspection, and these shifts could be noted easily, especially when he spoke English. If he became agitated, he would break into Bosnian, suddenly, because his mind was working too fast, with too much anger, to compose English sentences that made sense. He did not break into Bosnian when speaking about Owen; he knew Owen well, knew what to make of him and knew how to express his thoughts in a controlled way, unlike the Bosnian protesters who camped outside the Palais des Nations, outside coils of barbed wire, demanding, among other things, that Owen be put on trial as a war criminal.

"If David Owen did not exist, the Europeans would find another David Owen," Izetbegović smiled.

It was a statement that Owen might not quibble with. He had a relatively accurate riposte to accusations of being an appeaser. Don't pick on the mediators, Owen would say, we are just doing the job we have been asked to do—the Western world has decided not to

use force in this conflict, so we mediators have very little leverage
with the Serbs. It was true. Owen was a convenient whipping boy
for virtually all sides, even for the European governments that he
represented; they could keep their hands clean because he was more
than willing to dirty his. In the end, he was merely a cog in the
machine, albeit a very important, highly visible, easily despised and
scruple-free cog. Still, just a cog.

This became clear when, while I was in Geneva with Owen, an
episode of forehead-slapping appeasement occurred in Sarajevo.
With the Bosnian capital close to collapse, and with President
Clinton reluctantly considering military action to free it, the U.N.
spokesman in Sarajevo, Barry Frewer, declared, to everyone's
amazement, that the city was no longer under siege. At the time, the
most popular local joke went like this: "What is the difference between Sarajevo and Auschwitz? In Auschwitz, they had gas." My
Washington Post colleague, John Pomfret, wrote in his dispatch,
"Frewer described the Serb forces that ring the city with an estimated 1,400 heavy weapons as being in a 'tactically advantageous
position . . . but I won't call it a siege.' " Within hours, the Bosnian
government declared Frewer persona non grata.

The unstated reason for denying reality was simple: U.N. commanders wanted to stave off an attack by the Americans, because
such an attack might anger the Serbs and encourage the Bosnians,
which was the opposite of what the United Nations was doing. As
Pomfret wrote two days later, the U.N. commanders, rather than
admitting their unwillingness to lift the siege, decided to deny that
the siege existed. It quickly became clear that they were making a
mistake by aligning themselves so obviously with the Serbs—reporters and editorialists were mocking the United Nations with
renewed vigor—but, against all good sense, the "tactically advantageous" rhetoric continued, which showed that not only were U.N.
commanders deceitful, they were appallingly stupid.

Was Sarajevo under siege?

"May I suggest that you look up the word 'siege' in the English
dictionary . . . and then make up your own minds," said Lieutenant
Colonel Tricia Purves, a U.N. spokeswoman. "That is for you to
judge."

Owen, Redman, Frewer, Purves, they were cogs, some bigger than
others, some quite venal, others quite affable, a few well-intentioned

and helpful whenever they could be. Still, they were just cogs. They were not pulling the levers.

▶ *Three*

> *"We make no apology to those who would find it more convenient if we would just disappear rather than serve as a constant reminder to them of their betrayal of principles."*
> —Muhamed Sacirbey, Bosnian foreign minister

IN LOS ANGELES, a rainstorm is reason enough to keep children indoors, so on rainy days, when I was a boy, my seventh-grade exercise class would be held in a small gymnasium, where, inevitably, our coach would let us play dodgeball for the fifty-minute period. Dodgeball was the most elemental of adolescent games. One boy would stand against a wall, and the others would be fifteen yards away, throwing rubber balls at him. The object, if you were against the wall, was to duck the balls, and to do this, you would jump in the air, fling yourself to the left, to the right, up in the air again, fake a move to one side, then hit the ground, roll to your right, hop back on your feet, skip to your left, dodge to the right, hit the ground again and so on, until you got zinged, which, within a minute, was likely to happen, because only a young Nureyev could stay on his toes that long; everyone else was doomed to run out of energy and then, *boom-boom-boom*, three balls would slam into you.

The image of dodgeball is what comes to mind when I think of the way President Clinton reacted to Bosnia. The image may not be exact, perhaps inadequate, but it's the best I can come up with. Clinton was the boy against the wall. Month after month, year after year, he engaged in an array of acrobatics, ducking to his left, then his right, laying low on the ground, rising up again, jumping to one side, then the other, faking left before going right. These weren't physical movements, but political ones. Saying the fighting was a civil war, then saying it was a war of aggression; blaming the United Nations for getting in the way of NATO, then blaming NATO for getting in the way of the United Nations (even though he could dictate policy to either organization); portraying Slobodan Milošević and Radovan Karadžić as war criminals, then sending high-level envoys to meet with them; demanding that the arms embargo against Bosnia be lifted, but refusing to do anything about it, and then, later, *opposing* the lifting of the embargo. The list of dodges is lengthy.

Because President Clinton was not known for assertiveness on any issue, his dodges on Bosnia seemed to fit a lifelong pattern of flip-flopping, proving that he was incompetent rather than invidious. The poor guy just wanted to please everyone, he wanted to lead from the middle rather than the front, he couldn't win any votes by intervening in Bosnia, so of course his policy was incoherent, and of course it was a failure because it did not roll back the Serbs.

I would offer a different interpretation, which is that Clinton's policy was coherent and successful, though not in the ways he would wish us to believe.

Imagine the boy against the wall. He is jumping in every direction, up and down and to the side and back again, and he looks absolutely ridiculous, even comical. There is no sense to his movements, no planning, just improvisation, wild and thoughtless. But look closer. The boy's strategy *is* improvisation. He cannot plan his moves in advance, because he does not know when the balls will be thrown, how fast they will be thrown, who will throw them or what trajectory they might follow, and even if he did know all that, the variables would be much too complex to be neutralized with a move-by-move, second-by-second strategy. The boy merely keeps one thought in his mind, Dodge the ball, Dodge the ball, and he gets on with it. If he is lucky, he will succeed and be untouched when the coach blows the whistle.

The only way Bill Clinton could appease Serbs was to improvise with Americans. Consistency was impossible in such a situation—he could not stand still and announce he was letting the Serbs have what they wanted. This would have caused an uproar. Instead, he engaged in his acrobatics and deceptions, saying one thing and doing another, or saying two different things, one right after another, inconsistency after inconsistency. Duck left, move right; duck right, move left. He looked confused and inept, he got bruised, but this was the price he had to pay once he chose to appease rather than oppose. He succeeded, for he kept America neutral in the face of genocide, and avoided the outrage he would have attracted if America saw him as an appeaser. He proclaimed his good intentions and avoided real action; what America lost sight of was the fact that Chamberlain proclaimed good intentions, too.

I would like to argue the case against Clinton in this book, do it like Clarence Darrow would. For more than a year, with the help of an Apple computer and database program, I have trolled through the bottomless depths of on-line news services and downloaded thousands of articles about Bosnia. Perhaps I have been obsessive. At the touch of a button, I can conjure onto my computer screen a list of stories about Clinton, or Slobodan Milošević, or John Major, or François Mitterrand or whomever or whatever I choose. If, today, I type the word "Sarajevo," a list of 556 entries appears. For "Clinton," 234 entries. For "Hypocrisy," 100 entries. Then, by pushing another key, I can view any of the entries.

I want to write about how the Clinton administration, wanting to keep Bosnia out of the spotlight, refused to let journalists and even members of Congress fly into Sarajevo on Air Force relief flights, and that, for the same reason, it refused to provide transportation out of Sarajevo—on *empty* transport planes—for a group of Bosnian actors who had been invited to perform their touching version of *Hair* in America. I want to write about how the U.S. government demanded the Serbs release all prison camp inmates but refused to offer asylum to more than a token number of those wretched souls—an offer that came late and reluctantly. Where were the rest to go? Somewhere else, but not to America.

I want to write about that, to give names, dates, places, quotes, to answer all questions that might be raised. But I do not have the strength.

I want to explain that President Clinton threw dust in our eyes by saying, for example, that he had tried hard to get our allies to agree to lift the arms embargo against the Bosnians and carry out air strikes against the Serbs, but in fact he hardly tried. He sent Warren Christopher on a famous trip to Europe in May 1993, but Christopher did not argue or cajole when he stopped in Paris, London and Moscow, he merely listened and nodded his head, and then returned to Washington to say that, despite his supreme efforts, our European allies refused to budge, so the embargo would, regrettably, stay in place, and the F-16s would, regrettably, stay in their hangars. President Clinton passed on the message to the country. More than two years later, his real agenda became clear when Congress called his bluff and approved a bill to lift the embargo; Clinton vetoed it.

Names, dates, places, quotes.

It was easy to blame the West Europeans, for they were, indeed, the firmest apostles of appeasement. Just as David Owen did the dirty work for British Prime Minister Major and French President Mitterrand, Major and Mitterrand were doing the dirty work for Clinton. This was helpful. Clinton could criticize the Europeans obliquely, and his aides could criticize them directly, but he never stood in their way, he implicitly encouraged them and let them take a well-deserved beating for being appeasers. The leading-edge role of Europe's leaders deserves far more attention than I can give it in this book. Why did Major follow the politics of Chamberlain rather than the politics of Churchill? Why did Mitterrand follow the politics of Pétain rather than the politics of de Gaulle? There are specific reasons. Major, an uninspiring leader, had shallow support in his own Tory party and was focused on domestic affairs, while Mitterrand, at the end of fourteen years in office, was a tired old man fighting cancer of the prostate. There are other reasons, too, many others, but they are less important than the general observation that nations, like individuals, have the ability to be brave and the ability to be cowardly, and, when the war in Bosnia broke out, the leaders of Britain and France tapped the cowardly vein in the soul of their nations, lulling their people to sleep with soothing lies. It could have been otherwise, and perhaps next time, with a new set of leaders, it will be.

Dust in our eyes. Bill Clinton wanted us to forget about Bosnia, to write it off as an infinitely complex place in which nothing was as simple as it might seem, only the high priests of politics could figure it out, for the war was a matter of tribal rivalries and those Balkan people "have been fighting each other for centuries," blah-blah-blah. This was rubbish, and Clinton knew it. What people on this planet have not been fighting other people for centuries? Not the French and Germans, not the British and French, not the Koreans and Japanese, and not, for that matter, the citizens of the United States; if you consider the Civil War and the war against Native Americans and perhaps toss in the recent riots in Los Angeles and Liberty City, not to mention Harlem or Watts or the startling murder rate in Washington, D.C., Americans have been fighting *one another* for centuries. The point is this: If you can understand the intricacies of a draw play in football or the wild-card play-off system, as most Americans can, then you can understand Bosnia. Beginners might need fifteen or twenty minutes of instruction to grasp the basics of either subject. Unfortunately, most Americans got two-minute television stories or six-hundred-word newspaper articles that created more confusion than comprehension—on the one hand this, on the other hand that—and influential government officials, with their evasions and contradictions, made things cloudier, intentionally. In essence, Americans never had the chance to learn the rules of the game, and they were told by their government not to bother, because the game was too complex for ordinary mortals to understand.

I want to explain that in May 1993, after Clinton used the Europeans as an alibi for his own inaction, the foreign ministers of Britain, France, Russia, Spain and America met in Washington and put on another show of resolve. They put aside the troublesome question of rolling back the Serbs and decided, instead, to protect a few bits of territory held by the Bosnians. They created six "safe areas." The message to the Serbs was clear: Take everything else but not our little safe areas. Yet, illustrating that appeasement increases rather than fulfills an aggressor's appetite, the Serbs kept attacking the safe areas, restricting the amount of food delivered to them, and the world powers did little. "Mr. Clinton is going to be a great president," cheered Radovan Karadžić. The United Nations troops dispatched to the safe areas were not, it transpired, allowed to use their weapons to defend the safe areas. The troops could fire back only if their own lives were in danger, rather than the lives of the Bosnians whom, we erroneously assumed, the troops were there to defend. On occasion the world powers forgot to pretend they were serious, and in one case, hundreds of U.N. troops were sent to protect the Bihać safe area *without weapons*. Obviously, if you had the terrible misfortune to live in a United Nations "safe area," you lived in one of the most dangerous places on earth. It was not much of a surprise that U.N. soldiers surrendered their weapons when Serbs finally called the West's bluff in 1995 and mounted an earnest assault on the safe areas of Srebrenica and Žepa, capturing them.

I want to explain that Bill Clinton's rare displays of resolve were deceptions, no different from fakes in dodgeball, shifting left before leaping right. In February 1994, a Serb shell landed in a Sarajevo marketplace, killing 68 people, a number of little consequence in a war that had killed about 200,000, but camera crews recorded the carnage in the safe area, and this led to international outrage. Clinton had to do something; if he remained passive, *he* would have become the target of outrage. So he issued an ultimatum: The Serbs had to withdraw their heavy weapons from a twenty-kilometer radius around Sarajevo or face an attack from America. Simple. The Serbs complied, because they always complied when they sensed America was serious. You would think that after such success, Clinton would issue similar ultimatums to relieve the other safe areas bombarded by the Serbs, but he did not.

The story does not end there. The Serb tanks that had surrounded Sarajevo were moved to Goražde, another unsafe safe area, which the Serbs then blitzed, in April 1994. The Clinton administration reacted by saying it would not intervene to protect Goražde, and so the Serbs, understandably, revved up their offensive. The only intervention came from the news media, which gave the offensive front-page play, noting, among other things, that the Serbs were bombing Goražde's hospital. United Nations officials pleaded with the Serbs to stop the attack, which of course the Serbs promised to do, and then, as U.N. officials told the world not to worry, that a cease-fire had been arranged, the Serbs moved closer and closer to the heart of Goražde. A *Washington Post* dispatch noted that Clinton "had to be prodded by a reporter into offering a blunt condemnation of the Serbs' actions in Goražde."

Finally, when the humiliation became too obvious, air strikes were ordered on the Serbs, and American fighter jets dropped a total of seven bombs, two of which failed to explode when they hit the ground, one of which didn't hit the ground at all, because it snagged in the plane's bomb racks. Serb losses were minor, not much more than an old tank, an armored personnel carrier and a "command center" (a few tents, we later learned). Clinton, instead of warning of more retribution, let the Serbs know that he had not really wanted to bomb them. "I would remind the Serbs that we have taken no action . . . to try to win a military victory for their adversaries." As the dust settled, quite literally, the American ambassador to the United Nations, Madeleine Albright, palmed off blame for the mess on senior U.N. officials who had downplayed the offensive; those officials, in turn, continued to claim that the death toll from the Serb attack was not so large as believed, and they palmed off blame for the offensive on the Bosnians—yes, the Bosnians—for provoking the Serbs to attack. It was easy to lose sight of President Clinton in this forest of pointing fingers.

Was I too involved in Bosnia, am I biased, extreme in my judgments? No. There were many other people, respected and well-known, who came to similar conclusions.

Richard Nixon said: "The siege of Sarajevo can have a redeeming character only if the West learns two things as a result. The first is that enlightened peoples cannot be selective about condemning aggression and genocide. . . . The other lesson is that because we are the last remaining superpower, no crisis is irrelevant to our interests."

George Shultz, secretary of state in the Reagan administration, said: "The Serbs have made suckers out of the United Nations. They have said, 'We're negotiating so don't use force on us because you might upset the negotiations.' Meanwhile, they're throwing the book at the Muslims, murdering them and raping them and so on. . . . We should be prepared to conduct military strikes on gun emplacements, on supply lines, on weapons caches and ammunition depots and not just near the front lines but way back into Serbia."

Margaret Thatcher wrote: "Feeding or evacuating the victims rather than helping them resist aggression makes us accomplices as much as good samaritans." She also said, "I am ashamed of the European Community, for this is happening in the heart of Europe. It is within Europe's sphere of influence. It should be within Europe's sphere of conscience. There is no conscience."

I want to explain much more, not just to skim the surface of events, but I do not have the strength. It is enough, I hope, to mention these things, to cite a few eminent people, to mention, for example, that the Goražde scenario repeated itself six months later, when Serbs attacked the Bihać "safe area," and whittled it down to size while President Clinton and his partners in Western Europe fiddled once more. To bomb, or not to bomb? The answer they came up with was to bomb a little. They found a tiny airport that Serbs were using, at a place called Udbina, and they bombed the airport. Please don't get the wrong idea. They did not bomb the warplanes and helicopters that were parked at the airport, for they did not want to send the wrong message to the Serbs. They dropped a few bombs on the runway, creating a few craters that would take a few days to fill in, and then the warplanes and helicopters that were parked a few yards away and had not been touched could resume their attacks.

Clinton, Major and Mitterrand were trying to send two messages to two audiences. To their publics, they were saying, We are serious. To the Serbs, they were saying, We are not serious.

The Serbs were tired of getting slapped on the wrist, and wanted to be sure that F-16s would not be used to make holes in other airfields, so they took the precaution of taking 400 U.N. soldiers hostage and forcing some of them to lie down on the runway at their main air base in Banja Luka. One of the U.N. soldiers had a heart condition and was on the verge of dying, but he nonetheless had to do his face-down time on the tarmac, eight hours a day. The United Nations pleaded with the Serbs to let this poor soldier leave, and finally arranged a swap in which another U.N. soldier would take his place. The healthy U.N. soldier arrived in Banja Luka, alongside a third U.N. soldier who would drive the sick one back to Zagreb. The two new ones were promptly taken hostage without the sick one being released. The only people surprised at this turn of events were the U.N. officials who arranged the deal.

During these events, General Michael Rose, the U.N. commander, had a phone chat with a midlevel Serb official, Jovan Zametica, and a recording of the call was leaked to reporters. "Don't mess with us, Mike," the Serb said. "Don't fuck with us."

Clinton and his European allies, taking Zametica's advice to heart instead of telling *him* to fuck off, turned their attention toward further retreat. After the debacle in Bihać (which was eventually saved from collapse by a Croatian Army offensive that dislodged the besieging Serbs), the use of air power to punish the Serbs was abandoned, as was the general notion of trying to punish the Serbs or even, on occasion, slap their wrists. All of the humiliations heaped by the Serbs upon troops representing the world's major powers— the killing of scores of them, the hostage taking, the mock executions, the groping of female soldiers, the extortion, thievery and lying—it was all forgotten, filed away for historians to laugh or cry over. Clinton dropped the pretense of being assertive and joined Major and Mitterrand (replaced in 1995 by Jacques Chirac) in offering the Serbs virtually everything they wanted in a peace treaty, including the crucial privilege of linking their captured territory with Serbia proper. The matter of forcing the Bosnians to accept such a deal would be dealt with in a necessarily more discreet manner.

On August 28, 1995, the Serbs committed an atrocity that was too obscene for the West's leaders to overlook. A mortar shell landed in a Sarajevo marketplace, killing thirty-seven people. The television footage was ghastly. Once again, Clinton and his counterparts in London and Paris risked becoming the focus of public anger unless they did something. This time they really had no choice. On August 30, NATO warplanes began the largest air attack in the alliance's history, more than 3,500 sorties in two weeks, wave after wave of the world's most advanced military aircraft dropping the world's most advanced munitions. A salvo of Tomahawk Cruise missiles was even thrown into the assault. This was exactly the kind of intervention that, for more than three years, the West's leaders had said would not work, could not work. Of course it worked. The Serbs backed down, withdrawing their heavy weapons from the hills above Sarajevo and opening roads into it. They also softened their position on peace talks. Meanwhile, Bosnian and Croat forces took advantage of the Serbs' disarray and launched ground offensives that recaptured large chunks of territory. The Serbs were on the run. It looked like the story might have a happy ending.

If only. The West's goal had not changed, just the means to achieve it. Instead of using diplomacy to persuade the Serbs to accept half of Bosnia, the West was using force. The goal remained the same: Bosnia would be dismembered, with Serbia getting half. The Clinton administration, trying to get the partition completed as quickly as possible, even pressured the Bosnians and Croats to halt their offensives. This was remarkable. Instead of forcing a wider Serb retreat, Clinton opted to call off the air strikes and red-flagged the Bosnians and Croats, who faced "intense pressure" to stop their advances, according to the *Washington Post*. At the time, White House spokesman Michael McCurry bluntly said, "We have made it very clear that we wish they would suspend that fighting."

In the Balkans, as elsewhere, there is usually more to a given event than meets the eye. With the air raids, there was actually less than met the eye. The raids changed few things, aside from bringing Clinton and his partners in Europe closer to their goal of partitioning Bosnia. As always, the Bosnians would be pressured to accept whatever territory was offered to them. A month after the air raids, Clinton convened top-level negotiations at a military base in Dayton, Ohio, which resulted in an accord awarding 49 percent of Bosnia to the Serbs. Although Bosnia theoretically would remain a single country, in practice it would be split in half. Izetbegović, Bosnia's president, left Dayton a bitter man, saying the accord was unfair but better than continued warfare. Milošević, Serbia's president, could not contain his glee; he actually hugged an American general.

Finally, I want to explain that appeasement does not work. Forget about the moral objections to it, about the humiliations it has brought to our governments and to ourselves; just think of the practicalities. Clinton and his counterparts in Western Europe generally had their way against the "laptop bombardiers." They did nothing for more than three years and watched as more than 200,000 people were killed. It took a few weeks of bombing in the late summer of 1995 to let the Serbs know that there was, surprisingly, a limit to the forbearance of our leaders, that they really should settle for half of Bosnia, which they did. Our leaders could have demanded far more in the name of justice, could have done far more in the name of justice, but chose not to. In their desire to stop the war on terms acceptable to Milošević, they abandoned their promises never to reward ethnic cleansing. They appeased. They also overlooked an important lesson of history. Peace is not guaranteed by a thick treaty or enforcement troops; it is guaranteed by justice.

I have only a few words left in me about the tragedy of Bosnia. At the end of 1994, when everyone involved in the Balkan crisis knew that Bosnia was being left to twist in the wind, an unusual death notice appeared in *The New York Times*. Bordered in traditional black, and signed by more than seventy members of the Western world's political and cultural elite, it stated the following:

IN MEMORIAM

OUR COMMITMENTS,
PRINCIPLES, AND MORAL VALUES
DIED: BOSNIA, 1994
ON THE OCCASION OF THE 1,000TH DAY
OF THE SIEGE OF SARAJEVO

EPILOGUE

In the course of writing this book, many friends have asked me what it is about, and I have had a hard time coming up with a precise answer. It is about many things, about war, about Bosnia, about politics and hatred and demagogues and heroes and cowards and me and. . . . It is about many things. After spending a year writing more than 100,000 words, I have a better idea of what the book is about, and I think it is about the wild beast, which is not an animal, nor a person, but a spirit of evil that exists in all animals, all people, all societies. The understanding of what my book is about has helped me answer, at least in my own mind, a question asked thousands of times in America since the war began: Why should Bosnia matter to those of us fortunate enough not to live there? Here is my answer: Bosnia can teach us about the wild beast, and therefore about ourselves, and our destinies.

What happened in Bosnia was not a Balkan freak show but a violent process of national breakdown at the hands of political manipulators. The dynamics of fear and loathing between people of different backgrounds—ethnic or religious or economic—are not as unique or complex as we might like to believe. Violent breakdowns can occur in virtually any country during times of economic hardship, political transition or moral infirmity; such troubles create

opportunities for the manipulators, and the manipulators create opportunities for the wild beast. I would not dare predict that it could
happen in America, which is so different from Europe, but I would
suggest that we avoid placing bets on any predictions, whether optimistic or pessimistic. Rebecca West put it best: "I have been struck
again and again by the refusal of destiny to let man see what is
happening to him, its mean delight in strewing his path with red
herrings." Sometimes, destiny need not even waste its herrings on
us, for we can be incapable of seeing what is before our eyes.

In 1984, Sarajevo hosted the Winter Olympics. If you had been
there at the time, and if you had asked any Yugoslav—that's what
they called themselves back then, Yugoslavs—whether he could
imagine his city falling into war in eight years' time, he would have
laughed out loud and tried to detect slivovitz on your breath, and
if he didn't detect any, he might have excused himself and walked
to the nearest police officer to report a madman on the loose. Now
fast-forward to a year before the war began. Yugoslavia is falling
apart. A group of comedians make a short film for Sarajevo television in which the members of a mixed Bosnian family wage hand-
to-hand combat for ownership of their apartment; the biggest battle
is for control of the bathroom. Viewers laughed long and hard at
the film's absurd notion that the people of Bosnia would wage war
against one another. Fast-forward one more time, to just a few
months before the war started, when a colleague from my newspaper interviews Muslims, Serbs and Croats who live in the same
apartment building in Sarajevo, live right next to one another and,
in the case of mixed marriages, of which there were many, share the
same bed and gave their children a Serb first name, a Muslim last
name, and perhaps, in honor of their best friend, a Croat middle
name. These people said there could be no war, no, never, because
no one wanted it, and war would make no sense; how, after all,
could you divide up people who were so intertwined?

Not long ago, destiny played its games on me. In February 1991,
the *Post* sent me to the Soviet Union for a few weeks, and I spent
most of my time in the Baltic republics, Lithuania, Latvia and Es-
tonia, which were bogged down in a doomed effort (so we thought)
to become independent. Mikhail Gorbachev, beloved in the West,
had made it clear that the Soviet Union was not going to let any of
its republics break away, and lethal force had been used to back up

his point. In Moscow one evening, I had dinner with several colleagues who lived there. We talked, naturally, about politics, and I asked the usual newcomer's questions, including, What is going to happen? There was a silence, and then, one after another, my colleagues talked of a long period of darkness, years, during which the oppressive hands of the Red Army and KGB would rule the country, because Gorbachev was losing control, perestroika and glasnost had failed. I remember feeling depressed by their diagnosis, and glad that I worked in Eastern Europe, where the corner had been turned, the darkness had ended. If I would have suggested that, in six months, hard-liners might stage a coup against Gorbachev, and that the coup would fail and that the Soviet Union, which we all had grown up with and believed to be immortal, would die on the spot, breaking into bits and pieces with names like Kyrgyzstan and Uzbekistan, my colleagues would have laughed and wondered whether my water glass was filled with vodka.

My point is this: The gap between reality and science fiction has narrowed. One of the books I read during my travels in the Balkans was J. G. Ballard's *High-Rise*, the tale of a London apartment building in which the white-collar residents slip into war against one another. It was sparked by a dispute over a loud party and led to primeval combat in which men urinated and defecated in corridors to mark their territory and smeared their naked chests with the blood of others they had killed. The book begins with these sentences: "Later, as he sat on his balcony eating the dog, Dr. Robert Laing reflected on the unusual events that had taken place within this huge apartment building during the previous three months. Now that everything had returned to normal, he was surprised that there had been no obvious beginning, no point beyond which their lives had moved into a clearly more sinister dimension." Although the passage comes from a book of science fiction, it is not entirely irrelevant to today's America.

I was born in Los Angeles, and lived, until I left for college, fifteen minutes away (by car, the measure of distance in L.A.) from the sidewalk where Nicole Simpson's throat was cut from ear to ear. I don't know about the rest of America, but I know that Los Angeles is changing. Parts of it remain healthy, even vibrant, but other parts are rotting. You cannot jog along Ocean Avenue, which is on a lovely bluff in Santa Monica overlooking the Pacific, without passing by a pile of rags that is, in fact, the sleeping body of a homeless man, and there are days when beaches are closed because raw sewage is washing onto the sand. This is a yuppie's lament, but I am not looking for sympathy for myself, only for my hometown, which is different now, still containing greatness, but less of it, and less balance. A few years ago, a jury's verdict in the Rodney King case set off a major riot. Does this mean we are slipping into a sinister dimension? No one knows for sure these days, and that's what concerns me. The response of America's leadership (Republican and Democratic) to the ravaging of Bosnia has not been reassuring; politicians who accommodate evil abroad are not particularly well suited to defend us from it at home.

I cannot deny that a residue of caution has stayed with me after the time I spent in Banja Luka, Sarajevo, Belgrade and Geneva; the darkness of men and governments was quite strong in those places, and it cannot be forgotten easily. I remember how Colonel Bob Stewart, the British commander in Vitez, said Bosnia changed him more than any other experience in his life, but he did not know what the changes were. I am beginning to sense the ways in which Bosnia changed me.

My parents, whose main concern was academics rather than religion, sent me to the best secondary school in Los Angeles, which happened to be an Episcopal school with mandatory chapel once a week. This was no problem for me, nor for the many other Jewish students. The chaplain, Father Gill, a history teacher and model-airplane fanatic, was beloved by all students, and you counted yourself lucky if you were placed in one of his courses. I even served as his altar boy on one occasion, an honor I could hardly refuse, nor wanted to. I slipped into a white cloak in the vestry and performed flawlessly until, at the end of the service, Father Gill offered me communion. I had reached a boundary that I knew I should not cross, so I politely shook my head from side to side, a silent no. I remember the way one of his eyebrows shot up in surprise before he carried on and offered communion to the next boy. He never mentioned it afterward, and I received an A in his history class.

I had no formal training in Judaism, and I felt that being Jewish never mattered much in America; I never heard anyone say anything anti-Semitic in my presence, nor can I recall any instance in which being a Jew affected me academically or professionally. It seemed no more important than the color of my hair. After graduating from my Episcopal high school, I attended a Jesuit university, Georgetown, for two years; nobody cared, nobody asked, nobody whispered. I count this as a blessing, for I know, after living in Eastern Europe and reporting on Bosnia, that such things cannot be taken for granted by any minority group that has faced harassment through the ages. In Poland, for example, there is an amazing situation in which some Poles blame their economic problems on the Jews, even though, among Poland's nearly 40 million citizens, only a few thousand are Jewish. Such is the incoherence of hatred that it can exist in the absence of those who are hated.

This is what I have taken so long to say on the question of changes: I am now more aware of the fragility of human relations, and more aware of what being a Jew can mean. I learned this from the Muslims of Bosnia, who made two fatal mistakes. They thought that being a minority group no longer mattered in civilized Europe, and they thought the wild beast had been tamed. They failed to realize that although a person might attach little importance to his religion, other people might take notice one day; and just because your society seems stable does not mean it will always be so. Muslims versus Christians, Jews versus non-Jews, whites versus blacks, poor versus rich—there are so many seams along which a society can be torn apart by the manipulators. These are the lessons of Bosnia that have stayed with me and, perhaps, altered me. The wild beast is out there, and the ground no longer feels so steady under my feet.

Notes

CHAPTER 1: THE WILD BEAST

9   *"The Serbs took the prisoners"*: Blaine Harden, "Refugee 'Witnessed Massacres Every Day' at the Bridges on the Drina," *Washington Post*, August 7, 1992; and Blaine Harden, "The Yugoslav Gulag: Days in the Life of Bosnian Inmates," *Washington Post*, August 7, 1992.

10   *"Turks on the bridge"*: Ivo Andrić, *The Bridge over the Drina* (London: Harvill/ HarperCollins, 1994), p. 50. The meaning of Andrić's body of work has been the source of some debate, particularly in recent years. His novels and short stories about Bosnia, where he was raised in Višegrad by his Catholic mother, have been used by nationalists, primarily Serbs, to support their claim that Serbs, Muslims and Croats are doomed to fight one another and therefore should not live together. An opposing school of thought contends that Andrić, who died in 1975, admired the diversity in Bosnia and wanted to emphasize that people of different nationalities and religions possess the capacity to coexist in peace and should strive to do so.

11   *"The people were"*: Ibid., p. 282.

24   *He was delighted*: Brian Hall, *The Impossible Country: A Journey Through the Last Days of Yugoslavia* (London: Secker & Warburg, 1994), p. 30. Hall cited a passage from the memoirs of an Italian reporter, Curzio Malaparte, who interviewed Pavelić during the war. Here is what Malaparte wrote: "While he spoke, I gazed at a wicker basket on the Poglavnik's [leader's] desk. The lid was raised and the basket seemed to be filled with mussels, or shelled oysters. . . . 'Are they Dalmatian oysters?' I asked the Poglavnik. Ante Pavelić removed the lid from the basket and revealed the mussels, that slimy and jelly-like mass, and he said smiling, with that tired good-natured smile of his, 'It's a present from my loyal Ustashis. Forty pounds of human eyes.' "

30   *"We have evidence"*: Hugh Pain, "U.N. Commander Warns of 'Downward Spiral,' " Reuters dispatch, July 22, 1992.

31   *MacKenzie backed them*: See Tom Gjelten, "Blaming the Victim," *The New Republic*, December 20, 1993, in which Gjelten debunks MacKenzie's claim about the Breadline Massacre. MacKenzie, in his memoir of the war, *Peacekeeper: The Road to Sarajevo* (Vancouver: Douglas & McIntyre, 1993), wrote on p. 255 that he told French President François Mitterrand, "There is strong but circumstantial evidence that some really horrifying acts of cruelty attributed to the Serbs were actually orchestrated by the Muslims against their own people, for the benefit of an international audience." MacKenzie has since backed off the claim, but not entirely. He calls for thorough investigations. Regarding the issue of responsibility for the war, MacKenzie wrote, on p. 154, "There is more than enough blame to go around for all sides, with some left over."

32   *"One has killed"*: The congressional hearing was held on May 26, 1993. Based on his assessment that all sides bore blame for the conflict, MacKenzie called for redrawing Bosnia's borders so that Croats would get a share, Serbs would get a share and Muslims would get "a significant chunk of the center of the current

country." With soldierly bluntness, MacKenzie cast the carving up of Bosnia as an unappetizing necessity. "Critics will say this rewards force and sets a bad example. I can only say to them, read your history. Force has been rewarded since the first caveman picked up a club, occupied his neighbor's cave and ran off with his wife. The aim is not to right all the wrongs of the past, which is clearly impossible, but to stop the killing and to create the conditions for a lasting peace in Bosnia-Herzegovina."

32–33   *In a front-page article:* The CIA report, one of the most authoritative assessments of war crimes in Bosnia, was disclosed in Roger Cohen, "C.I.A. Report Finds Serbs Guilty in Majority of Bosnia War Crimes," *The New York Times*, March 9, 1995. The *Times* quoted a Clinton administration official as saying, "To those who think the parties are equally guilty, this report is pretty devastating. . . . The scale of what the Serbs did is so different. But more than that, it makes clear, with concrete evidence, that there was a conscious, coherent and systematic Serbian policy to get rid of Muslims, through murders, torture and imprisonment." (A month later, the *Times* published another story by Cohen in which a senior member of the Serbian secret police leaked official documents that linked Milošević to the camps.)

A "Commission of Experts" set up by the U.N. Security Council to investigate war crimes arrived at the same conclusions as the CIA. In its final report, delivered to the Security Council on May 24, 1994, the commission stated that the ethnic cleansing was "systematic" and "influenced, encouraged, facilitated and condoned" by Serb leaders. The commission added, "It is clear that there is no factual basis for arguing that there is a 'moral equivalence' between the warring factions." Every respected human rights group I know of agrees that the vast majority of atrocities were committed against Muslims, mainly by Serbs and to a lesser extent by Croats. My own investigations in Bosnia, though not exhaustive, provided me with what I believe is an accurate picture of the scale of atrocities, and this picture coincides with the one sketched out by the CIA and the U.N. Commission of Experts. For more on the subject, see chapters two and three.

CHAPTER 2: GROUND ZERO

37   *the notorious Jasenovac slaughterhouse:* The information about Kovačević's birth at Jasenovac comes from Ed Vulliamy, *Seasons in Hell: Understanding Bosnia's War* (London: Simon & Schuster, 1994), pp. 9 and 100.

38   *Mladić invented a new military argot:* Slobodan Lekić, "Controversial Serb General Crucial for War or Peace," Associated Press dispatch, April 8, 1994.
     lengthy investigative story: Mary Battiata, "A Town's Bloody 'Cleansing,' " *Washington Post*, November 2, 1992.

45   *Omarska was an abandoned:* My description of the killing process at Omarska comes from a variety of sources, including my own interviews with prisoners, reports from the United Nations and State Department, reporting by Roy Gutman of *Newsday* and a thorough description in the book by Vulliamy, one of the first correspondents to visit Omarska.

50   *"They forced me":* Roy Gutman, "Genocide Case: Germany Nabs Serb in Camp Crimes," *Newsday*, February 15, 1994.

53–54   *"Three days after her arrival":* The testimony was contained in a report submitted by the State Department to the United Nations Security Council on March 9, 1993, for use in collecting information on violations of the Geneva Conventions.

54   *acts of decency:* Roy Gutman, "Mass Rape: Muslims Recall Serb Attacks," *Newsday*, August 23, 1992.

56   *executing Argentineans:* The book, *Excursion to Hell*, by Lance Corporal Vincent Bramley, was published in 1991. Bramley, after retiring from the army, told a reporter from the *Los Angeles Times*, "I only wrote the book to tell people what

the war and battle was like from an ordinary soldier's viewpoint. There are plenty of senior officers who knew what happened."

57 *Private Brown was sent home:* The courts-martial of Private Brown and other soldiers involved in the killing were covered widely in the international media. See Charles Trueheart, "Canadian Guilty of Killing Somali," *Washington Post*, March 18, 1994; and "Canadian Soldier Gets 90 Days in Somali's Killing," Reuters dispatch, May 1, 1994.

"The Bush administration": George Kenney, "See No Evil, Make No Policy," *Washington Monthly*, November 1992.

60 *belittled the Holocaust:* See "Undignitary," *The New Republic*, May 3, 1993; and Robert Kaplan, "Croatianism: The Latest Balkan Ugliness," *The New Republic*, November 25, 1991. The book was published in 1988, when Tudjman was an amateur historian. Under pressure, he has backpedaled from a few of its most odious assertions, which include the following statement about the Holocaust: "The estimated loss of up to six million dead is founded too much on both emotional, biased testimonies and on exaggerated data in the postwar reckonings of war crimes and squaring of accounts with the defeated. . . . In the mid-'80s, world Jewry still has the need to recall its 'Holocaust' by trying to prevent the election of the former U.N. Secretary General Kurt Waldheim as president of Austria!"

63 *"I talked to":* Later, Kenney's viewpoint evolved in a new direction as he began criticizing Bosnia's leaders for continuing to wage a stalemated war they could not win. Kenney urged them to accept an imperfect peace for the sake of avoiding further death and destruction. This placed Kenney relatively close to prevailing U.S. government policy, but he remained critical of the U.S. government's hands-off stance at the start of the war, when Serb atrocities were at their height.

CHAPTER 3: COUNTRY OF HEROES

69 *"I've probably just written":* David Rieff, *Slaughterhouse: Bosnia and the Failure of the West* (New York: Simon & Schuster, 1995), p. 93.

78 *"This is Serbia":* Alec Russell, *Prejudice and Plum Brandy: Tales of a Balkan Stringer* (London: Michael Joseph, 1993), p. 251.

82 *"Gather the courage":* Roy Gutman, "Town's Mayor Pleads for Bombing to End Misery," *Newsday*, April 21, 1994. Gutman listened to Briga as he made his extraordinary plea, which included this statement: "We cannot stand these massacres. You may not understand what I am describing here. I urge you to ease our pain. Bomb Goražde and the citizens of Goražde. . . . I appeal to [U.N. Secretary General] Boutros Boutros-Ghali. We cannot hold out any longer. Let him take just half the aircraft the U.N. used in Iraq not to bomb Serb positions but to bomb the citizens of Goražde. Bomb the city to allow a faster and less painful death. The citizens of Goražde will forgive him and the world for that. At least let them die in dignity. This is no empty phrase. It is from the heart."

A doctor who had survived: Jonathan C. Randall, "Serbs Batter Goražde, Disregarding Cease-fire," *Washington Post*, April 21, 1994. Surgeon Goran Askamija made these remarks in a shortwave broadcast.

85 For a description of the mosques' destruction, see Jonathan C. Randall, "Bosnian Serbs Increase the Pressure on Muslims, Croats in Banja Luka; Demolition of Two Historic Mosques Perpetuates Climate of Fear," *Washington Post*, May 11, 1993. Information about the detention of UNHCR personnel came from Canadian diplomat Louis Gentile, who was on temporary assignment for the UNHCR in Banja Luka. He wrote a letter that was published in *The New York Times* on January 14, 1994. The relevant passage: "When the remains of two mosques (including Ferhad Pasha) and two Muslim cemeteries were blown up, and bulldozers sent to desecrate and remove the debris, several of my staff and I were arrested and temporarily detained by the Bosnian Serb police for attempting to investigate and stop the desecration."

87   *"The trouble with Eichmann"*: Hannah Arendt, *Eichmann in Jerusalem: A Report on the Banality of Evil* (New York: Penguin, 1977), p. 276.

90   *"Millions of people"*: Rebecca West, *Black Lamb and Grey Falcon* (Edinburgh: Canongate Classics, 1993), p. 582.

    "It is like some fantastic": Ibid., p. 585. My description of the outbreak of the war and the retreat of Serbia's army is drawn from West's book, which is widely regarded as the most comprehensive and compelling account of the history of the Yugoslav people.

104   *"We shall be smart"*: Ed Vulliamy, *Seasons in Hell: Understanding Bosnia's War* (London: Simon & Schuster, 1994), p. 235.

105   *"I love Warrior"*: Ibid., p. 240.

110   *A well-known Russian writer*: The scene is contained in an offbeat and effective documentary entitled *Serbian Epics*, by Paul Pawlikowski.

CHAPTER 4: MERRY CHRISTMAS, SARAJEVO

132   *"You know how"*: Michael Herr, *Dispatches* (London: Picador/Pan Books, 1978), p. 23.

154   *"all measures necessary"*: The first step was taken by the U.N. Security Council on August 13, 1992, when it adopted Resolution 770, which called on member nations to use "all measures necessary" to deliver aid "wherever needed" in Bosnia. The terminology was understood to authorize military action. Resolutions 836 and 844, adopted on June 4, 1993, and June 18, 1993, respectively, authorized U.N. troops "to take the necessary measures, including the use of force" in defense of six U.N.-declared "safe areas." The resolutions explicitly authorized air attacks.

158   *"That is how they wish"*: Christopher Isherwood, *Prater Violet* (New York: Farrar, Straus & Giroux, 1945), p. 47.

159   *"In Serbia, the media"*: Cited by Tom Gjelten in *Sarajevo Daily: A City and Its Newspaper Under Siege* (New York: HarperCollins, 1995), p. 77.

166   *Michael Herr described*: Herr, *Dispatches*, p. 173.

172   *"The concern is that"*: Eckhard's statement was contained in a Reuters story, Kurt Schork, "Moslems Prepare Offensive, Serbs Talk Tough," December 28, 1992. The Magnusson quote comes from my own notes at his briefing.

175   *Sarajevo was filled with*: For an in-depth description of the Archduke's assassination and the events leading up to it, see Rebecca West, *Black Lamb and Grey Falcon* (Edinburgh: Canongate Classics, 1993), pp. 331–61. Her description is detailed and colorful but suffers, in rhetorical excess, from her obvious dislike of the Austrians.

184   *Colonel Sartre's mediation effort*: Colonel Sartre claimed that the doors were open when he arrived on the scene. However, his account was disputed by British Army Captain Peter Jones, the senior officer on the scene before Sartre arrived. Jones, whose version of events seems more credible than Sartre's, told a number of journalists, including myself, that the bullet-proof doors were locked shut at the time of Sartre's arrival. Sartre soon ordered Jones to leave the scene, and it was after Jones's departure that, apparently, the doors were opened and Turajlić assassinated.

188   *most desperate places*: Information about the conditions in Srebrenica comes from a variety of sources, including my interviews with refugees evacuated from the enclave, and published accounts by U.N. soldiers and aid workers who spent time there. Useful articles include Jonathan C. Randall, "Serb Guns Punish Bosnian Enclaves; U.N. Physician Says Trapped Muslims Dying in 'Huge Numbers,' " *Washington Post*, March 15, 1993, in which Simon Mardel, a doctor working for the World Health Organization, explained how, in Srebrenica, he had to perform amputations with a garden saw, and that nurses performed major surgery because doctors could not handle the large number of incoming casualties.

The Associated Press ran a useful eyewitness account on April 6, 1993, by Haris Nezirović, a Bosnian journalist who spent several weeks in Srebrenica. Here is how he describes the scrambles for parachuted food:

> During the first month of airdrops, at least 15 people were crushed, stabbed or shot to death in the nightly fights for food. On March 11 alone, five people were reported killed. Two days later there were three more deaths—a mother suffocated in a crush, a woman killed when a bundle landed on her and another person stabbed to death. The hunt for food begins every night as darkness falls. Crowds stream from the town into the nearby hills—elderly hobbling on sticks, soldiers who have deserted the front lines, wounded men on crutches, entire families. They traverse muddy or icy paths, cross streams and struggle up steep, slippery slopes. Some trek from villages 15 miles away and return home in the morning. Reaching the hilltops, they disperse among the trees, light fires for warmth and wait. Exhausted elderly people sit with their faces contorted in pain as they struggle to catch their breath. There is no way of knowing where the parachutes will drift down, and the wait can be for nothing if the bundles land too far away. Some families separate to boost the chances that one member will be in the right place.

188 *undergone a conversion:* Robert Fox and Michael Montgomery, "The General Who Refused to Go Away," *Daily Telegraph*, March 16, 1993. Their profile, based in part on the account of a U.N. officer who accompanied Morillon to Srebrenica, provides useful information about the general's experience in the enclave and his brief speech announcing his intention to stay.

189 *his tenure in Bosnia would be cut:* See Jonathan C. Randall, "France Likely to Recall General Leading U.N. Troops in Bosnia," *Washington Post*, April 14, 1993.
     On July 11, 1995, Serb forces conquered Srebrenica and cleansed the tens of thousands of people sheltering there. Following orders from their superiors, U.N. soldiers stationed in the "safe area" did not resist the final Serb onslaught. Survivors of the forced exodus told of widespread atrocities, including women being taken away, presumably to be raped, and men being executed. Two weeks later, the Serbs conquered the Žepa "safe area." U.N. soldiers there offered no resistance.

189–90 *"It is difficult for me":* Briquemont's resignation was preceded by a series of interviews in which he bluntly accused the U.N. Security Council of incompetence at best, and hypocrisy at worst, by passing resolutions without providing the means to carry them out. In an interview carried by Reuters (Kurt Schork, "U.N. Commander in Bosnia Slams Security Council, EC," December 30, 1993), Briquemont said, "I don't read the Security Council resolutions any more because they don't help me. . . . There is a fantastic gap between the resolutions of the Security Council, the will to execute those resolutions and the means available to commanders in the field." Briquemont cited Resolution 836, which established six "safe areas" without providing enough troops to protect them. "The resolution contains beautiful words, but it was a little bit of hypocrisy. . . . To manage a crisis you must have clear political objectives and a military strategy supported by the contributing nations. When we study the case of Yugoslavia, we see all the errors we shouldn't make."

CHAPTER 5: MR. SUICIDE

194 *His funeral a:* Blaine Harden, "Fast Life, Flashy End for Belgrade Mobster," *Washington Post*, November 21, 1992. Harden notes that Knežević followed the footsteps of his father, Dušan. "According to several Belgrade residents who grew up around the central train station where the senior Knežević practiced his trade,

extortion was then a harsh but simple business. Dušan Knežević sold bricks to well-dressed people who walked by him on the street. If a passerby could not be bullied into buying a brick, residents say, Knežević would hit him with it."

199   *Some are criminals:* Laura Silber, "Serbia's Ultranationalist Leader Emerges as Formidable Political Force," *Los Angeles Times*, August 3, 1993.

202   *His family background:* My account of Milošević's background is pieced together from a variety of sources, including research I conducted in Belgrade (primarily interviews with Serbian journalists and academics) and readings of a number of books and articles. Although some basic facts of his life are well-known, precise details are hard to come by, such as where and when his parents committed suicide, and there are many conflicting versions. I have done my best to toss out the least credible tales (including a statement by Milošević's wife, in an interview with *Vanity Fair*, that his parents did not commit suicide) and present a good-faith sketch of his life.

205   *"The breakup of ":* Warren Zimmermann, "The Last Ambassador: A Memoir of the Collapse of Yugoslavia," *Foreign Affairs*, March/April 1995.

206   *The industrialists who ran HAPAG:* My account of the HAPAG speech is drawn entirely from Ron Chernow, *The Warburgs: The Twentieth-Century Odyssey of a Remarkable Jewish Family* (New York: Random House, 1993), pp. 380–81. Other details I give about Max Warburg's life are drawn from the same book.

208   *"Nationalism is the":* Blaine Harden, "Serbia's Treacherous Gang of Three," *Washington Post*, February 7, 1993.

      His colleagues say: Stephen Engelberg, "Carving Out a Greater Serbia," *The New York Times Magazine*, September 1, 1991. Engelberg's excellent profile of Milošević's rise to power includes the following description of his epiphany in Kosovo:

> "It was a spontaneous reaction," says Slavoljub Djukić, a journalist who was there that night. "His close associates said that when he came back to Belgrade, he was like a heated stove. He was full of emotions. He could not control his feelings. He could not calm down." Friends and enemies alike agree this was a critical moment of passage for Milošević, the first time he felt his power over crowds. [Former Belgrade Mayor Bogdan] Bogdanović watched the performance on television and was aghast. "Something happened there, something like what happens to the character in the Charlie Chaplin film *The Great Dictator*, when they wave the flags and he realizes his power," Bogdanović says. "He came to realize he could govern by the use of the masses. He experienced it."

209   *"Everyone knew that":* Joseph Heller, *Catch-22* (New York: Dell, 1990), p. 364.

214   *"Milošević makes a stunning":* Zimmermann, "The Last Ambassador." Zimmermann was recalled from Belgrade in 1992 as a protest against Milošević's government. Two years later, Zimmermann resigned from the State Department. Regarded as an apologist for Milošević while stationed in Belgrade, Zimmermann is now sharply critical of Milošević and admits that Washington's passive Balkan policy, which he helped shape, was a failure. His lengthy article in *Foreign Affairs* is a concise account of Milošević's pivotal role in the collapse of Yugoslavia.

215   *"I can't do":* The documentary, part of the *Frontline* series on Britain's Channel Four, aired in August 1993.

220   *A wily jack-of-all-trades:* Dragan is not his real name; in this case, for reasons of safety, I have used a pseudonym.

227   *State television maintained:* Warren Zimmermann, "The Captive Mind," *New York Review of Books*, February 2, 1995. Also see Mark Thompson's excellent book, *Forging War: The Media in Serbia, Croatia and Bosnia-Hercegovina* (Avon, Eng.: The Bath Press, 1994).

      Milošević, like a drill sergeant: Radio Free Europe/Radio Liberty Research Report,

"Government Control over Serbia's Media," by Stan Markotich, February 4, 1994. The article includes statistics on the turnaround in public opinion on the Vance-Owen plan.

228 *After showing a series:* Dušan Stojanović, "Ahead of Elections, Milošević's Propaganda in Full Swing—Again," Associated Press dispatch, December 15, 1993.

Yugoslav Statistics Bureau: Slobodan Lekić, "Inflation at 286,125,293,792—and Climbing," Associated Press dispatch, December 1, 1993.

CHAPTER 6: PULLING OUT

238 *Croats began doing the same:* The Croat offensive was a mirror image of the Serb one. The main Croat militia in Bosnia, the HVO, was armed and supplied by Croatia proper; they cleansed the towns they conquered, just as Serbs in Bosnia were armed and supplied by Serbia and cleansed the towns they conquered. The Croat siege of the Muslim sector of Mostar was as brutal, if not more so, than the Serb siege of Sarajevo. Tudjman justified the offensive by using the same sort of propaganda used by Milošević—that Muslims wanted to enslave Christians and create an Islamic state. Ambassador Zimmermann recalled in his *Foreign Affairs* article ("The Last Ambassador: A Memoir of the Collapse of Yugoslavia," March/April 1995) a private meeting in which Tudjman erupted into a diatribe against Bosnia's Muslims: "They're dangerous fundamentalists and they're using Bosnia as a beachhead to spread their ideology throughout Europe and even to the United States. The civilized nations should join together to repel this threat. Bosnia has never had any real existence. It should be divided between Serbia and Croatia." This outburst occurred before the war in Bosnia had started.

It is worthwhile to note that Tudjman's control of the media in Croatia was even stricter than Milošević's control of the media in Serbia. Whereas Milošević at least tolerated an impotent opposition media, Tudjman would not. After turning state television into a virtual adjunct of his HDZ (Croatian Democratic Union) political party, Tudjman orchestrated the seizure of newspapers and magazines that refused to support his nationalist line. This gave rise to an ironic joke in which Tudjman meets Hitler and says, "If only I had your army, I would have defeated the Serbs long ago." Hitler responds, "If only I had your media, the Germans still would not know they had lost the war." For an excellent and in-depth analysis of the manipulation of the media by Tudjman and Milošević, see Mark Thompson's *Forging War: The Media in Serbia, Croatia and Bosnia-Hercegovina* (Avon, Eng.: The Bath Press, 1994). As many commentators have noted, the difference between the Croatian and Serbian leaders is that Tudjman is an inflexible nationalist while Milošević is a clever opportunist.

239 *When the Croats attacked:* The Bosnian Army fought the Croats to a standstill, and the standstill was turned into a shaky peace after America issued a quiet ultimatum to President Tudjman: Call off the offensive or face the same sanctions and isolation as Serbia. Tudjman, unlike Milošević, wanted to be accepted into the "family" of Western nations, and therefore relented. Britain and France were not nearly as robust as America in trying to end the Croat offensive, presumably because they saw it as a useful form of pressure to force Bosnia's leaders to accept defeat.

CHAPTER 7: THE APPEASERS

250 *"Did you have any misgivings":* The briefing was held on August 13, 1993, at the U.S. Mission to the United Nations in Geneva.

252 *"I can no":* A copy of the resignation letter was provided to the author.

In July 1995, the top U.N. official investigating human rights abuses in Yugoslavia, Tadeusz Mazowiecki, resigned his post as a gesture of protest. Mazowiecki, a respected intellectual and Poland's first post-Communist prime minister, told journalists that he could not "continue to participate in the pretense of the protection of human rights." He accused the United Nations of hypocrisy for "claiming to defend [Bosnia] but in fact we are abandoning it." See Marcus Kabel, "U.N. Yugoslavia Investigator Quits over 'Hypocrisy,' " Reuters dispatch, July 27, 1995.

252 *a private report:* See Daniel Williams, "Ex-Official Accuses U.S. of Being Soft on Serbs," *Washington Post*, February 4, 1994; and Saul Friedman, "Official: U.S. Downplayed Bosnia Genocide," *Newsday*, February 4, 1994. Johnson wrote the report while on leave at the National War College. He revealed that Clinton administration officials privately admitted that domestic political considerations outweighed the benefits of taking a stronger stance in Bosnia. The following excerpt from Williams's article is useful:

> Johnson recounted one unusually candid conversation that took place over lunch last spring involving Holocaust survivor Elie Wiesel, Undersecretary for Political Affairs Peter Tarnoff and department counselor Timothy E. Wirth. Wiesel argued that mass killing of Muslims by Serb forces and creation of concentration camps were cause "for decisive outside intervention." Tarnoff pointed to the political risks for President Clinton of intervening and failing, saying that "failure in Bosnia would destroy the Clinton presidency," according to Johnson. Wirth added that the "moral stakes" in Washington were higher: "Survival of the fragile liberal coalition represented by this presidency." Johnson was present at the lunch. Another witness said the report was accurate and a group of department officials had laughed in outrage after the conversation.

254 *"At his birth":* As quoted in Noel Malcolm, "Lord Fraud: The Real Story of David Owen," *The New Republic*, June 14, 1993.

257 *"We are being":* As quoted in Eve-Ann Prentice, "Bosnian Muslim Leader Gambles on a Waiting Game," *The Times* (London), August 3, 1993.

     battle of Muslim on Muslim: Owen's hand was involved in a larger outbreak of fighting in early 1993. Owen and his then co-mediator, Cyrus Vance, drew up a peace plan to partition Bosnia into ten autonomous provinces controlled by Serbs, Croats or Muslims (with the exception of a jointly controlled Sarajevo province). The Vance-Owen plan had the disastrous effect of sparking a new Serb offensive against the Bosnians and enticing Croat nationalists to withdraw their wavering support for the Bosnian government.

     The Croats were delighted because the plan would give them control over a surprisingly large number of provinces. The Croats viewed the plan as a green light for their militia to take immediate and complete control of areas shared with the Bosnian Army but slated for their control under the plan. This led to the Croat-Bosnian war and meant the Bosnian side became more purely Muslim and more bitter. In addition, the plan, which would have required Serbs to withdraw from large patches of territory, sparked an offensive by them in eastern Bosnia. Trying to forestall implementation of the plan, Serbs attacked several areas that Bosnians still held and were slated to control under the plan. Several towns fell to the Serbs. In the end, the Vance-Owen plan was abandoned after the Serbs refused to accept it. Its ill-fated introduction only worsened the plight of Bosnia's government.

     On May 31, 1995, Owen announced his resignation as the European Union's mediator, citing fatigue and a lack of progress in the peace talks. He had been on the job for nearly three years.

260 *"I was fourteen or fifteen":* As quoted in Ian Traynor, "Wrong Man in the Wrong Place," *The Guardian*, August 2, 1993.

261 *a 1970 tract:* The tract is, among cognoscenti of the Bosnian conflict, one of the

most talked-about and least read documents. In its call for Muslim solidarity and for Muslims not to wander from the teachings of their faith, *Islamic Declaration* offers Christian propagandists an opportunity to paint Izetbegović as a fundamentalist. But the declaration has another side in which, for example, Izetbegović shows clear admiration for Western capitalism: "its dynamism, its ability to set science and the economy in motion while ensuring a high degree of political freedom and legal security." Bosnia is never mentioned—not once—in the document.

262 *"Frewer described"*: John Pomfret, "U.N. Shifting Bosnian Focus from Protection to Partition," *Washington Post*, August 17, 1993. Pomfret also noted that the U.N. command appeared to be depriving Bosnians of food in order to pressure them to surrender. An excerpt:

> Bosnian government officials and U.S. military sources said the lead U.N. agency in Bosnia is fighting a plan to begin airdrops of food into the besieged Muslim city of Mostar. U.S. military officers first proposed adding Mostar to the list of airdrop sites in a meeting in Sarajevo on June 9. So far, however, officials from the U.N. High Commissioner for Refugees have not approved the plan. Mostar, the main city in southeastern Bosnia, has been cut off from the world for more than two months by Croat forces. An estimated 40,000 people are trapped there with little food, water or shelter. Mugdin Pašić, an official with the Bosnian Ministry of Foreign Affairs in charge of coordinating with the U.N. aid agencies, said U.N. officials told him that only negotiations, not airdrops to Mostar, would solve the humanitarian problem. "The UNHCR is supposed to be engaged in humanitarian aid, not politics," Pašić said. "Their meaning is: Sign away your country and we'll give you a little food."

"May I suggest": The Purves quote is contained in Giles Elgood's Reuters dispatch from Sarajevo, "When Is a Siege Not a Siege?," August 20, 1993.

263 *"We make no"*: Quoted by Evelyn Leopold, "Bosnia Rebukes West, Says It Will Not Fade Away," Reuters dispatch, December 17, 1993.

265 *Air Force relief flights*: For example, Senator Joseph Biden, in an April 19, 1993, report to the Foreign Relations Committee, said the Pentagon refused to let a congressional delegation he led fly into Sarajevo on an Air Force transport plane. The delegation traveled on a U.N. plane instead. Biden accused the Pentagon of trying "to discourage congressional travel to Bosnia."

265 *refused to offer asylum*: A release of thousands of prisoners was postponed in October 1992 because Western countries refused to offer asylum to them; the prisoners had nowhere to go, so they stayed in prison, and this time it was not the Serbs' fault. The International Committee of the Red Cross issued an unusually blunt statement criticizing Western countries. In my story, "West Reportedly Refuses to Accept Freed Bosnians," *Washington Post*, October 22, 1992, the Red Cross official who negotiated the release, Pierre Gassmann, said, "It's total hypocrisy. The Western countries have made promises [to take the prisoners] but aren't delivering on them." Belatedly, the U.S. agreed to resettle 3,000 Bosnians.

President Clinton passed: For useful analyses of Christopher's trip to Europe and the evolution of American policy, see the Bosnia chapters in Elizabeth Drew's book, *On the Edge: The Clinton Presidency* (New York: Simon & Schuster, 1994); and John Newhouse, "No Exit, No Entrance," *The New Yorker*, June 28, 1993.

In a major speech on February 10, 1993, Christopher adopted a rhetorical hard line that was never backed up with action. "The continuing destruction of a new United Nations member challenges the principle that internationally recognized borders should not be altered by force. . . . Bold tyrants and fearful minorities are watching to see whether ethnic cleansing is a policy the world will tolerate. If we hope to promote the spread of freedom, if we hope to encourage the emergence of peaceful ethnic democracies, our answer must be a resounding 'No.'" Three months later, after returning from Europe, Christopher reversed himself and called Bosnia a "quagmire." In testimony before the House Foreign Affairs Committee on May 18, he said, "It's been easy to analogize this to the Holocaust, but I never heard of any genocide by the Jews against the German people. But here you have atrocities on all sides." The historical record does not support his suggestion that the Bosnians had been, or were, committing genocide against the Serbs. His remark about "atrocities on all sides" is an example of wrongfully equating victim and victimizer; it has no factual basis. Please see the last note for chapter one, p. 280.

266   *"have been fighting each other":* The quote comes from a May 14, 1993, presidential press conference and was cited in Fred Barnes, "Safe Haven," *The New Republic,* June 14, 1993.

267   *"Mr. Clinton is":* Cited in Misha Glenny, "Demilitarize Bosnia or the Storm Will Spread South," International *Herald-Tribune,* July 31, 1993.

   hundreds of U.N. troops: In late 1994, 1,200 Bangladeshi peacekeepers were sent to defend the Bihać "safe area." They had 300 rifles at their disposal.

268   *"had to be prodded":* Ruth Marcus and Daniel Williams, "U.S. Backs NATO Shift in Bosnia: Clinton Plan Seeks Broader Authority to Conduct Airstrikes," *Washington Post,* April 21, 1994.

   "I would remind": Cited in Ann Devroy and Daniel Williams, "Treating U.N. and NATO as Enemy Is a 'Mistake,' Clinton Warns Serbs," *Washington Post,* April 15, 1994.

   U.N. officials who had downplayed: General Michael Rose, then the commander of U.N. forces, said of the Bosnians in Goražde, "They think we should be fighting their wars for them. They basically turned and ran and left us to pick up the bits." According to an American congressman who was briefed by Rose, the U.N. commander claimed that an estimate of 700 dead and 2,000 wounded, which came from the U.N. High Commissioner for Refugees, was a wild exaggeration. Rose repeated the claim in briefings with reporters; he never offered any evidence to back it up. See Giles Elgood, "U.N. Commander Says Muslim Troops Ran from Serbs," Reuters dispatch, April 28, 1994; and Maud S. Beelman, "How Many Really Died in Goražde? General's Doubts Spark Furor," Associated Press dispatch, April 30, 1994.

269   *"The siege of Sarajevo":* Richard Nixon, *Beyond Peace* (New York: Random House, 1994), p. 154.

   "The Serbs have made suckers": Carol Giacomo, "Shultz Says U.N. Failed in Bosnia, Urges Air Strikes," Reuters dispatch, April 26, 1993.

   "Feeding or evacuating": Margaret Thatcher, "Stop The Serbs. Now. For Good," *The New York Times,* May 4, 1994.

   "I am ashamed": William Drozdiak and Peter Maass, "Western Anxiety Deepens over Bosnian Crisis," *Washington Post,* April 15, 1993.

270   *400 U.N. soldiers:* The events in Bihać and the bombing of the Udbina airport were covered widely in the American media. For the hostage incident, see Carol J. Williams, "Bosnian Serbs Renege on Hostage Deal, Seize 2 More Peacekeepers," *Los Angeles Times,* December 7, 1994.

   "Don't mess with": Quoted in Anna Husarska, "A Serbian Christmas," *The New Yorker,* December 26, 1994.

271   *"intense pressure":* John Pomfret, "Bosnians, Croats Say They Will Halt Sweep Against Serbs," *Washington Post,* September 19, 1995.

   "We have made it very clear": Dana Priest, "Croat, Muslim Offensive Raises Concerns," *Washington Post,* September 19, 1995.

272   *Milošević, Serbia's president:* Elaine Sciolino, Roger Cohen and Stephen Engelberg, "In U.S. Eyes, 'Good' Muslims and 'Bad' Serbs Did a Switch," *The New York Times,* November 23, 1995. In its behind-the-scenes reconstruction of what hap-

pened during the final days and hours of the negotiations, the *Times* reported that the Bosnian delegation faced severe pressure to agree to the pact. According to the *Times*, when the deal was completed, Milošević "shook hands with the secretary of state, and raised his left hand in triumph. Tears came to his eyes, and the bearish, balding Mr. Milošević impulsively hugged Brig. Gen. Donald Kerrick, an Army general on the National Security Council Staff. As for Mr. Izetbegović, he paused and accepted the deal—reluctant to the end. 'Well, it's not a just peace, but my people need peace,' he told Mr. Christopher."

EPILOGUE

274 *"I have been struck"*: Rebecca West, *Black Lamb and Grey Falcon* (Edinburgh: Canongate Classics, 1993), p. 1128.

275 *"Later, as he sat"*: J. G. Ballard, *High-Rise* (London: Triad/Panther, 1977), p. 7.

Bibliography

Almond, Mark. *Europe's Backyard War: The War in the Balkans.* London: William Heinemann, 1994.

Andrić, Ivo. *The Bridge over the Drina.* London: Harvill/HarperCollins, 1994.

———. *The Days of the Consuls.* London: Forest, 1992.

Arendt, Hannah. *Eichmann in Jerusalem: A Report on the Banality of Evil.* New York: Penguin, 1977.

Ballard, J. G. *High-Rise.* London: Triad/Panther, 1977.

Chernow, Ron. *The Warburgs: The Twentieth-Century Odyssey of a Remarkable Jewish Family.* New York: Random House, 1993.

Drakulić, Slavenka. *Balkan Express: Fragments from the Other Side of War.* London: Random House, 1993.

Drew, Elizabeth. *On the Edge: The Clinton Presidency.* New York: Simon & Schuster, 1994.

Enzensberger, Hans Magnus. *Civil War.* London: Granta, 1994.

Giovanni, Janine di. *The Quick and the Dead: Under Siege in Sarajevo.* London: Phoenix House, 1994.

Gjelten, Tom. *Sarajevo Daily: A City and Its Newspaper Under Siege.* New York: HarperCollins, 1995.

Glenny, Misha. *The Fall of Yugoslavia: The Third Balkan War.* London: Penguin, 1992.

Gutman, Roy. *A Witness to Genocide.* New York: Macmillan, 1993.

Hall, Brian. *The Impossible Country: A Journey Through the Last Days of Yugoslavia.* London: Secker & Warburg, 1994.

Heller, Joseph. *Catch-22.* New York: Dell, 1990.

Herr, Michael. *Dispatches.* London: Picador/Pan, 1978.

Isherwood, Christopher. *Prater Violet.* New York: Farrar, Straus & Giroux, 1945.

Kaplan, Robert D. *Balkan Ghosts: A Journey Through History.* New York: Vintage, 1994.

Karahasan, Dzevad. *Sarajevo: Exodus of a City.* New York: Kodansha America, 1994.

MacKenzie, Lewis. *Peacekeeper: The Road to Sarajevo.* Vancouver: Douglas & McIntyre, 1993.

Maclean, Fitzroy. *Eastern Approaches.* London: Penguin, 1991.

Malcolm, Noel. *Bosnia: A Short History.* London: Papermac/Macmillan, 1994.

Morillon, Philippe. *Croire et Oser: Chronique de Sarajevo.* Paris: Bernard Grasset, 1993.

Nixon, Richard. *Beyond Peace.* New York: Random House, 1994.

Reed, John. *War in Eastern Europe: Travels Through the Balkans in 1915.* London: Phoenix, 1994.

Remarque, Erich Maria. *All Quiet on the Western Front.* London: Picador/Pan, 1991.

Rieff, David. *Slaughterhouse: Bosnia and the Failure of the West.* New York: Simon & Schuster, 1995.

Russell, Alec. *Prejudice and Plum Brandy: Tales of a Balkan Stringer.* London: Michael Joseph, 1993.

Silber, Laura, and Little, Allan. *The Death of Yugoslavia.* London: Penguin/BBC, 1995.
Thompson, Mark. *Forging War: The Media in Serbia, Croatia and Bosnia-Hercegovina.* Avon, Eng.: The Bath Press, 1994.
Vulliamy, Ed. *Seasons in Hell: Understanding Bosnia's War.* London: Simon & Schuster, 1994.
West, Rebecca. *Black Lamb and Grey Falcon.* Edinburgh: Canongate Classics, 1993.
West, Richard. *Tito and the Rise and Fall of Yugoslavia.* London: Sinclair-Stevenson, 1994.

Acknowledgments

The best way to understand how this book came into being is to imagine a pyramid composed of people rather than stones. If one person had stepped out of line, anywhere, anytime, the pyramid would have collapsed, and the book would not have been written. There are hundreds of shoulders upon which I stand. No matter what I say here, I cannot fully express my gratitude to my family, friends and colleagues. But I will give it a shot.

At the *Washington Post*, the door was opened in 1983 by Jim Hoagland and Karen DeYoung, who hired me as an intern and inspired me to pursue an overseas career. In 1987 Michael Getler brought me back to the paper in South Korea and gave me more opportunities than I could have hoped for. His support and patience have been the pillars of my career. I had the great luck to work in Asia with Fred Hiatt and Margaret Shapiro, who became mentors and friends. Blaine Harden assumed those roles in Eastern Europe. From way above, Donald Graham, Ben Bradlee, Leonard Downie and Robert Kaiser offered the kind of personal encouragement that means very much to a young reporter. I would also like to thank Jackson Diehl, David Ottaway, Christine Spolar, Peter Harris and the foreign desk staff.

In Eastern Europe, I depended on the companionship and counsel of dozens of colleagues. My friendships with Allan Little and Kevin Sullivan more than compensated for all the difficulties of covering a Balkan war. I also drew sustenance from the company of Meriel Beattie, Joel Brand, Marija Fekete, Alan Ferguson, Janine di Giovanni, Cathy Jenkins, Jonathan Landay, Charles Lane, Adam LeBor, James Mason, Alec Russell, Kurt Schork, Ian Traynor and Carol Williams. It would have been impossible to emerge intact from Bosnia without their help. The staff of *Vreme*, especially Miloš Vasić and Petar Luković, generously shared their insights with me. Nicholas Denton created a computer database program that brought order to the chaos of my files and notes. I cannot mention, in the space at my disposal, every colleague whose friendship or advice helped keep me going; they know who they are, and they have my lasting gratitude.

It is no secret among war correspondents that we owe virtually everything to our interpreters. They are our eyes and ears and they often save our lives. I can think of few stories I filed from the Balkans that were not the result of a partnership with an interpreter. My mainstays were Džemal Bećirević, Vlatka Mihelić and Sasha Radas. The perilous work they performed on my behalf went beyond the call of duty and beyond friendship. It is because of brave people like them that the truth of what happened in Bosnia has emerged. I cannot thank them enough.

For every year of my life I have been encouraged and encouraged again by my mother, my father and my five siblings. It is hard to feel lonely or forgotten in this world when you have such a supportive family. In Europe, Daphne and Micky Astor made me feel that I was never far from home. As I wandered from one continent to another, I have been blessed, too, with the presence of Kyo Choi in my life. She has influenced this book.

I would like to give special thanks to three people who helped transform my manuscript into a book. Ernest Beck read the earliest drafts and stripped them of much sloppiness, indulgence and irrelevance. His comments were invaluable. I am saddened that Diane Cleaver, who believed in my work at an early stage and took me under her wing, passed away so suddenly. She was an agent dedicated to books and to writers. Lastly, I suspect that Jonathan Segal, my editor, understood the manuscript better than I did. From the day it landed on his desk, he poured his energy and intellect into it, nurturing it, and this made a supreme difference.

This book is a personal rendering of stories told to me, and lessons taught to me, by the people of what used to be called Yugoslavia. I drank their coffee and brandy, ate at their tables, slept in their homes, used their telephones, borrowed their cars. Whatever favor a traveler could ask, I asked, and I rarely heard the word "no." I am unable to thank all these people by name. There are too many of them, and the justice of mentioning a few names would be counterbalanced by the injustice of not mentioning others. In some cases, the names are unknown to me. Strangers came into my life, helped me and then drifted away. I have tried to tell their stories, and the story of their terrible war, in a way they would approve of. If I have succeeded, that is my way of thanking them, feeble as it is. I hope I have succeeded. It is the most I can do, even though they need and deserve so much more.

Index

A NOTE ABOUT THE AUTHOR

Peter Maass worked as a foreign correspondent from 1983 to 1995, based in Asia and Europe. His articles have appeared in the *Washington Post*, *The New York Times*, *The Wall Street Journal* and *The New Republic*. His wartime dispatches from the Balkans led to his selection as a finalist for the 1993 Livingston Award for International Reporting. Maass is currently a staff writer for the *Post* and lives in Takoma Park, Maryland.

A NOTE ON THE TYPE

The text of this book was set in Sabon, a typeface designed
by Jan Tschichold (1902–1974), the well-known German
typographer. Based loosely on the original designs by
Claude Garamond (c. 1480–1561), Sabon is unique in that
it was explicitly designed for hot-metal composition on
both the Monotype and Linotype machines as well as for
filmsetting. Designed in 1966 in Frankfurt, Sabon was
named for the famous Lyons punch cutter Jacques Sabon,
who is thought to have brought some of Garamond's ma-
trices to Frankfurt.

Composed by PennSet, Bloomsburg, Pennsylvania
Printed and bound by Berryville Graphics,
Berryville, Virginia
Frontispiece map by George Colbert
Designed by Anthea Lingeman